I0606437

Nadia Boulanger

War Years in America and Her Last Decades

Literature Art Music

Nadia Boulanger

War Years in America and Her Last Decades

James Whipple Miller

With more than two hundred previously unpublished letters exchanged with American disciple
Ruth Robbins

and exclusive interviews with Turkish pianist
Idil Biret

Foreword by
Rémy Stricker

Literature Art Music

www.chestnuthillpress.com

ISBN (hardbound): 978-1-312-38573-3

Philadelphia, Pennsylvania

Companion website: www.ruthrobbinsmusic.com

Contents

Idil Biret (lower center), Nadia Boulanger (at piano), and Ruth Robbins (far right) in Fontainebleau, 1953 [Idil Biret Archive]

FOREWORD

This exchange of letters between Nadia Boulanger and Ruth Robbins is valuable in many ways. First, we have the chance to preserve the letters of both parties. The letters also show the mastery of the English language acquired by Nadia Boulanger during her exile and stay in the United States during the Second World War and tell of her intense activity growing out of remorse for not having remained in France.

But we also discover the fabric of friendships she created there. Ruth Robbins is a good example. She indeed rendered many services to her revered teacher and continued to send her gifts immediately after the war and during that difficult period. Boulanger knew how to maintain the dedication of her pupil with her characteristically punctilious communications on holidays and anniversaries. We also see how she returned to the United States in the 1950s to reconnect with her goals of teaching and performing concerts.

Many of her letters reveal her tireless energy as well as her resignation when facts hinder her. Thus, when the two women fail to meet,

"It is a beautiful hope gone—but it has been a dream—and has given me joy. So, am still grateful" (April 20, 1965). Or again, "And life goes on, rather tragic in its implications but . . . we would fall into despair if we did not concentrate on our own duty. And there, it is simple, evident, and it is as we can act still with some use" (April 5, 1959).

Hence this correspondence, beyond its wealth of biographical information, draws the portrait of a great personality, her relationship with a student, and at times her intimacy, a not insignificant prize.

— RÉMY STRICKER

Preface

The subject of this book is Nadia Boulanger's internal life from 1941 until her death in 1979, viewed from the perspective of two postwar students with whom she had close relationships. Previously unpublished resources provide new windows on Boulanger's personality and emotional landscape: her exchange of more than two hundred letters with American disciple Ruth Robbins and recollections provided by Boulanger's beloved postwar student, Turkish pianist Idil Biret.

Although scholars may find these new resources of use, my aim is to provide the general reader interested in biography or music incisive portraits of three extraordinary women. All three put music at the center of their lives. They shared a worldview that placed aesthetics far above and far beyond the everyday realms of commerce and politics. Each had close emotional ties with the other two. The common language of music bound together the master, Boulanger (1887–1979), with disciples Robbins (1910–2005) and Biret (b. 1941), passing the torch across three generations and three cultures. We are fortunate to have, in their own words, a record of the relationships between these three lovers of music.

Those who value aesthetics, as a rule, are appalled by war. They realize great art transcends chasms of language, gender, geography, and time. It transmits the best of civilization to coming generations. But if this transmission is interrupted—by an invasion of Goths, for example—civilization can fall into centuries of darkness.

Nadia Boulanger, composer, conductor, and perhaps the most influential teacher of music of the twentieth century, witnessed cultural devastation in the buildup to the Second World War. The lives of creative people she loved were twisted and threatened. The European musical world was shattered. Many Jewish artists and musicians fled to England or America. They were the lucky ones. She could not bear to think about what was happening to those who stayed.

In late 1942, as Nazi invaders laid siege to Stalingrad, Boulanger wrote, "Knowing that our whole civilization is in mortal danger . . . only each of our wills can help to save it, in being really ready to die for the values in which we ought to believe."

Despite Boulanger's charming English grammar—she wrote flawless, elegant French, but notes or letters in English frequently have unusual grammar and usage—her message is clear: only we can save civilization—and only if we are prepared to die for our values. "There is no more time to waste," she wrote. We must "be alive" to the value and beauty of culture if we are to counter "the primitive destructive and accumulated strengths to destroy what centuries have, at the price of a great labor and great honor, created."[1]

This book is the story of a four-decade exchange of letters between Nadia Boulanger and my aunt Ruth Robbins. It also tells how

---

1 Letter 42-9. In Part 3 below, the Boulanger–Robbins letters are arranged in sequence; thus, this letter was the ninth exchanged in 1942.

their lives and values were intertwined with another extraordinary woman, pianist Idil Biret, who studied with Boulanger in Paris as a child. In 1953, when she was eleven, Biret met Robbins, who was to prove a warm, nurturing presence in the stiff and formal atmosphere of Boulanger's salon.

These lifelong relationships were based on the love of beauty, specifically beauty as described by philosopher George Santayana: a "manifestation of perfection . . . the ultimate justification of being . . . a conformity between the soul and nature, and consequently a ground of faith in the supremacy of the good."[2] Boulanger, the mentor, was a worldly trailblazer with extraordinary talent and drive who overwhelmed all barriers. Before Robbins met her, Boulanger was already famous, at least in the feminist and classical music worlds: the first woman to conduct the Royal Philharmonic Orchestra of London, the New York Philharmonic, the Philadelphia Orchestra, and the Boston Symphony Orchestra, among others, and a teacher of many outstanding composers and performers.

Robbins, the thirty-year-old student (Boulanger was fifty-three when they met in 1940), was an unworldly Midwesterner seeking validation and understanding. Idil Biret, a child prodigy born in 1941, was sent at age seven to study under Nadia Boulanger by a unanimous act of the Turkish Parliament passed shortly after Biret's impromptu piano performance in Ankara, Turkey, awed President İsmet İnönü and assorted diplomats.

The three met in Paris. Biret had a childlike resistance to the fierce discipline of Boulanger's style of teaching and, in the 1950s' found a sympathetic listener in Boulanger's American friend Robbins. Robbins's and Biret's lives were further entwined when Şefik Büyükyüksel, my Yale classmate and friend, married Biret in 1976.

2 George Santayana, *The Sense of Beauty: Being the Outlines of Aesthetic Theory* (New York: Dover, 1955), 164.

Thus, I am connected to Biret through my aunt Ruth and my friend Şefik Büyükyüksel. I've heard her perform in Guangzhou, Beijing, Bayreuth, Istanbul, Carnegie Hall, and, on July 9, 2005, my aunt Ruth's cottage in Berkeley, California.

Robbins once asked Boulanger how to live with the evils of the world. Boulanger responded eloquently: "There must be men to fight, making the gift of their best years, of their life," she wrote, adding that "the one who cannot fight, or women must defend of not less precious treasury."[3] The "not less precious treasury" is civilization itself. Her message applies equally now, as today's barbarians—corporate lobbyists, oligarchs, antigovernment funders, media potentates, and philistine politicians—assault cherished institutions and values.

Boulanger wrote, "Done to escape is awful; done to develop is what has to be, if one fights not only against, but also for what is more than life, and what gives real meaning to Victory." Victory—over the "primitive destructive and accumulated strengths" destroying a world we value—must come equally from frontline warriors and from those who fight behind the lines: those who value, uphold, and pass down the finest fruits of each generation to the next. If the torch of civilization is not carried forward, victory is meaningless.

In the battle for civilization, Boulanger views the artist as an equal to the soldier. Indeed, she argues, true victory cannot be achieved unless the artist leads by example, upholding values worth fighting for. She saw herself, her protégés, her colleagues, and her students as a cultural battalion needed for victory over the forces of chaos and destruction.

Boulanger ignited a passion for the beautiful, offering a vision of music and art at the center of what is civilized. She connected

---

3 Letter 42-14 from Nadia Boulanger (NB), mid-September 1942. Note: for smooth reading, in the main text I have quietly corrected a few anomolies that are preserved in the letters themselves.

Robbins to a higher purpose: the very preservation of culture. This torch, passed from earlier mentors to Boulanger, went from Boulanger to Robbins and Biret. Nadia Boulanger, Wilhelm Kempff, and Alfred Cortot nourished the flame in Idil Biret, who in turn brings it to her master students, audiences, and listeners. One individual at a time, mentor to apprentice, teacher to student, artist to aesthete, generation to generation, the love of beauty protects civilization from the dark forces of chaos.

These letters provide insight into the values and vision lovingly conveyed from a brilliant musician to a sensitive and expressive acolyte. Boulanger and Robbins are lost to us now, but this record of their relationship enables lovers of beauty, as William Wordsworth wrote, to "grieve not, rather find strength in what remains behind."

Acknowledgments

Let me first express my deep appreciation for the overwhelming generosity of musicians and music lovers who have helped me in this endeavor.

Alexandra Laederich, general delegate of the Nadia and Lili Boulanger International Center, provided immense support that made this project possible. The Center preserved and curated both sets of letters, from Ruth Robbins to Nadia Boulanger, and from Boulanger to Robbins. Beyond that, Laederich provided countless additional resources, recommendations, responses to questions, and referrals. *Merci infiniment!*

Infinite thanks are also due to the late pianist, musicologist, and educator Rémy Stricker, who kindly provided a brief appreciation of the value of the Boulanger–Robbins letters in the foreword. We all owe him a debt of gratitude for his lifelong contributions to our understanding and appreciation of music.

Sylvia Kahan, professor of music at the College of Staten Island of the City University of New York and author of *Music's Modern Muse:*

A Life of Winnaretta Singer, Princesse de Polignac, went out of her way to give me excellent advice about the manuscript. My debt of gratitude to her is deep.

Jan Krzywicki, professor of composition at Temple University, has given his time to help me understand my aunt Ruth Robbins's compositions and exercises, set when she studied with Nadia Boulanger in the mid-1940s and with Francis Poulenc in the mid-1950s. He also volunteered to engrave Robbins's compositions, which can now be heard on the companion website ruthrobbinsmusic.com.

Composer, violist, and vocalist Hannah Selin kindly recorded Robbins's voice compositions, never before performed, miraculously bringing her long-silent notes to life. These, too, can be heard on ruthrobbinsmusic.com.

Tenor Sean Christensen reviewed the compositions and gave me many valuable insights from the perspective of a performer.

Roy Rudolph, head librarian of the Longy School of Music in Cambridge, Massachusetts, kindly produced bulging folders from the archives of the early 1940s, when Robbins was a student there, and the late 1950s, when she taught at Longy. The archival materials Rudolph furnished—including applications, registrations, grade reports, letters, and a magnificent photograph of Robbins in Boulanger's 1943 advanced composition class—provide unique personal perspectives of both Boulanger's and Robbins's roles at the school.

Sarah J. Adams, the Richard F. French Librarian at Harvard University's Eda Kuhn Loeb Music Library, patiently explained to me the allocation of Boulanger materials among Harvard's various libraries and collections. Adams guided me to the Isham Memorial Library, a special collections library, where I was welcomed by Josh Kantor and Christina Linklater. There I was able to photograph a variety of letters Nadia Boulanger wrote to sponsors and friends. Kantor also provided scans of three of Ruth Robbins's compositions from the 1940s that were preserved in the Isham library's collection of works by Boulanger's students.

Gretchen Vogel, my cousin Wendy Robbins's daughter, took the delightful photograph of Idil Biret and Ruth Robbins beaming at each other at Biret's performance for Robbins in July 2005. Gretchen produced the video of that memorable performance, providing her great-aunt with soothing music in her last days as well as a record for posterity.

Nedim Gery-Büyükyüksel did a yeoman's work deciphering and transcribing the original handwritten letters. He helped resolve many questions. Needless to say, without his many hours of labor, this book would not exist.

Nor would it exist without my niece Gabby Miller, who brought to the family's attention the importance of Ruth Robbins's letters from Nadia Boulanger. Robbins delighted in reading her favorites aloud to her great-niece. Does Gabby Miller's conceptual art reflect lessons on beauty, truth, and morality she indirectly absorbed from Boulanger? The letters Robbins shared and the values she embodied were part of Gabby Miller's upbringing.

My dear friends Şefik Büyükyüksel and Idil Biret provided the inspiration for writing this book and provided much encouragement along the way. They read drafts and made innumerable suggestions and corrections. Biret and Büyükyüksel are my cultural heroes. Their lives are devoted to bringing the best in classical music to audiences and listeners around the globe. They carry the torch of civilization through the chaos of our age.

And what can I say about the support of my wife, Alden Mellor Heck? To thank her for her good humor, patience, insights, and countless ideas and corrections hardly does her justice. Franz Schubert is supposed to have said, "Happy is the man who finds a true friend, and far happier is he who finds that true friend in his wife."

I concur wholeheartedly.

Three Lovers of Music

Nadia Boulanger with Idil Biret in Fontainebleau, 1952 [Idil Biret Archive]

Ruth Robbins and Idil Biret
in Berkeley, California, in 2005 [Ruth Robbins Archives]

Nadia Boulanger (1887–1979)

"It is easy to see her as the most influential teacher since Socrates," composer Ned Rorem.[4] Or, as music critic and former Boulanger student Don Campbell expresses it, "To measure the potency of Boulanger's influence is impossible. As a tree is rooted firmly to the earth, she was rooted in the history and grammar of Western music."[5] Or from violinist and composer Yehudi Menuhin, "In a world of such fluctuating and relative values . . . Nadia Boulanger is a fixed point—in itself an unbelievable achievement. But beyond this, she is a beacon and a guidepost for the many new generations which have flocked to her side during the course of her ninety years."[6]

Nadia Boulanger was an energetic force of nature devoted to teaching musicians—especially younger musicians—truths about creativity in musicianship, composition, and interpretation. Her letters

4 Ned Rorem, "The Composer and the Music Teacher," *New York Times: Sunday Book Review,* May 23, 1982.

5 Don G. Campbell, *Master Teacher: Nadia Boulanger* (Washington, DC: Pastoral Press, 1984), 1.

6 Yehudi Menuhin, introduction to *The Tender Tyrant, Nadia Boulanger: A Life Devoted to Music; A Biography*, by Alan Kendall (Wilton, CT: Lyceum Books, 1977), xv.

to Robbins reveal how, in her personally conservative way, Boulanger lived by clear philosophical principles.[7]

Among the soloists, conductors, composers, and arrangers who flocked to her side—and were significantly influenced by her—were Daniel Barenboim, Leonard Bernstein, Idil Biret, Elliott Carter, Aaron Copland, David Diamond, Roy Harris, John Eliot Gardiner, Philip Glass, Jean Françaix, Quincy Jones, Dinu Lipatti, Igor Markevitch, Astor Piazzolla, Léo Préger, Roger Sessions, and Virgil Thomson. In addition to so many well-known conductors and performers, other Boulanger disciples went on to be music department chairs or music professors at Harvard, Wellesley, the Longy School of Music, Vassar, Mills College, and other colleges and universities.

Boulanger's strong personality, musicianship, and active life have been well chronicled in many books,[8] not to mention in countless radio interviews, newspaper articles, and magazine profiles. Her close friends included Igor Stravinsky, for whom she arranged a commission from Mr. and Mrs. Robert Woods Bliss to compose his Concerto in E-flat, "Dumbarton Oaks," and Leonard Bernstein, who sat at her bedside on her last birthday, September 16, a month before she finally slipped away at age ninety-two on October 22, 1979.[9]

Before the Second World War, with an outstanding reputation as a conductor, organist, choral director, and teacher, Nadia Boulanger

7 See in Part 3, for example, the 1942 exchange of letters between Nadia Boulanger and Ruth Robbins (hereafter "NB" and "RR" in footnotes) at the height of the Second World War.

8 Bruno Monsaingeon, *Mademoiselle: Conversations with Nadia Boulanger*, trans. Robyn Marsack (Manchester, UK: Carcanet Press, 1985); Jérôme Spycket, *Nadia Boulanger*, trans. M.M. Shriver (Stuyvesant, NY: Pendragon Press, 1992); Kimberly Francis, *Teaching Stravinsky: Nadia Boulanger and the Consecration of a Modernist Icon* (New York: Oxford University Press, 2015); Jeanice Brooks, *The Musical Work of Nadia Boulanger: Performing Past and Future between the Wars* (Cambridge: Cambridge University Press, 2016); Jeanice Brooks, ed., *Nadia Boulanger and Her Work* (Chicago: University of Chicago Press, 2020).

9 The moving account of Leonard Bernstein's (1919–1990) last conversation with NB is reproduced in Campbell, *Master Teacher*, 11–13. He asks her if she hears music in her head. Barely able to speak, she responds, "Tout le temps. Tout le temps" (All the time. All the time). Curious, he asks, "Do you hear it now, at this moment? Mozart, Monteverdi, Bach, Stravinsky, Ravel?" After a long pause, she responds, "Une musique ni commencement ni fin" (A music without beginning or end).

was a highly influential arbiter of aesthetic taste in the Paris salon culture. She moved among the aristocratic, the wealthy, and the famous. Countess Marie-Blanche de Polignac and Winnaretta Singer, Princesse Edmond de Polignac were among the great patronesses who provided funds for needy students, commissions for work, and support for musical events.

After the Second World War, the prewar salon culture had disappeared. Winnaretta Singer, Boulanger's most important patroness, died in 1943. Musical taste moved from the neoclassicism Boulanger espoused to contemporary modernism. These changes meant Boulanger would never again have the prominence she once enjoyed, yet some continuity remained. Her post at the American Conservatory in Fontainebleau became her base of operations, and she hosted a one-woman salon on Wednesday afternoons in her spacious Paris apartment on rue Ballu. She often spent a restful summer week or two at the palace of Prince Pierre of Monaco, nephew of Winnaretta Singer, and prepared the music for the marriage of his son, Prince Rainier, to American actress Grace Kelly. She continued to be an active supporter of great talent and to direct a coterie of people who had substantial means or influence—American, British, and European—to support students and composers with scholarships, referrals, and commissions.

She was famous in the musical world, deeply engaged with four generations of outstanding classical musicians, and a friend of the noble, the wealthy, and the talented; what did Nadia Boulanger see in Ruth Robbins? How did this American Midwesterner, whose musical talent was self-admittedly modest and who was of relatively modest means,[10] become a trusted friend and close companion? Their four decades of correspondence give us an intimate view of two independent

10 Although RR's means were limited, she once gave NB a car (referred to as "Peugie" in their letters) and twice provided $500 scholarships for other students.

women during and after the Second World War and reveal aspects of Nadia Boulanger's life and character that otherwise would be lost to us.

The French Socrates?

"Education is the kindling of a flame, not the filling of a vessel."
"There is only one good, knowledge, and one evil, ignorance."

These are sayings of Socrates, but they represent one of Nadia Boulanger's fundamental beliefs: excellence is not easily obtained; it is earned through the hard work of learning. In a January 1943 card to Robbins, she hand-copied a quote from Charles Péguy:[11]

> Nothing is obtained without pain, and
> life is perpetual work. —Education can-
> not be conferred; it is obtained by work,
> and is communicated. —It is by reading
> that a man shapes himself and not by
> reciting hand-books. And it is also by
> working, modestly—

In his incisive book *Lessons of the Masters*, George Steiner holds that "the only honest, verifiable license for teaching, for didactic authority, is by virtue of example. The teacher demonstrates to the student his own grasp of the material." He emphasizes the moral nature of teaching: "In regard to morality, only the actual life of the master has demonstrative proof. Socrates and saints teach by existing."[12]

11 Poet, essayist, and editor who espoused socialism and French nationalism.

12 George Steiner, *Lessons of the Masters: The Charles Eliot Norton Lectures*, 2001–2002 (Cambridge, MA: Harvard University Press, 2005), 3–4.

Whether Nadia Boulanger was either a Socrates or a saint may be up for debate, but she certainly lived her life according to strongly held moral and social values. Alone in the world when her mother, Raissa Myshetskaya, died in 1935, Boulanger learned to value and nurture friendships. The earliest extant letter from Boulanger to Robbins, dated August 13, 1941, reveals that the two already had a relationship.[13] After discussing sharing a house in Cambridge for the upcoming school year, Boulanger then responds to unspecified help Robbins has offered: "But I already thank you deeply. I cannot possibly do all what ought to be done, and your help means a great deal to me."

A few days later, on August 18, 1941, Robbins writes to explain that the plan had fallen apart since the third party, another student, Julie, had backed out in part because she feared her social life would be constrained. "From the social point of view—well, I haven't any," Robbins comments wryly. "What is very important to Julie means very little to me." In this letter, the clarity, honesty, and detail with which Robbins explains a sticky situation are exemplary. She alludes to her self-doubt and how if she is not adequate for a musical career, she would welcome facing the truth now "and stop trying to be a musician," for she is "searching for something solid to stand on" and "does not count the cost."

Robbins acknowledges she may be oversharing, as we would put it today, but adds, "It is so easy to write to you about such things, and since I started, I could not stop. If I keep telling you that I feel you understand so deeply, it is because I am not used to it, and it overwhelms me." Boulanger's prompt response, dated August 20, 1941, is honest and to the point about a practical matter—housing. Her

13 The letters preserved by the two correspondents are a rich trove, but there are lacunae, and several are undated; I have endeavored, with occasional guesswork, to place these in their original sequence. See the full text of the letters in chronological order with additional footnotes in Part 3.

response exemplifies Nadia Boulanger's laser focus on moving ahead to accomplish goals without looking back or to the side. She does not touch upon the looming emotional issue in Robbins's letter: wondering whether she should even attempt to be a musician.

Robbins clearly seeks reassurance from Boulanger. Instead, Boulanger offers, "Am not less happy to have you this winter in Cambridge, even if not so near. It means very much to me" and an apologetic "Hastily, affectionately yours" to reassure Robbins that the letter was written in haste to put the housing issue behind them while placing a bookmark on personal matters.

The 1941–1942 academic year, spent at the Longy School under Boulanger's tutelage—even though they did not share a house—had a tremendous impact Robbins wrote about in a May 1942 letter. Her style is noticeably more relaxed than in previous letters. Robbins writes that she is "bursting with something," then humorously adds, "If I do not get it out of my system, I shall probably turn into a camel and grow humps on my back which will be the result of unsaid things."

What she absolutely has to get out of her system is her deep gratitude:

> There is no way for me to describe to you what this year's work has meant to me (and music is only a small part of it), but it has created quite a problem. All my life I have dreamed of having such an experience and of working with someone in whom I had absolute confidence, and now that I have had it, and am having it, I do not know what to dream about anymore!

She describes an explosion of love for her teacher—not adolescent or sexual love but a spiritual connection similar to the love students felt for Socrates, who awoke in his followers a sense of deep virtue connected with living ethically and thoughtfully. To describe her gratitude, Robbins then writes,

> I often wonder why I, of all the millions of people on this earth, should be one of those fortunate few to have been let out of the mist and shown where I am and why, and where I must go, and to be helped along the way. It is such a wonderful discovery.

Robbins was not the only one to explode with love for Boulanger. Two decades earlier, in 1922, when Boulanger was in her mid-thirties, Melville Smith was a recent Harvard graduate on a scholarship to study music in France. He wrote to his college friend Bernard DeVoto,

> The incomparable Nadia is as incomparable as ever. One day about a month ago, when my feelings were again at a zenith, I had the courage to profess the extent of my affection for her. Since then my feelings towards her have lost much of their sexual stimulus and retained a deep love which I hope will endure. She understood me completely—she always does—and assured me that she is "extremely fond of me," but added "in a sort of maternal way" (was she serious?). At any rate, my former torment is gone, and if the sure fact of having stated what I thought was a deep emotion has diminished it, far better to have done so. Between us now exists a deep friendship and comradeship which is incomparable. What a woman![14]

---

14 Mark DeVoto, "Melville Smith: Organist, Educator, Early Music Pioneer, and American Composer," in *Perspectives on American Music, 1900–1950*, ed. Michael Saffle (New York: Routledge, 2000), 268. Melville Smith (1898–1962) later became director of the Longy School of Music in Cambridge, Massachusetts, where NB taught during the Second World War.

Like Robbins, Melville Smith felt completely understood by Boulanger and enjoyed an incomparable friendship and comradeship with her. He then went on to explain why he believes that any sort of romantic love with Boulanger would never be possible for him—or for anyone.

> Perhaps when I see her again in Gargenville next summer[15]—where I am to spend it, as last summer—a new stage will arrive in my feelings towards her. But at present, all is calm. It transpires—or rather I have verified what I had always heard—that the celestial Nadia has had the grand amour and with her characteristic decisiveness has banished it from her life forever (from the point of view from which the word "amour" is regarded in France). He was Raoul Pugno, the great French pianist, who died at the beginning of the war. To say that I admire her even more since knowing this is not necessary, to you! She is dead right—and the less French—for her mode of action. "Faire l'amour" is a common French expression—but unknown, I expect, to great souls.

One cannot help but draw a parallel to Alcibiades's response when his attempt to seduce Socrates is laughingly rejected:

> What do you suppose to have been my state of mind after that? On the one hand I realized I had been slighted, but on the other I felt a reverence for Socrates' character, his self-control and courage; I had met a man whose like for wisdom and fortitude I could never have expected to encounter.[16]

15 NB maintained a summer home in Gargenville, near that of Raoul Pugno (1852–1914), a family friend thirty-five years her senior. He became NB's mentor and collaborated with her in writing an opera, *La ille morte*, 1910–1913.

16 Plato, *Symposium*, trans. Walter Hamilton (Harmondsworth, UK: Penguin Classics, 1951), 107.

Similarly, Melville Smith saw Boulanger as a great soul, above casual romance, living life on a higher plane. He was swept away by this powerful woman embodying clear moral and artistic values.

Was Nadia Boulanger the most influential teacher since Socrates? We cannot know, but certainly, for many people she opened doors of understanding, awakened a passion for the beautiful, and offered perspective on how to live a moral life.

War Years

In the autumn of 1940, Nadia Boulanger fled the Nazi invasion to the south of France. In November, after obtaining a visa and an exit permit in Vichy, she sailed to the United States to take up a hastily arranged job at the Longy School of Music in Cambridge, then under the directorship of her former student Melville Smith. Ruth Robbins was among the twenty students in the advanced theory class she taught that year.

Nadia Boulanger in her mid-fifties

Boulanger felt guilty about leaving France. She had left behind friends, fellow musicians, and students. It was not until the Nazis swept across northern France that she was finally persuaded that departure was the only course of action.[17] Her reluctance to leave was moral. She believed it was her duty to remain, to protect friends, to keep music alive. She weighed this patriotic duty against what she believed was an ultimately higher one: to preserve the fruits of civilization

17 NB left Lisbon for the United States in 1940. She arrived in New York on November 6 and was late for the fall semester at Longy.

by passing understanding to younger generations. She could do this only by teaching, and the United States was her best option. Earning a living from teaching and conducting was not a problem. She already had many American students and was welcomed by elite universities, music schools, and orchestras. She would be among the many fellow musicians who had also fled Europe, including her dear friend Igor Stravinsky.

All these issues are touched upon in the letters she wrote to Robbins during the Second World War. Boulanger often reflected on civilization, war, the welfare of those she left behind, and the moral justification for music and art.

In the summer of 1942, Robbins and Boulanger again discuss sharing a house in Cambridge for the next academic year. In August 1942, Nadia wrote,

> Strange, in such a time, to find time for such questions. But, that is just life. The mind knowing that our whole civilization is in mortal danger. That only each of our will can still help to save it, in being really ready to die for the values in which we ought to believe, and here, one of these foolish (and rather honest) human beings, weeping for the loss of a little dream. But I do, without forgetting for a minute that there is no more time to waste, and that we must really be alive, if we are not to help (to give our consent) to complex and primitive destructive and accumulated strengths to destroy what centuries have, at the price of a great labour and great honour, created.
>
> Dear Ruth, thanking you again—for old as I am, the only hope and consolation is found in you, the young ones, and your affection and your confidence are great comfort.

Boulanger's perspective on the war is broad and deep: Western civilization is in mortal danger, and her greatest responsibility is to fight to make certain the fruits of civilization created over centuries "at the price of a great labour and great honour" are understood and held precious by younger generations.

Robbins picks up on this theme in a September 4, 1942, letter:

> So many times I wonder if it is not just selfishness that makes me return to Cambridge to have another year of music as full and rich as last year. I love it so, but realize that I have contributed nothing and probably will contribute very little along that line, and would probably be much more useful as a worker in an airplane factory or as a nurse.
>
> But I keep seeing past the war, and know that no matter how bitter and furious a struggle it is now, it cannot go on forever. When it is over, there will be plenty of work to do in the search and establishing of better values, and if I have not learned to believe in myself in the meantime, I will be just as useless then as I always have been. If it were only development in music that would be gained from another year's study, I might really hesitate, no matter how much it means to me. But already, in one year, you have helped me so much to find my own convictions, and to have the courage of my own convictions, that I cannot even imagine what another year will bring forth. There has always been a great chasm between my imagination and everyday life, but you have flung a bridge across, and all I have to do is take the necessary steps to cross it. So in the face of every doubt and criticism, I can only look forward to the coming year with great joy.

Instead of being a worker in an airplane factory or a nurse, Robbins justifies her choice with the emotional growth Boulanger inspires. In an undated response likely written days later, in September 1942, Boulanger reinforces Robbins's justification for studying music in the midst of war:

> And this problem of values, of education, of tradition, of thought, of art is so great, that we have only to stop for a minute to think of history, to have the answer. With high intellectual standards, you can ask any sacrifice. With lower standards spiritually or intellectually, you meet selfishness, weakness, and despair. There must be men to fight, making the gift of their best years, of their life to save what the one who cannot fight, or women must defend of the not less precious treasury. . . .
>
> So, do not feel troubled. What you prepare yourself to do and to give will be more than badly needed.

Two years later, on August 25, 1944, eleven weeks after the D-Day invasion, Boulanger was reflective, measuring burgeoning hope against sacrifice, fear, loss, and sadness—and measuring her guilt about leaving France against the close friends "so necessary to my inner life" she made during her four-year sojourn in the United States.

> Understanding, feeling each nuance of what makes life so complex, in these highly significant days! Enjoy, one cannot, for the sacrifices are too terrible. Though there is light in the darkness, once the hope is seen, a new, still unknown fear arrives; now, it is no more an awful

> nightmare one is going through: Who is still alive? What will we hear? Killed by the Germans, dead through suffering—gone because it was the time marked by God
>
> . . . But . . . what friends I would have lost had I not come here for so many years. Friends so close to me, so necessary to my inner life, and having given so much of their heart, as I gave thence so much of mine.

During 1943 and 1944, Boulanger and Robbins developed a true friendship that went beyond yet never supplanted a master disciple relationship. Robbins felt privileged to be in Boulanger's company. She was glad to schedule Boulanger's Chicago-area students, to drive her up to St. Clara Convent in Sinsinawa, Wisconsin, or to send her thoughtful gifts. The stimulation and enjoyment of being with Boulanger were more than enough recompense.

Throughout the 1942–1943 academic year, Boulanger overextended herself, teaching both at Longy and at the Peabody Institute in Baltimore, commuting back and forth each week. Exhausted, in October 1943 she finally informed her former student Melville Smith that she would not return to Longy for the 1943–1944 academic year.[18] Instead, she would stay in Santa Barbara, California, as a guest of Arthur and Georgette Sachs to rest and recuperate.[19]

It was a regenerative year. Her great friend Igor Stravinsky, now based in Los Angeles, often visited, and he briefly contemplated moving to Santa Barbara. On October 6, 1943, Boulanger instructed Robbins to join her. "Go tomorrow to the ticket office. . . . Retain a bed for Los Angeles, and let me know when you are to arrive."

18 Alex Powell, "Organizational Identity in the History of the Longy School of Music" (PhD diss., Boston University, 2014), 85–87.

19 In the 1930s, Arthur Sachs (1880–1975) retired from his partnership in the family firm, Goldman Sachs, to devote himself to charity and art collecting. His French wife Georgette's family had a large villa in Uzerche, where NB first took refuge in 1940 when she fled south from Paris and Gargenville.

Robbins was delighted to accept this invitation. She was able to continue her individual lessons with Boulanger and at the same time was welcomed into the heady social environment at the Sachs ranch. Robbins was proud of her role as page-turner when Stravinsky and Boulanger sat to play piano together as they rehearsed his new works.[20]

When Robbins returned to Chicago after a four-month sojourn, Boulanger would at times ask her to find items and send them. Robbins started sending her care packages containing inexpensive yet thoughtful gifts. On September 17, 1944, Boulanger thanked her for one of her packages:

> The ingenious, thoughtful, amused, and amusing box. Everything in it is as beautiful as the books I shall read with such interest. The illustrated one is already appreciated by the eyes—then bath, mail, ranging, counting, fishing. What cannot be accomplished with its contents?
> Really, you are too kind. And I do thank you very very much.

Most of the contents of this box will remain a mystery, but they were selected with good humor and great thoughtfulness, as one can tell from Boulanger's reaction. In addition to the books Boulanger mentions, one imagines that "bath, mail, ranging, counting, fishing" could allude to a bar of soap, a postage scale, hiking socks, a miniature

20 Stephen Walsh, *Stravinsky: The Second Exile; France and America, 1934–1971* (Berkeley: University of California Press, 2008), 161–162. In October 1955, three new Igor Stravinsky (1882–1971) works (Sonata for Two Pianos, *Scherzo à la russe*, and *Circus Polka*) were introduced by the duo at a lecture/recital at Mills College in Oakland, California. The performance was reviewed by Alfred Frankenstein (1908–1981) in the *San Francisco Chronicle*: "It was interesting to hear Stravinsky do the talking while Miss Boulanger sat silently by to assist only in the playing. She has one of the most formidable musical intellects of the century, and is one of the most articulate and influential theorists of this era, but Wednesday night she was content to provide profound and fluent performances at the first piano while the composer played the second piano with his customarily mordant virtuosity." See full review, handwritten by RR, in Part 3, October 25, 1944.

abacus, and, perhaps, a package of fishhooks. The items would relate to activities she knew the recipient was involved in or had spoken of. The thoughtfulness and humor resided in Robbins's explanations of how these inexpensive items—often found around the house rather than purchased—could be used by the recipient. This type of gift giving was a lifelong practice. Robbins's family members knew they would never receive something expensive from Robbins, but whatever she gave would provoke a laugh and still be useful.

Boulanger and Igor Stravinsky reviewing the score of his Concerto in E-flat ("Dumbarton Oaks"), 1941 [Courtesy Archives Nadia Boulanger, Conservatoire National Supérieur Musique et Danse de Lyon]

Nadia Boulanger's 1941–1942 music theory class included Ruth Robbins (1910–2005); Harold Shapero (1920–2013), American composer and pianist; Robert Middleton (1920–2016), chair of the music department at Vassar College from 1974 until his retirement in 1985; Paul Des Marais (1920–2011), composer; Claudio Spies (1925–2020), composer on the music faculty at Harvard and the Juilliard School; and composer Irving Gifford Fine (1914–1962). [Longy School Archives]]

Postwar France

Victory in Europe was declared May 8, 1945.[21] Boulanger, and indeed the entire populations of every allied nation, felt overwhelming relief. The despair of civilization mortally threatened by forces of evil suddenly ended. Great joy rang from church bells, was shouted on the streets, and resounded from auto horns. At the same instant, deep melancholy for lives lost and cities destroyed as well as practical

21 May 8 is known as VE Day in Britain and North America. The surrender agreement was signed by Germany on May 7, 1945. The agreement stipulated that hostilities would stop at 23:01 (CET) on May 8, 1945, just an hour before midnight. The appointed time was already the morning of May 9 in Russia. Bells rang and people cheered on other days as well; for example, May 5 was the day of liberation for Holland and Denmark, and Parisians had cheered their liberation months earlier—on August 26, 1944.

concerns about how to relaunch lives so sorely interrupted for years were unavoidable.

The war's end, in fact, presented Boulanger with entirely new priorities—to assess damage and loss, reconnect with those dear to her, and take steps to rebuild her shattered musical environment. Understandably, Boulanger sought to return to France as soon as possible, but military and government priorities made it difficult to book a passage. Month after month passed as she pulled strings in her network of influence. Finally, on Christmas Day 1945, she sent a telegram to Robbins:

> Do miss you profoundly not for too long however for expect impatiently next meeting sailing now 31st wishes to you all gratitude and love = Nadia Boulanger.

After four years of proximity to Robbins, Stravinsky, the Sachses, and other American friends, Boulanger left for France. Yet even before departure, she anticipates seeing Robbins again soon: "expect impatiently next meeting." In an undated letter written within weeks of her return, in the early spring of 1946, Boulanger thanks Robbins for a thoughtful gift, then again asks Robbins to join her in Paris:

> Really, you ought to come this summer. Such events. Menuhin, all the original works, Jean Françaix's little opera. You would have to take care of food and room, but the rest we could arrange. A kind of scholarship—after all, it will not happen another time!

Although Boulanger is delighted to be home again, life is challenging. The complications of moving her life back to France are compounded by shortages on all sides. Robbins helps out by sending boxes of household items not readily available in France.

Robbins's ambiguous March 23, 1946, salutation "Dearest Teacher (?!)" hints at a transition from student to friend. In the letter, Robbins expresses concern about conditions in France.

> Dearest Teacher (?!)
>
> Ever since I came home, I have avidly read any reports I can find about conditions in France. But reports have been so contradictory that it is hard to get a clear picture. At first the reports stated that the food situation was really desperate, so I have been sending boxes to various people with food that was not very inspiring but the most nourishing I could think of. But in the last week there have been several reports saying that bad conditions have been exaggerated a great deal and that it is possible to get good meals in almost any restaurant . . .
>
> Do you still think I should try to go to Paris in the fall? Perhaps now that you have been there for a while, it does not seem such a good idea to you anymore.

Boulanger acknowledges receipt of packages from Robbins in her letter of April 27, 1946.

> Here are the bundles, so wonderfully chosen. How shall I ever thank you? When you are to be here, you will at once understand what we all feel.
>
> When are you arriving? Can hardly wait. It will be so good to see you again. Let me know and do not come too late.

> . . . Paris is in its spring loveliness, speaking for the future through its past.

Boulanger never hesitated to ask wealthy patrons to provide scholarship funds for needy talents. In the same vein, she sends Robbins lists of what she needs, even suggesting in her letter of June 8, 1946, that she purchase a car for their mutual use.

Robbins went to France in September and stayed until early February 1947. This sojourn solidified their friendship. Robbins's March 23, 1947, letter, written on her return from France, is chattier and more relaxed than previous correspondence. Robbins freely critiques a musical performance she attended. She has confidence in her discernment and is torn by the difference in intensity and sophistication of life in France compared to her life at home:

> I had a very nice visit in Boston from Wednesday to Sunday. Winnie rounded up several of your ex-pupils, and they came to tea on Saturday to hear news of you. Shapero, Middleton, Allanbrook, Pinckam, Griselda (Tony could not come), Paul Demarais, Spies, and Leonard Fine . . .[22]
>
> Returning home seems to be a harder adjustment for me to make each time I do it. Life here is so far removed from that which I have become accustomed to, and instead of arriving anywhere, I am always right back where I started from. It is as though I were two separate persons living two

22 Students of NB's at the Longy School of Music, 1941–1943: Harold Shapero (1920–2013), American composer and pianist; Robert Middleton (1920–2016), chair of the music department at Vassar College from 1974 until his retirement in 1985; Paul Des Marais (1920–2011), composer, Claudio Spies (1925–2020), composer on the music faculty at Harvard, Vassar, Swarthmore, Princeton, and the Juilliard School. Leonard Fine is no doubt RR's mistaken name for composer Irving Gifford Fine (1914–1962). "Winnie" is Winifred Johnstone, another Longy classmate who was to be a lifelong supporter of NB's North American activities.

> lives, and the one here has nothing whatever to do with the other.

In her response, Boulanger shows a maternal understanding of Robbins's dilemma of living in two worlds:

> Just a line, full of love, full of the sadness of your going. What you feel I partly understand, and so goes life! But you will finally fulfill, here or there, your own wishes, and make of your life what you, rightly I think, want.

The Fontainebleau faculty and students, summer 1953; close-up: Ruth Robbins, upper left; Nadia Boulanger, lower left; Annette Dieudonné, lower right. [Ruth Robbins Archives]

The 1950s: Peace and Melancholy

The French economy boomed during the 1950s and into the 1960s. In 1979, demographer Jean Fourastié published *Les trente glorieuses, ou la révolution invisible de 1946 à 1975.*[23] The content called attention to the growth decades of 1945 through 1975. The title alludes to Les Trois Glorieuses, the three days of July 27 through July 29, 1830, when King Charles X of France was overthrown and sovereignty through inheritance was replaced with a new principle: sovereignty by popular will. The significance of this fundamental change was forever romanticized in Eugène Delacroix's iconic painting, *Liberty Leading the People* (1830). Liberty was indeed recovered in 1945. During the 1950s, relief from the exigencies of war as well as constant economic growth and the restoration of French culture created positivity and hope perhaps equal to what Delacroix's image represented.

The 1950s were a period of recognition and relative stability in Boulanger's life. In 1946, she was appointed professor of *accompagnement au piano* at the Paris Conservatory, and in 1953, she became director of the Fontainebleau School. These positions put her at the center of Parisian musical life and established her firmly as the leader of Franco-American musical relations—at least as far as classical music was concerned. In 1956, she had a moment in the glare of global television lights in her role as chapel master for her lifelong friend, Prince Pierre of Monaco, when she led the choral and musical programs for the marriage of his son, Prince Rainier, to American actress Grace Kelly.

In America as well, economic growth, artistic flourishing, and postwar optimism were part of the culture. Despair and worry are largely absent from their correspondence during this period. Robbins, now confident of her musical ear, opines freely on performances she attends:

23 *The glorious thirty, or the invisible revolution from 1946 to 1975.*

> M and Mme Casadesus[24] played Mozart's Double Piano Concerto in E♭ last week. It was such a pleasure to hear it that it was disappointing to have it end. And very unfortunately (to my ears anyhow), Rodziński[25] followed it immediately with the Strauss Till Eulenspiegels, which completely wiped out the impression of the delicacy and refinement of the music and the excellent taste of the performance of the Casadesuses. By the time the concert was over (after the intermission, a Beethoven symphony) it was hard to remember that the Mozart had been played at all. [March 30, 1950]

Growing into her role as both friend and confidant, Robbins also shares personal frustrations:

> We are still trying to find the right person to stay with Mother so I can have a little freedom. It has been like trying to go through a solid rock of resistance, but I have made an issue of it this summer, as I insist that I must be free to carry on my work. If it were a matter of Mother not being able to afford to have someone to look after her, that would be entirely different, but that is not the case, so I am fighting for a chance to carry on a more normal life. [August 1, 1951]

Boulanger ages into her mid- to late sixties enjoying a full life, but melancholy notes appear in her correspondence. She witnesses

24 Pianists Robert (1899–1972) and Gaby Casadesus (1901–1999) both taught at Fontainebleau, Robert beginning in its first year, 1921, and Gaby joining him on the faculty in 1939.

25 Polish conductor Artur Rodziński (1892–1958).

the inexorable march of time marked by illnesses and the deaths of loved ones. During the fall of 1950, Boulanger was on a restorative stay in La Moubra in the Swiss Alps when she heard that one of her favorite young artists, the piano prodigy Dinu Lipatti,[26] was declining. Boulanger writes in a letter to Robbins,

> Came here for a rather necessary rest, intended to stay eight days more, but my dear, poor Lipatti is again very sick. He always is, alas, but in a greater danger. And if I can see him, will return for a few days to Geneva. The struggle for his life is unbelievable, and his resistance miraculous, but . . . how long can an organism stand such a strain? Well, we must all pray. He is one of the greatest artists I have ever known, and an angel. When he is worse, he is worried for all of us, not for himself! Forgive me, you do not know him, but if you have any of his records, you know. [September 22, 1950]

Two months later, on December 2, Lipatti died at age thirty-three. In a Christmas card to Robbins, Boulanger says,

> Am so distressed by Dinu Lipatti's death that I feel out of reality. But just in his memory, loving more the ones I really love. And you are so profoundly amongst them. [Christmas 1950]

In a birthday note, two weeks later in January 1951, she is still absorbed by this early death:

26 Romanian pianist Dinu Lipatti (1917–1950) became NB's student in 1934 as a teenager.

> And as life goes and the time shortens, it is harder. You may have heard of Dinu Lipatti's death—a disaster and such a profound, heavy sorrow. As great an artist, as great a soul. One finds it difficult to overcome such a blow!

Boulanger's sorrow at Lipatti's death was deep and genuine. As amply evidenced in her correspondence with Robbins, when she liked people, Boulanger formed intimate and affectionate relationships, especially with those who, like herself, were sensitive, honest, and morally upright.

In a May 1, 1950, letter about the pageantry marking the end of the reign of her dear friend Prince Pierre of Monaco, Boulanger waxes nostalgic. She evokes the majesty of the ceremonies with a poetic appeal for Robbins to "build a fairy tale" with her imagination.

> Am seeing the end of a dream—'tis rather sad. We were in Monaco for the fests given in honor of the accession to the sovereignty of the son of Pierre de Monaco. Do you remember him? And it has been so beautiful, as well in the cathedral as in the Court of the Palace. Had I a little time would I be defeated by myself, for I cannot evocate these ceremonies for you, but . . . no time, and so you must enter into our dream, let your imagination build a fairy tale, and if you let it grow, you will perhaps approach reality.

In Boulanger's romantic sensibility, love and loss are inextricably bound. Inevitably as we age, loss increases its foothold in our lives. Yet loss can be countered by cherishing more those we love, and by using the imagination to create beauty that "will perhaps approach reality."

That said, Boulanger never loses her rootedness in the concrete and the practical, as is evident in her September 29, 1951, letter of recommendation for Robbins, who sought a teaching position:

> Miss Ruth Robbins has studied with me for years, and I could not recommend her too highly for the teaching of Solfeggio and harmonic basis. She is born to help, to transfer her knowledge to bring people to love what they understand.
>
> Excellent teacher, Miss R. Robbins is a person of high moral value. She is understanding, and her pupils are indeed well guided and inspired. She knows what mean these elements without which one never becomes a good musician. Nadia Boulanger

Robbins's delight with the recommendation is expressed with humorous self-deprecation:

> If I was a pauper a few hours ago (before your letter came), now I am a millionaire with such a recommendation! The great danger now is that I will have such a plethora of pupils that I will never be able to get away from them! And aren't you a clever woman! To recommend me to teach solfège! Now I will have to work like the devil to live up to such a reputation! [October 18, 1951]

Boulanger pinpointed the best use of Robbins's knowledge and skills. Robbins did not have the natural talent or musical sensibility to succeed as a teacher of composition or advanced piano technique, but she knew the basics of harmonics and solfège (a music education method used to teach pitch and sight singing). The virtues Boulanger cites that make Robbins a good teacher include generosity, love of beauty, and "high moral value." Musicianship is not mentioned.

Nor is Robbins's gentle sense of humor highlighted in the recommendation, yet Boulanger clearly appreciated it. In 1956, she was in charge of preparing the musical program for the marriage of Prince Rainier to Grace Kelly. Days before the ceremony, Boulanger received this from Robbins:

> You must be all excited about your forthcoming concerts in Monaco. A nice newsy letter from Annette about a month ago told me all about your plans for the concerts for the coronation. Please, when newsreel pictures are being taken, stand right out in front and do not let the prince hide so much as the toe of your shoe! Perhaps some miracle will occur, and I will be able to go to the movies and see you there! Really, you owe it to us poor creatures to whom you have given a taste for such a glorious life only to have it snatched away at midnight, so to speak, like poor little Cinderellas. [March 29, 1956]

You can almost hear Boulanger's chuckle in her response, written on a postcard on April 18, 1956, the eve of the church ceremony:

> Dear Ruth,
> Here is my word: I will do it! And it is worth [it].

November 22, 1963

At 2 p.m. on November 22, 1963, Boulanger's student Idil Biret was to have her United States debut as the piano soloist with the Boston Symphony Orchestra. Biret wrote,

> My birthday is the 21st of November, so the orchestra played "Happy Birthday" to me at the rehearsal and everything was going perfectly. The afternoon of the concert I felt something was unusual, but I didn't know what it was. Mr. Leinsdorf, looking very pale, came into my room and said, "Ah, there you are," and then walked out. His secretary came in and sat down, she was in a very strange state, but she didn't say anything either. Then my father came in and told me that President Kennedy had been shot and that there was some question about whether we would continue with the concert or not. But Mr. Cabot, the chairman of the board of the orchestra, went out onto the stage and said that the day he lost his father he attended a concert and found consolation in it, and hoped the audience would find solace in this music. Everyone was in a terrible state, but we played the concerto anyway; it was a very tragic debut.[27]

27 The recording of the WGBH live broadcast of Biret's November 22, 1963, concert, including the announcements by Erich Leinsdorf (1912–1993) and Henry B. Cabot (1895–1974), was added to the National Registry of the Library of Congress. It is one of few instances where the initial shock of the news was recorded, where the immediate reaction has been forever preserved. See a comprehensive Library of Congress descriptive essay here: https://www.loc.gov/static/programs/national-recording-preservation-board/documents/WGBH-Boston-Symphony-JFK-Assassination.pdf.

Idil Biret with Erich Leinsdorf and the Boston Symphony Orchestra, November 22, 1963. [Idil Biret Archive]

Biret's reminiscence comes from an interview with music critic Richard Dyer published in 2000.[28] Dyer continues, "The BSO added the funeral march from Beethoven's Eroica symphony to the program." Margo Miller, writing in the *Boston*, praised the twenty-two-year-old pianist for her depth of touch, dynamics, lyricism, and "rapture of youth. Despite the circumstances and Leinsdorf's precipitous tempi, Biret's pianistic equilibrium is never disturbed, and her emotional fires blaze away, unbanked."[29]

On November 24, 1963, a year and a half after Robbins's and Boulanger's visit to the White House, Robbins wrote to Boulanger,

> I have been sitting before my television set for several hours trying to take in the events of this incredible moment in

28 Richard Dyer, "Pianist Idil Biret Is Unparalleled in Playing and Recording," *Boston Sunday Globe*, September 24, 2000, M2.

29 Margo Miller, "Tribute to Kennedy Is Solace in Music," *Boston Globe*, November 23, 1963. An audio recording of the concert confirms Miller's opinion.

> history. At this moment, officials are awaiting the arrival of President de Gaulle. The prime minister of Japan has just arrived. Dignitaries from all over the world are expected to continue to arrive all night. I am absolutely drained emotionally from all I have seen. What looms more and more in my mind is the greatness and nobleness of Mrs. Kennedy, the president's widow. Her fortitude is overwhelming. Within two hours after the slaying of the president she stood calmly at the side of Lyndon Johnson in her bloodstained clothing for his swearing in ceremony as the new president.
>
> At no time in the long, sad, two and a half days since the murder has she lost her composure. It has just been announced that she wishes to walk behind the cortège to the funeral rites tomorrow.

Boulanger's luncheon with Jackie Kennedy eighteen months before, a shared experience that highlighted their distinct roles as master and acolyte, is a subtext. Then Robbins writes of the impact of the events of November 22, 1963, on Idil Biret:

> Poor Idil! Her debut in the States has been completely pushed into the shadows by the momentous events . . .
>
> I have thought so often these last two days of the happy occasion a year and a half ago when I drove up to the White House door with an important and renowned passenger in my little VW. What a contrast to the scenes of today!
>
> I am worn out, but cannot tear myself from the TV screen. And tomorrow will be another tearful day, the official day of mourning. After that, life will return to

"normal"—but who knows what the consequences of this dreadful tragedy will be?

With all my love and gratitude for the many, many happy times with you.

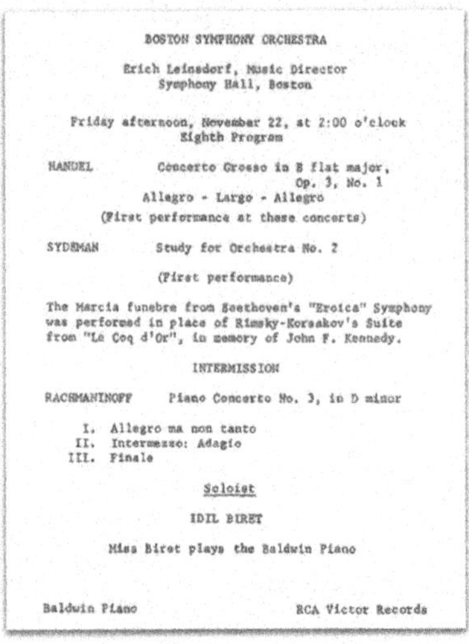

BOSTON SYMPHONY ORCHESTRA

Erich Leinsdorf, Music Director
Symphony Hall, Boston

Friday afternoon, November 22, at 2:00 o'clock
Eighth Program

HANDEL — Concerto Grosso in B flat major, Op. 3, No. 1
Allegro - Largo - Allegro
(First performance at these concerts)

SYDEMAN — Study for Orchestra No. 2
(First performance)

The Marcia funebre from Beethoven's "Eroica" Symphony was performed in place of Rimsky-Korsakov's Suite from "Le Coq d'Or", in memory of John F. Kennedy.

INTERMISSION

RACHMANINOFF — Piano Concerto No. 3, in D minor

I. Allegro ma non tanto
II. Intermezzo: Adagio
III. Finale

Soloist

IDIL BIRET

Miss Biret plays the Baldwin Piano

Baldwin Piano — RCA Victor Records

November 22, 1963, program revised to include the funeral march from Beethoven's Symphony no. 3 in E-flat Major ("Eroica") [Idil Biret Archive]

Biret did, in fact, perform on November 22, the day Kennedy was shot. The chairman of the Boston Symphony Orchestra, Henry B. Cabot, spoke to the audience to confirm the terrible news and welcomed everyone to find solace in the coming performance. Erich Leinsdorf opened the program with the funeral march from Beethoven's Symphony no. 3, (*Eroica*). Then, as originally planned, Biret performed Rachmaninoff's Piano Concerto no. 3 in D Minor with the orchestra. The next night, November 23, the orchestra performed a special memorial service for Kennedy that included Beethoven's entire Symphony no. 3. On November 24, the orchestra returned to scheduled programming, and Biret resumed her piano soloist role with the orchestra.

Nostalgia and Decline

The early 1960s were an era of positivity and new beginnings in both France and the United States. Young, handsome Massachusetts senator John F. Kennedy had been elected in November 1960 and was inaugurated as the United States president in January 1961. He promised a new era of progress and goodwill. Progress was famously demonstrated with a highly visible space program that put America's first man into space in 1961 (Alan Shepard) and America's first man in orbit in 1962 (John Glenn). Goodwill and idealism were actualized with the formation of the Peace Corps in 1961, dedicated to spreading United States know-how globally through all-volunteer programs in education, medicine, business, and agriculture. Kennedy's glamorous wife, Jacqueline Bouvier Kennedy, was a dedicated Francophile with a degree in French literature. She devoted herself to supporting music, the arts, and fashion, and, in particular, promoting French culture.

In 1958, with the collapse of the Fourth Republic in France, General Charles de Gaulle, the towering figure of French resistance to the Nazis, ended his voluntary retirement from political matters. He led France in the creation of a new constitution and the formation of the Fifth Republic, with support from 86 percent of the French electorate in a referendum. He was loved and admired by the French people, even in the colonies. Given a choice of accepting the new constitution or leaving the French umbrella for independence, every colony except Guinea chose to stay.

Ultimately, the 1960s in France and the United States were not without conflict. The Algerian independence movement brought with it the exodus of nearly one million French settlers in 1962. President Kennedy was assassinated in November 1963. In 1968, worker and student movements in both the United States and France revealed deep discontent with traditional social mores and the perceived repressiveness of government.

All the same, the optimism at the beginning of the decade was borne out by continuing strong economic growth. One might even say that the idealistic demands of students and workers in 1968 were a direct consequence of the optimism at the beginning of the decade.[30]

Boulanger was seventy-two when the 1960s dawned. Still full of energy, she admits to a frantic way of life, almost as if by going this fast she could outrun Father Time.

> Am leaving Sunday. Disorder is at its top and agitation exemplar. Hope however to be ready! Problem—reduce the size and the number of luggages and bring all the usual and useless things to Varsovie![31]
>
> So, it is your turn to guess how looks the rue Ballu[32] and its inhabitants.
>
> Pray for me! [February 26, 1960]

Robbins studied with Boulanger at Fontainebleau the summers of 1960 and 1961 and enjoyed her time there tremendously. Yet her interest in teaching piano to youngsters was beginning to wane. In a

30 The year 1968 was one of global unrest and disillusionment. On January 5, Alexander Dubček was elected the first secretary of the Czechoslovakian Communist Party to lead a brief period of liberalization and reform known as the "Prague Spring," only to see, within months, Soviet forces occupy the country and reinstitute hard-line Communist rule. At the end of January, the Tet Offensive in Vietnam demonstrated clearly that United States claims of progress in the war were illusory, strengthening the antiwar movement. In April, the Reverend Martin Luther King was assassinated. In May in France, huge student demonstrations led to clashes with the Parisian police, resulting in hundreds of injuries, followed by widespread worker strikes, dissolution of the National Assembly, and President Charles de Gaulle's threat to bring in military intervention. In June, United States presidential candidate Robert Kennedy was assassinated. In August, the Democratic Party's national convention in Chicago was disrupted by thousands of students led by protest groups like the Yippies, Students for a Democratic Society, and the Black Panthers.

31 Warsaw.

32 36, rue Ballu was where NB lived, taught private lessons, and had Wednesday "afternoons," or "gatherings at which pupils and invited guests heard music old and new, and discussed and analyzed." Allen Hughes, "Nadia Boulanger, Teacher of Top Composers, Dies," *New York Times*, October 23, 1979.

February 1, 1961, letter, after describing summer travel plans to France, she writes,

> I have been having a very enjoyable winter with my sculpturing class. Our teacher this year is a M. Moranon, from somewhere in the South of France, I am sure. He has such a thick accent that it is difficult to understand him, but he is very witty and keeps us amused all the time. As my musical life consists entirely of teaching youngsters, many of whom do not want to study, and practically none of whom do any work, it is not very inspiring. The reason I enjoy the art work so much is that I myself am actively making "art" (??), and that is the most deeply satisfying thing in my life. That is why I miss you so much, and all the musical activity that goes with you. I hope that you do not mind that I enjoy sculpturing so much!!

In response, Boulanger expresses delight at the news that Robbins would return to Fontainebleau in the summer. She again describes a frantic pace of life before she thanks Robbins for the Valentine's decorations she drew on her letter:

> What a letter—wonderful, and with such happy news. Do not change now. How would I stand another deception? Seeing you again will be such a joy.
>
> Am in Paris in May, about June 1 to 12, gone Sept. 1 for Romania, God willing, back in November from Moscou. The Valentine makes me quite cheerful and your letter so glad. [February 4, 1961]

Before that Fontainebleau summer session began, however, Boulanger toured the United States with Robbins, who served as her chauffeur and companion. She drove Boulanger to the White House for a luncheon with Jackie Kennedy, during which Robbins waited with her old VW bug alongside the black limos and black-suited drivers of the limo pool.[33] Boulanger was grateful for the close companionship of Robbins. Aboard the *Queen Mary* on her return from the United States, Boulanger wrote,

> Which words would be adequate! You know I hope, what I do feel, so deeply. When I say thank you, so many things are meant. You have to have open ears and a receptive mind!
>
> How strange it will be to go on without you—and how sad—but these weeks will always remain with me. Such a gift of one self is a blessing, and it has given to all these journeys a character of confidence, of rest, of intimacy quite unique.

Later in the letter, however, Boulanger returns to dark thoughts:

> Hope Annette is not as sick as Marcelle makes me fear. This fear has rendered this trip full of anxiety.
>
> And, may I confess, with Tasha gone—well, dear Ruth, why would I darken your thoughts with my darkness? [May 7, 1962]

---

33 Robbins family anecdote.

Tasha was Boulanger's beloved Russian blue cat. When Idil Biret first met Nadia Boulanger, Tasha played an important role. In a 2021 interview on Radio France, Biret recalled that first meeting:

> I had always heard about "Mademoiselle Boulanger" who was very severe, and my professor in Ankara, Mithat Fenmen, had said to me "Be careful! If she receives you, you must be really really good, or else she will lock you up in a dark little room in the apartment." (laughs) So I always went looking for this dark room that was . . . but I never found it, of course. So I arrived at her place, wondering who I was going to find. And I was thrilled, as there was a cat there. Because since my earliest childhood cats have been—let's say that I had a very special relationship with cats. So there was this cat called Tascha. It was a gray cat, a Russian Blue. Very timid, very—but I was delighted to see it. And Mademoiselle Boulanger immediately offered me chocolate, which had the effect of cajoling me—well not cajoling but . . . (laughs). And I played for her.[34]

A month later, disturbed by the illness of former student and professional partner Annette Dieudonné, Boulanger writes from the Palais de Monaco, "How a long letter is needed, but I can hardly send

---

34 J'entendais toujours parler de « Mademoiselle Boulanger » qui était très sévère et mon professeur à Ankara Mithat Fenmen m'avait dit « Attention ! Si elle te reçoit, il faut que tu sois vraiment très très bien, autrement elle va t'enfermer dans une petite pièce noir qu'il y a dans l'appartement» (laughs) Et alors j'ai toujours cherchée cette pièce noir qui . . . mais je ne l'ai jamais trouvée, naturellement. Alors je suis arrivée chez elle, en me disant « qui vais-je trouver ? » Et j'était ravis, il y avait un chat. Parce-que les chats, depuis ma plus jeune enfance, ont été—disons, j'avais une relation tout à fait spéciale avec les chats. Alors il y avait ce chat qui était Tascha. C'était un chat gris, un bleu de Russie. Très timide, très—mais j'était ravis de le voir. Et Mlle. Boulanger tout de suite m'a offert du chocolat, ce qui a eu le don de (laughs) de m'amadouer—pas m'amadouer mais . . . (laughs). Et j'ai jouée pour elle. [Transcription of the relevant section of the radio interview by Nedim Gery-Büyüyüksel, www.francemusique.fr.

these feverish lines—really difficult time—and so little help, in spite of Annette struggling more than she can." (June 5, 1962).

A few days later, Boulanger again seems fatigued by her frantic pace of life and wishes Robbins were with her:

> Indeed wish to write but have so much to do and so little help that the problems are unsolved—queer period, under, for all, such a pression! But everything remains present and I still bless "my" VW!
>
> How big is our shrinked world—everywhere is everywhere—but you are there, and I am here! It makes the whole difference. Going Tuesday to England: London —> Bath —> London —> Bath —> London —> around —> London. . . .
>
> And when I think how easy it could be! Pray for me—pray for these weeks to come. So heavy! And realize how much I have left in my VW. [June 9, 1962]

"How easy it could be" with Robbins as driver and companion. "How much I have left in my VW," she writes. Her heavy burden of engagements was lighter with Robbins by her side in the VW, as she could relax and chat with her humorous friend in the intervals between commitments.

Old Age

In September 1967, Boulanger's eightieth birthday was celebrated by students and friends. On December 10, Robbins writes a nostalgic letter about the travels they shared, both in Europe and in the United States:

> I also think of you all the time, with so much gratitude for all the enlightenment in music and teaching that you have given me. I do not know exactly how to say what I mean, but I think it is the attitude towards all the arts—the sense of craftsmanship, the sense of honesty, the sense of the essential, and of course, the sense of beauty.
>
> All my studies with you and all those wonderful excursions with you—the Pyrenees, Rome, Angoulême, Poitiers, Tours (mostly in the middle of the night!), Dumbarton Oaks, the White House (at least to the door)—too many places to recall at this moment. Oh dear! I will have to stop writing about all those wonderful times. I cannot stand it!

What Robbins gained from Boulanger—"the sense of craftsmanship, the sense of honesty, the sense of the essential, and of course, the sense of beauty"—is an apt summary of what many received from this twentieth-century master. Boulanger's influence was only in part due to consummate musicianship. She expressed her beliefs by how she lived. Boulanger opened people's minds and senses. She connected her students to a purpose higher than personal success. She found beauty congruent with the morally good. Craftsmanship, honesty, beauty, and a sense of the essential were learned not from her lectures but from the standards to which she held herself, standards that made being a musician inseparable from living a life of virtue and quality.

Their correspondence became less frequent as the years wore on. They did not see each other. Their friendship was not over, but it was now something that had happened in the past. In a letter dated January 7, 1974, Boulanger—now eighty-six—again looks back at former times and considers how memory can bring joy into the present. Yet one feels her deep melancholy, one that cannot quite be banished by thoughts of the past and hopes for the future:

> What a joy brings your letter!
>
> I also keep present our adventures, the vain search for one pleasant place to have lunch on the highway, and hundreds and hundreds of details, always present. Alas! Many sad memories exist, as well. You probably did not hear of the passing of Barbara Trask, which causes me great sadness.
>
> With her, too, so many evocations of the past have abolished the distance between California and Paris.
>
> With you, I keep on and keep on dreaming that you will announce your arrival tomorrow, for just half a day, but it would mean seeing you and going on hoping and thinking of you so profoundly, so tenderly, so affectionately, so faithfully.
>
> I remain your poor old half broken,
>
> Nadia Boulanger

Two years later, in a birthday letter to Robbins, Boulanger gives an idea of her inner life and her view of how to live in a world of turmoil:

> Soon it will be the 21st of January,[35] and I fear I shall be late, and it causes me real trouble, for you know you are so often on my mind.
>
> Life goes on here as usual, unbearable to everybody, even for me, but I still survive. . . .

35 RR's birthday.

> Seem to be dominated by a hope to have the mail in order, all answered, and that enters already in the field of impossibility, but the mind remains free, and I am often with you, thinking, hearing, remembering, and it would not be fair to say that you are absent. Unseen, yes—but absent, no, by no means. And with deep affection I send you wishes. I hope you go through the turmoil spread over the whole world, sufficiently absorbed in your own activities, that you perceive the necessity to pursue our own efforts more than ever. [January 1976]

Life seems unbearable. The best she can do is to keep herself busy while letting her mind freely wander to the happiness she has known in the past. She keeps lifelong friends close to her by "thinking, hearing, remembering." This enables her to feel that friends are "unseen, yes—but absent, no, by no means."

By 1977, Boulanger was dictating brief letters to friends, no longer writing them in her own hand. However, in her last communication with Robbins, a Christmas greeting in 1978, she wrote in her hand "Happy Christmas, Faithful wishes" and signed her complete name. The rest of the note was dictated and is written in another hand:

> Thank you so much for your letter, dear Ruth. It is so good to hear from you, though it would be so much better to see you. Well, dreams sometimes come to realization!
>
> With love and hopes

Robbins's last letter to Boulanger was a birthday note for Boulanger's ninety-second birthday. In it, Robbins details how she is moving from Massachusetts to California, throwing away as much as possible—but not the stones that Boulanger collected in Santa Barbara:

> I am in a tremendous upheaval as I decided to move to California to be near my sister and her family. The movers will be here next week, and I have been frantically going through things to dispose as much as possible.
>
> Among the wonderful treasures are so many reminders of you! Programs, letters, photos, music, and, yes, a bowl full of stones you collected in Santa Barbara.
>
> I am very reluctantly giving up rocks I have collected from Montana, Colorado, and California, but yours I will keep to be reminded of so many wonderful times with you. [September 4, 1979]

Boulanger died six weeks later, on October 22.

Throughout the next several decades, Robbins kept the memories of Boulanger deep in her heart, sharing favorite letters with her grandnieces who lived across the lawn in California. Then, on July 9, 2005, Boulanger's beloved student Idil Biret, whom Robbins first met in 1952, spent the afternoon playing for Robbins, bringing to life "the sense of craftsmanship, the sense of honesty, the sense of the essential, and of course, the sense of beauty" that Boulanger embodied and shared with so many.[36]

Immersed in the beauty of Biret's videotaped performance during her last months, Robbins was able to drift back to memories of the lifelong friendship she had been so fortunate to experience. With windows open to the fresh scents of California redwoods and

---

36 Letter 67-6.

canyon oaks, the video played throughout the morning. Listening to Biret play Chopin, Robbins died peacefully at age ninety-five at 11 a.m. on December 10, 2005, having outlived her beloved mentor by more than a quarter century.

The music had finally stopped for both of them, but their love of beauty lives on in the words they left behind.

Idil Biret plays for Turkey's president İsmet İnönü in 1946. [Idil Biret Archive]

Left to right: Narcís Bonet, Annette Dieudonné, Idil Biret, Nadia Boulanger, and Jean Françaix at Fontainebleau in 1952. [Idil Biret Archive]

IDIL BIRET (B. 1941)

At her twelfth birthday party, celebrated at Nadia Boulanger's salon on rue Ballu, Idil Biret was round-faced, lighthearted, and fun, her corkscrew curls dark and bouncy. She wore a pink dress and giggled as she held Tasha, Boulanger's beloved and spoiled cat. After cakes and tea were served, Biret—at Boulanger's request—went to one of the two grand pianos in the large living room of "Mademoiselle" (as Boulanger was often called). Biret sat poised, serious, silent. She took a breath and drew her hands up from her lap. Her tiny fingers seemed to elongate, then they flew—no, soared—into Mozart's Piano Concerto in C Minor. She played with tenderness and joy. Awestruck, adults in the room ceased conversation. All heads turned as they realized something miraculous was occurring. How could a small child play with this mature, refined, and indeed extraordinary artistry?[37]

In her native Turkey, Biret has been a cultural avatar from the moment in 1946 when President İsmet İnönü requested an unplanned

37 My sister Susan L. Miller provided this description of the party. Fourteen at the time and living with RR in Paris that year, she was invited by NB to provide a youthful companion for Biret in a salon of serious adults.

performance following a concert attended by diplomats and political leaders in Ankara. She was five. Her mother, Leman Biret, described this extraordinary event:

> When Hasan Ali Yücel [minister of education] told Idil that Inönü wanted her to play, her reply, as though she had awaited this for a long time—"I will play after the concert"—made everyone laugh. When her turn came, she was taken to the piano and seated on top of a pile of musical scores so that she could reach the keys. Her teacher, Turkish composer and pianist Mithat Fenmen, stood near her and introduced the pieces she would play. We waited to see what she would do and the reaction she would get from playing in this surprise situation. As confident and natural as if she were at home, she played the Prelude in C Major from Bach's *Well-Tempered Clavier* in one go, then moving on to the C Minor Prelude. Idil was not finding the thunderous applause unnatural . . . and continuing as though performing was something she had been doing forever. Here she was, bringing down the house and causing people to wipe tears from their eyes, but she was as oblivious to this as if she were eating at the kitchen table or playing with her toys.[38]

Idil Biret with Mithat Fenmen [Idil Biret Archive]

38 Dominique Xardel, *Idil Biret: A Turkish Pianist on the Concert Stages of the World* (Idil Biret Archive, 2009), 183. Private English translation of *Une pianiste Turque en France* (Paris: Buchet-Chastel, 2006).

Child Wonder

The five-year-old's performance had a tremendous impact on Turkey's political elite. At the next session of the Turkish Parliament, a special act was passed—Idil's Law—providing for her training abroad. Mithat Fenmen, her first teacher, had trained in Paris as a teenager at the École normale de musique under Alfred Cortot and Nadia Boulanger. It was natural that Biret would follow in his footsteps.

In 1948, at age seven, Biret went with her parents to Paris, where her genius was immediately recognized. Like Fenmen, she, too, studied with Cortot and Boulanger. Wilhelm Kempff, amazed at her talent, also took her under his wing.

"Biret was a pupil and protégé of three of the greatest musicians of the last century . . . and her legacy of recordings is worthy of her heritage," wrote Richard Dyer in a *Boston Globe* review of her recordings.[39] "She played regularly for the German pianist, but he did not want to interfere with her preparatory studies, telling her he would work with her after she had graduated," he notes.

Nonetheless, when she was eleven, Kempff did invite her to perform the Mozart Concerto for Two Pianos with him, along with other works by Haydn, Bach, and Mozart, at the Théâtre des Champs-Elysées. They were an unprecedented duo—the fifty-eight-year-old master at the top of his game, with the eleven-year-old child by his side.

Under Boulanger's tutelage, at fifteen Biret graduated from the Paris Conservatory with three firsts (roughly the equivalent of a master of arts summa cum laude), an extraordinary accomplishment

39 Dyer, "Pianist Idil Biret."

for anyone but unprecedented for someone so young. She then began her studies with Cortot and Kempff.[40] "What both Kempff and Cortot had was this wonderful breathing through deep legato," Biret said in her interview with Dyer. "I am still working to achieve that—practicing always without pedal, then the pedal must come in like the 'third hand,' giving a certain sound that is magic. . . . Kempff hated hard, harsh sounds, and his way of using the pedal was unique and refined. I remember once I played Beethoven's *Hammerklavier* for him, and he said, 'It's too bombastic—always be careful to leave something more, to give the feeling that you can do more.'"[41]

Mature Artist

At sixteen, Biret began a career as a soloist with the most distinguished orchestras in the world, including the London Symphony, the Philharmonia, the London Philharmonic, the Boston Symphony, the Leningrad Philharmonic, the Leipzig Gewandhaus, the Staatskapelle Dresden, the Orchestre de la Suisse Romande, the Tokyo Philharmonic, the Warsaw Philharmonic, the Orchestre national de France, and the Sydney Symphony.

Nadia Boulanger inscription: "To my little Idil, Christmas 1959. May the Angel guide and protect her on the beautiful and perilous path she has started upon." [Idil Biret Archive]

In 1971, at age twenty-nine, Biret was named a State Artist of Turkey for

40 Xardel, *Idil Biret*, 49–62.

41 Dyer, "Pianist Idil Biret."

her outstanding contributions to Turkish culture. Biret had learned well from her masters.

Her 15-CD Chopin set won her a Polish Grand Prix du Disque Frédéric Chopin in 1995 and praise from Mahler biographer Henry-Louis de la Grange, who applauded her "authority, epic sense, rigor, power, emotion, poetry, and daring." In his *Boston Globe* review, Dyer notes that her complete Rachmaninoff is "unsurpassed for aristocratic, passionate pianism, and exacting musicianship."

Scholar and music critic Bernard Jacobson wrote,

> As the author of a book about Brahms, I do not think I can praise Idil Biret's set of his piano music more highly than by acknowledging that her performances have transformed my understanding and intensified my love for it. . . . Her achievement is a triumph, and calls for a resounding bravo from all lovers of Brahms.[42]

For broad scope and sheer quantity, Biret's recording output is extraordinary. Her more than one hundred records since the 1960s include the first recordings of Liszt's transcriptions of the nine symphonies of Beethoven for EMI (recorded at the Church of Chaumont-Gistoux in Belgium in 1986), Berlioz's Symphonie Fantastique for Atlantic/Finnadar, and for Naxos, the complete piano works of Brahms, Chopin, and Rachmaninoff; the three sonatas of Boulez (the recording received the Diapason d'or de l'année award in France in 1995); the Études of Ligeti; and the *Firebird* piano transcription by Stravinsky, with a Marco Polo disc of the piano compositions and transcriptions of her mentor Wilhelm Kempff. Other recordings include Beethoven's thirty-two

42 Henry de la Grange and Bernard Jacobson quotes are from Dyer, "Pianist Idil Biret."

sonatas and five piano concertos and the many LPs she made for Decca, Vega, EMI, and Atlantic Records in France, Germany, and the United States, as well as recently recorded concertos of Grieg, Liszt, Ravel, Saint-Saëns, Schumann, and Tchaikovsky. Her recording of the five Hindemith piano concertos with the Yale Symphony Orchestra was released worldwide by Naxos in October 2013 to commemorate the fiftieth anniversary of the composer's death.[43]

Şefik Büyükyüksel

A key factor in Biret's continued productivity and creativity has been the support of her husband, Şefik Büyükyüksel. He was born on the European side of the Bosphorus Strait, he likes to point out. Büyükyüksel's mother, who dealt with depression, found solace at the piano, and he grew up with his mother's love for music. In 1961, he came to live with our family for a year as an exchange student. He gladly accepted my father's offer of piano lessons, considering it a great privilege.

The author with Şefik Büyükyüksel, Aspen, 1961

That Christmas, Büyükyüksel traveled with the family to Aspen for a ski vacation. There, at a family reunion of twenty-odd aunts, uncles, cousins, and in-laws, Şefik first met Ruth Robbins. He played the old upright in the lodge common room, and she stopped to listen, encouraging him. Another evening he met famed aviator Charles Lindbergh, whose son Jon had married a cousin. Büyükyüksel sat alone outdoors, apart from the family bustle. Charles Lindbergh came

43 Idil Biret official website biography: www.idilbiret.eu.

out on the porch, saw him on the steps, and asked how he was doing. They talked for fifteen minutes; Lindbergh was curious about this lonely Turk and his plans for the future. The brief encounter made an impression on Büyükyüksel. When he joined the management of Turkish Airlines and later the Association of European Airlines, he kept on his wall the signed photo of the most famous plane in aviation history, the *Spirit of St. Louis*.

Büyükyüksel and I were classmates at Yale. He enjoyed playing the baby grand in the Davenport common room and would travel most weekends to Greenwich Village to collect classical recordings in secondhand record stores. Fellow music lovers frequently came to his room, where they would share records.

During college and his army years, Büyükyüksel successfully resisted the advances of matrimonially inclined women, but once his career was established, he was able to think expansively about a partner in life. His vision quickly narrowed to only one woman, Idil Biret, a distant cousin, who by the time she was in her early twenties was already the most famous musician in Turkey, where she performed regularly between her world tours as a concert pianist.

Büyükyüksel's management position with Turkish Airlines meant that on his days off he could get free standby tickets anywhere the airline flew. Thus was he able to pursue Biret concert by concert not only within Turkey but around the world. Whether he stood at the stage door with a bouquet of flowers after every performance is uncertain, but eventually, Biret saw him for the man he was. They have now been married over forty-five years.

It may be that no marriage is truly made in heaven, but some achieve a balance that serves the parties well. Büyükyüksel is Biret's guardian against the vicissitudes and distractions of contracts and tax authorities, and he arranges her tours and recordings. Biret provides him entry to a sublime realm of beauty, the breadth and depth of which are experienced only by the few and the very fortunate.

Idil Biret and Şefik Büyükyüksel playing chess, Istanbul, 1976
[Idil Biret Archive]

Biret the Person

Biret is a delight to be with, frequently smiling, no doubt in part because her imagination is constantly filled with beautiful passages she loves as she toys with tones, tempos, crescendos, and diminuendos in her mind. Extraordinarily gentle and sensitive, Biret is keenly aware of others. Her facility in music also extends to language. She has maintained close friendships over the decades in Turkish, French, and English and enjoys completing crosswords in all three languages.

Biret loves to swim in the ocean, so every June she and Büyükyüksel charter a boat out of Fethiye, Turkey, to meander around Aegean isles and inlets off the southern coast of Turkey. They also try every winter to spend a couple of weeks in Honolulu, where Biret can swim at her beloved Waikiki Beach. Guests on Büyükyüksel's boat are varied: professors, musicians, former business colleagues, relatives, and childhood friends, but all have decades of shared experience with Büyükyüksel and Biret. These friendships have endured over the years, and each June they are renewed once more, marking off yet another year on the clear blue waters of the Aegean.

It is a movable feast from inlet to islet, idling in picturesque coves, swimming, eating, conversing, reading, napping. Biret plays an eighty-eight-key digital keyboard below deck, next to the galley, smiling and nodding as she skims over passages for upcoming performances. The cook and deckhand listen in silent reverence as they shell beans or peel potatoes.

When Biret swims, she is a sight to behold. She dons a dark dry suit, miniflippers, hand webs, goggles, and a bright red tasseled bathing cap Büyükyüksel insists she wear so she can be easily sighted by passing boats as she paddles through the sea. She swims at a slow, steady pace for an hour or more at a time, achieving a distant point, then returning. I can only imagine the music coursing through her imagination, tempo kept by the slow rhythm of her swimming and the staccato wavelets lapping against her red cap.

Unlike most classical pianists, Biret does not have a fixed repertoire. With her photo- and audiographic memories, she can sight-read and simultaneously hear a full orchestration in her head, creating her interpretations and emphases on the fly. She has often filled in for other pianists when needed because she can play anything at the highest standards simply by reviewing the piece and running through it before a performance.

No matter how sublime her classical pianism may be, Biret

knows how to thoroughly enjoy the casual musical performance as well. She loves to improvise spontaneously and plays the keyboard for her brother-in-law Ibraham's rock-and-roll band reunions. Once, a Yale classmate who had given up his legal career to play jazz and blues in nightclubs sat at the digital keyboard to teach Biret blues rhythms and chords. Biret stared at his fingers, cocked her ear, and within a few seconds joined him, laughing as she played enthusiastic two-handed blues riffs over my classmate's bass line.

Biret and Turkish Culture

Biret was born into a bright day of outward-facing secularism and open-mindedness in a nation looking abroad for the best practices and ideas to adopt into Turkish culture. She was sent to Paris by a Turkish legislature enthusiastic about embracing Western culture so she could learn from the most renowned teacher in the musical world. It was this same cultural expansiveness that brought Büyükyüksel and other Turks of his generation to the United States and Europe not just as students but as lifelong global citizens loving the best of all cultures.

Idil Biret with Wilhelm Kempff, 1982
[Idil Biret Archive]

The amazing trajectory of Biret's life embodies the ideals of the Turkish cultural renaissance initiated by Kemal Atatürk, founder of the modern Turkish republic as a means of bringing his young republic out of the grips of the sclerotic, self-absorbed Ottoman conservatism and into the full daylight of Western civilization. Wilhelm Kempff had been a key figure in Turkey's cultural expansion and modernization. In a Bayerischer Rundfunk public service radio program recorded in 1995, Biret describes the first meeting of the great German pianist with the great Turkish revolutionary and statesman as Kempff related it to her in June 1982, when she was visiting with Kempff at his villa overlooking the Mediterranean in the village of Positano on the Amalfi coast.

> Later, after dinner, the question of his first visit to Turkey was posed. Was it in the 1930s? "No, much earlier" was Kempff's reply. "I first visited Turkey in 1927. I gave a recital in Ankara at the Halkevi.[44] Kemal Pasha then invited me for dinner with his friends at the Presidential residence. There was a large gathering of people in the evening and the dinner lasted until about 11:00 p.m.
>
> As the guests were leaving, he asked me to stay behind, and when everyone was gone, we passed into his study. There, Kemal Pasha started the conversation by saying that as part of a drive for modernization in Turkey he was introducing many reforms in law, education, and other areas affecting the public life.
>
> He continued to say that classical music was an integral part of the Western culture, the source of his reform movement. He therefore felt the necessity of the widespread introduction of classical music in Turkey as part of the drive towards modernization in the country.
>
> Kemal Pasha said he was afraid that without also parallel reforms in music in Turkey, his reforms in other areas would remain incomplete. Kemal Pasha then asked my thoughts

44 A hall for public concerts, theater, and the like.

> on how this could be achieved, the schools, institutions to be formed for this purpose and the eminent musicians and musicologists I may recommend for invitation to Turkey to help build the foundations of classical music.[45]

There can be no revolution without music, Atatürk believed. Classical music was integral to Euopean culture, and European culture was the source of his reform movement. Kempff brought Paul Hindemith to Atatürk's attention. The rising star of composition was promptly engaged by Atatürk to help found the state conservatory in Ankara and to organize Turkey's system of musical education.

The Turkish cultural revolution went far beyond music. Never hesitant to take sweeping measures, Atatürk took advantage of the fact that the Turkish population was largely illiterate and in 1928 personally introduced his newly alphabetized Turkish language to the country. Thereafter, the Arabic script of written Turkish—never a good fit—was eliminated, and fifteen million illiterate Turks learned to read and pronounce their native language using the Western alphabet.

Educated and cultured Turks rejoiced at the opening of the country toward the best of what Europe had to offer, and even common people could take pride in sending this enormously talented curly headed girl to represent Turkey on the European stage. The legislature was unanimous in its vote to provide funds. For many, Biret was an expression of the "natural joy" of the Turkish people.[46]

Nadia Boulanger showed her support of classical music in Turkey; after all, she had been entrusted with the education of Turkey's

---

45 Xardel, *Idil Biret*, 56–57.

46 "The nation has shed its blood to correct its errors: It is now at peace and can give vent to its natural joy," Atatürk exclaimed in 1928, maintaining that traditional Ottoman music, "this simple music, can no longer satisfy the highly developed soul and feelings of the Turk." Andrew Mango, *Atatürk: The Biography of the Founder of Modern Turkey* (New York: Overlook Press, 2000), p. 466.

most outstanding musical prodigy. After Biret graduated from the Paris Conservatory, Boulanger, with the help of Mithat Fenmen, arranged for Biret to play in two concerts in September 1958 in Istanbul and Ankara. The program consisted of three concertos: Mozart's Piano Concerto no. 24 in C Minor, K. 491; the Symphonic Variations of César Franck; and Schumann's Piano Concerto in A Minor, op. 54. At sixteen, Biret found the tour schedule demanding and, frankly, would have preferred to use the beautiful September weather to swim in the refreshing waters of Moda Bay below her family apartment instead of practicing for her performances.[47] Years later, Biret recalled,

> The rehearsals with the orchestra had begun and also the socializing (dinners, cocktail parties, et cetera). I was not looking forward to these gatherings, as I was of an age where I didn't quite belong to the adult world but was not anymore a child. During one of these parties, I started to drink what I thought was a lemonade. After two or more of these delicious nectars, we were invited to join the dinner table. I felt wonderful, a little weightless maybe.
>
> . . . .Nothing mattered anymore. . . . The piercing looks of Nadia Boulanger and my mother were immediately on me. I was then trying to explain to my neighbor, a nice elderly gentleman, that I was feeling slightly bizarre, as I had some of the tasty lemonade before. The gentleman exclaimed, "You had not lemonade but a white ladies' cocktail, you poor thing!" Neither my mother, nor Mademoiselle Boulanger, was amused by this incident.
>
> Throughout the tour, the strict control I experienced

47 Xardel, *Idil Biret*, 45–46.

> continued to function in daily life and in music. My teacher was even conducting the cadenzas, where I was supposed to be free. . . . So I didn't keep fond memories of this Turkish tour in general. Nadia Boulanger was visiting museums, attending parties and dinners, meeting officials with her usual boundless energy. In Ankara, she found a great new friend in the person of Mr. C. M. Altar, an extremely cultured, refined musicologist who was under-secretary at the Ministry of Culture. Whenever a problem arose, Mlle Boulanger would say, "I trust my dear Mr. Altar will find the right solution." And she was right. One of the great moments occurred when Mlle Boulanger met my grandmother: two formidable women facing each other! They were only able to communicate verbally through the help of a translator, but they could understand and feel far better in a sort of telepathic way when they were in the presence of each other.[48]

Boulanger accompanied Biret on another tour of Turkey in 1962, Boulanger conducting the orchestra and Biret the piano soloist. "The Turkish government treated Boulanger like visiting royalty, assigning her a lady-in-waiting and rooms in the most elegant hotels," notes Biret.[49] The relationship between Boulanger and Biret was deep yet fraught. "God sent me this child who is the soul of my sister Lili. It's unbelievable!" Boulanger confided to a friend. She once gave Biret a card picturing an angel with these words: "To my little Idil, Christmas 1959. May the Angel guide and protect her on the beautiful and perilous path she has started upon."

48 Idil Biret, interview with James Miller, Cordes-sur-Ciel, France, December 2019.

49 Idil Biret, *Idil Biret: Life and Music* (Philadelphia, Chestnut Hill Press, Fall 2023).

Yet Biret felt uncomfortable with Boulanger's strictness and inflexibility: "In spite of my great affection and respect for Mlle. Boulanger, I felt somewhat cramped under her direction. She disciplined me and would not allow me any freedom, even in the cadenzas."[50]

Biret continues to bring brilliant pianism to audiences around the world, gives master classes, and records. In April 2020, Istanbul's Bosphorus Bridge connecting Europe with Asia was closed by the Turkish government for COVID lockdown. A concert grand piano was placed at its exact center. There, at the precise spot Europe and Asia meet, Biret played Liszt's piano transcription of "Ode to Joy" from Beethoven's Ninth Symphony. This highly symbolic performance was recorded by the Directorate of Communications of the Presidency of the Republic of Turkey and released on its YouTube channel as "A call for love and unity . . . to the whole world."[51] Who could better represent the unity of Asia with Europe, of Turkey with the world, than Idil Biret?

Despite this propaganda piece (or conceptual art, if you prefer), the cultural revolution started by Atatürk—Turkey's embrace of European civilization, which Biret carried forward so magnificently for seven decades—is now in its demise.

The start of Turkey's turn to the West and toward European civilization was symbolized by Atatürk's conversion of Hagia Sophia from mosque to museum in 1935, six years before Biret's birth.

The magnificent Hagia Sophia, a domed architectural masterpiece, was built by the Roman emperor Justinian I over five years, from 532 to 537. For more than nine hundred years, it was the largest cathedral in Christendom—until, in 1453, Constantinople fell to attacking

50 Xardel, *Idil Biret*, 46.

51 Beethoven's "Ode to Joy," with lyrics by Giscard Rasquin, is the anthem of the European Union and of the Council of Europe, representing the whole of Europe; its purpose is to honor shared European values of freedom, peace, and solidarity. "Promotional video released for the Presidential concert on April 23," https://www.youtube.com/watch?v=r8SvyfZWOFY.

Ottoman forces. When Sultan Mehmed entered the city, he performed the Friday prayer and khutbah (sermon) in Hagia Sophia. This marked the official conversion of Hagia Sophia into a mosque and cemented the role of Ottoman sultans as preeminent leaders of both Islam and the empire.

Atatürk's 1935 rejection of Islam as a state religion to form a secular state was reversed on July 10, 2020, less than three months after Biret's symbolic performance precisely on the border of Asia and Europe. The Turkish Council of State, under the thumb of President Recep Tayyip Erdoğan, decreed that Hagia Sophia can be used only as a mosque and not for any other purpose. This blatant imitation of Sultan Mehmed's conversion of church to mosque in 1453 made Erdoğan's rejection of secularism absolutely clear. He attempts to cloak himself in a mantle of Ottoman supremacy, harking back to long-lost days of glory, when much of the Muslim world was under the central command of the reigning Ottoman sultan.

Time will tell whether Turkey's Islamist leadership can successfully eradicate from Turkish culture this eighty-five-year opening to European cultural values.

Long ago, in a review of Biret's November 22, 1963, Boston performance of Rachmaninoff's Third Piano Concerto, Margo Miller commented that "the fiery qualities of the piece . . . Idil Biret attacked with the rapture of youth." She highlighted Biret's touch ("Round sounds in the opening allegro were as pleasing and apt as the glittering tones she drew later in the finale"), then praised her dynamic range and unerring sense of phrasing.[52] Nearly six decades later, Biret plays with the same "rapture of youth," albeit with a more nuanced understanding derived from years of attuning her sensibilities to the essence of composers she has loved all her life.

52 Miller, "Tribute to Kennedy," 22.

Nadia Boulanger dedicated her life to passing the torch of the great tradition of European classical music; she guided her students to be aware of the craftsmanship, honesty, beauty, and essence of the works of art they were playing or composing. Idil Biret took what she absorbed from Nadia Boulanger, Wilhelm Kempff, Alfred Cortot, and the host of musicians she studied with or listened to and transformed it into the highest expression of the Western musical tradition. She has brought extraordinary gifts to audiences and students throughout the world and preserved them in recordings that will be available for generations to come.

Idil Biret at Woolsey Hall, Yale University, 2012 / photo: Harold Shapiro

Ruth Robbins (1910–2005)

Berkeley, California

The midmorning mists of December 10, 2005, dispersed when sunlight poured over the Berkeley hills. Spread out to the west was a triptych: to the left, towering insurance and banking edifices against a blue sky; at the center, reddish curves hanging between the two towers of the Golden Gate Bridge; and to the right, the graceful wooded slopes of Mount Tamalpais. The foreground was defined by the broad San Francisco Bay itself; the backdrop was the endless Pacific. Inside a cottage in a family compound that looked out on this view, Ruth Robbins faintly inhaled, then allowed a final sigh to escape and blend with the scents of the eucalyptus, redwoods, and canyon oaks outside her open window. Ruth Robbins died as she had lived: in peace, immersed in the music she loved.

In her last weeks, Robbins rested more than usual. She spent hours, eyes closed, listening to a videotape made five months earlier, on July 9. Idil Biret and Şefik Büyükyüksel traveled to California to celebrate the one hundredth birthday of Robbins's older sister, Helen Robbins Miller, the matriarch of Millerama, a family compound of three homes on a Berkeley hillside above the University of California campus.

Büyükyüksel had first met my aunt five decades earlier, when he was an exchange student, but Biret had known Ruth Robbins a decade longer. The extraordinary child prodigy, at age seven, left Turkey with her parents to study at the Paris Conservatory under the tutelage of Nadia Boulanger. There, at a 1953 Fontainebleau summer music program,[53] Biret met Ruth Robbins. By then, Robbins had grown from a student into a friend of Boulanger. Biret remembers how—in the salon culture of formal and polite discourse under the strict supervision of Boulanger—Ruth Robbins stood out as the one warm person who related to her as she was, a child in the present, not as a talent to be guided and shaped for a future she never chose.

Once, Biret injured her finger riding a bike. Fearing reprimand for endangering herself, she did not dare tell anyone for days—until she found Robbins, who hugged the child and told her everything would be OK as she cleansed and bandaged the wound. In an interview, Biret described the event as follows:

---

53 During the First World War, by order of General John "Black Jack" Pershing, who wanted to improve the quality of United States military band music, the then conductor of the New York Philharmonic, Walter Damrosch (1862–1950), was asked to organize a school in Chaumont, where United States troops were headquartered. It would be led by composer and teacher Francis Casadesus (1870–1954). After the war, in 1921, Damrosch and Casadesus decided to continue this successful operation. With the full support of French authorities, the American Conservatory—as it was called—was granted permission to open in the Louis XV wing of the Château de Fontainebleau. The American Conservatory (Conservatoire Américain de Fontainebleau) aimed to offer the best French musical education to young, promising musicians. NB, then a young composition/harmony professor, was among this distinguished faculty from the beginning. Her energy, knowledge, and spirit guided the school until her death in 1979. See http://fontainebleauschools.org/about.

I always wanted to learn how to ride a bicycle. My parents, concerned about the risks—falling down, hurting my hand, etc.—opposed, with a strong veto, what they thought was a childish whim. But I had made my mind up, so I started practicing under the supervision of a charming and patient young student, Eleanor Caluori, in the forest of Fontainebleau. Of course, this was done without telling my parents. In one fall I had while riding, I hurt my finger. I didn't dare speak about it to my parents. The only person I felt would be able to help me was Miss Ruth Robbins. I had a real trust in her natural way of behaving with N. Boulanger—completely different from other people, who reminded me of rabbits paralyzed with terror, fixed in the headlights of an approaching car at night. She and Winifred Johnstone[54] took me to a doctor, who asked me when this accident had happened.[55] Childishly, I replied, "Two days ago." In fact, a week had already elapsed since the accident, and my finger was quite swollen. I was supposed to act in the role of a child prodigy in a satirical opera that Jean Françaix had written about Parisian intellectual snobbery. With my bandaged finger, I played a short virtuoso piece and sang a song titled "Messire Yvain est Toujours à la Fenêtre."[56] The day following my operatic debut, I went back with Misses Robbins and Johnstone,

54 Spycket, *Nadia Boulanger,* 98–99. Winifred Hope Johnstone "became a very close friend . . . helping [Nadia] in many ways and even acting as her secretary when Boulanger had to stay in the States during the war."

55 Eleanor Caluori (b. 1943) went on to attend Wellesley and wrote her senior thesis on the Italian Baroque composer Luigi Rossi (1598–1653), graduating in 1965. She is the author of *The Cantatas of Luigi Rossi: Analysis and Thematic Index*, Studies in Musicology, (Ann Arbor: UMI Research Press, 1981).

56 Jean Françaix's (1912–1997) comic opera appears to have been based on Chrétien de Troyes's (1135–c. 1191) *Yvain ou le Chevalier au lion* and includes the lines, "Messire Yvain était toujours à la fenêtre, d'où il la regardait; plus il la contemplait, plus elle lui plaisait, plus il l'aimait. [M. Yvain stood fixed at the window, whence he looked out; the more he viewed her, the more she pleased him, and the more he loved her]."

> this time to a clinic, where I was immediately operated on. I had quite a serious form of paronychia. Fortunately, my finger soon improved, and even better, I had to spend the next ten days in bed, which meant no practicing and no stern critiques. My parents brought me tea and cookies, and I read whatever I wanted. To this day, I vividly remember the Jack London adventures I read: *Call of the Wild* and *White Fang*. And I will never forget the support Miss Robbins gave me during this period. She was a rock of optimism, reassuring my horrified parents and equally horrified Nadia Boulanger.[57]

In 2005, when Büyükyüksel and Biret decided to join our extended family to celebrate the one hundredth birthday of my mother, Helen Miller, they looked forward to seeing Ruth Robbins as well. Biret valued being able to spend time with the woman who had befriended her as a child and for whom, so many decades later, she still had the warmest of feelings.

July 8 was Helen's day. Some eighty or so friends and relatives congregated that evening, holding aloft one hundred candles—some with one in each hand—as they sang "Happy Birthday" to her from the lawn below the terrace of the main house. My mother beamed and held her hands high. She felt honored.

But the next day, July 9, was my aunt Ruth Robbins's day.

Biret sat beside my aunt at the cottage's grand piano, playing Liszt's Beethoven symphony transcriptions, Rachmaninoff, Chopin, and works of other composers familiar to so many who had been swept into the Boulanger circle. She played for one hour, then another. Ruth was radiant at her side, smiling with happiness, white hair backlit into a halo by

57 Idil Biret, interview by James Miller, Fethiye, Turkey, June 13–14, 2018.

the afternoon sun behind her. Dozens of nieces and nephews, grand-nieces and grandnephews, children of her grandnieces, and friends of the family sat and stood in the cottage or outside on the lawn, transfixed by the beauty of the music and the magic of the moment.

One grandniece, Gretchen Vogel, a professional videographer, captured this rare and expressive family event. After the performance ended and guests departed, my aunt Ruth treasured Gretchen's video. She watched it and listened to it over and over. It provided the background music to her increasingly quiet days. Listening, she re experienced the deep love she had felt—and still felt—for beautiful music and the people who create it. Sixty-five years earlier, this love had exploded and turned into a passion when Ruth Robbins first came under the influence of Nadia Boulanger at the Longy School of Music.[58]

In her last days, my aunt said few words. She was fading. She had the company of family members, who would sit beside her and listen with her to Biret's playing. You could look down at the pale, peaceful countenance of the aging woman in her bed, then look up to the video screen. You would see the same face, flushed with joy, beaming a wide smile, nodding in time to the music.

At her side when she breathed her last breath was Yangchen, the Tibetan woman who lived in the family compound and was a constant companion to Ruth and Helen. She ran up to Helen's house and said, "Please, you need to come to Ruthie now. I think the end is near." Although she had already witnessed Robbins's death sigh, she wanted Helen to believe that Ruth was still alive, that she could be at her sister's side at the last moment.

Yangchen then called me to tell us Ruth had passed away. My wife, Shiwei, and I went to my aunt's cottage, where she lay still and

58 The Longy School of Music was founded in 1915 by Georges Longy (1868–1930), a French-born oboist and graduate of the Paris Conservatory who had joined the Boston Symphony Orchestra in 1898. Between 1938 and 1943, NB taught advanced courses in harmony, composition, and counterpoint at Longy.

silent on her bed. The room was not silent, however. On the video, Biret was smiling and playing Chopin nocturnes. We kept the video running. It was early afternoon. My mother sat at Ruth's side, looking at her sister and wordlessly listening to Biret play. Our daughter Julia was soon to return from school, and other family members would arrive. We placed a large red-and-green silk scarf around her neck and draped it over her torso. Yangchen straightened the bed and draped a multicolored Tibetan cloth over Ruth. Shiwei found a lipstick and with her finger rubbed color onto Ruth's cheeks, saying, "I don't want Julia to be shocked when she sees her." Over the next two days, Ruth lay in state. Family members gathered to pay their respects and say farewell before the Neptune Society was called to retrieve her remains for cremation. Now her ashes lie in a garden bank amidst the rose bushes that she viewed every day from her cottage door.

• • •

Ruth Robbins led a fulfilled life, a life made more meaningful by the understanding of beauty, culture, values, morality, and strength of purpose she learned from her mentor and friend Nadia Boulanger. Twenty-three years younger than Boulanger, Robbins became one of her favorite companions. Boulanger appreciated Robbins's generosity, honesty, gentle wit, and lack of pretension. Biret, a full generation younger than Ruth, was also a special favorite of Boulanger's, perhaps because Biret's extraordinary talent reminded Boulanger of her beloved younger sister, Lili Boulanger, the gifted composer and pianist whose life tragically ended at age twenty-four. So on that July day in 2005, a silent yet powerful presence in the room was the spirit of Nadia Boulanger, a strong woman who found deep meaning in her personal relationships and who had character-forming influence on both Biret and Robbins.

Weeks after Ruth Robbins's passing, when family members sorted through her possessions, her grandniece Gabby Miller pulled a wooden box from the bookcase. "This is important," she said. "She used to read these to me." The box was filled with letters her great-aunt had treasured.

Gabby and her sister, Nathalie, had grown up across the lawn from Robbins's cottage. They were daily—sometimes several times a day—visitors to the cottage. Their great-aunt listened, read them stories, provided them with art materials and books, taught them music, or just let them be, offering a quiet and calm haven where Gabby and Nathalie were always welcome.

Almost all the letters in the box were handwritten by Nadia Boulanger, with a sprinkling of notes from Annette Dieudonné or Marcelle de Manziarly.[59] Gabby wrote on her website,

> Ruthie and I were extremely close. I grew up across the lawn from Ruthie's cottage. A lot of my teenage years were spent digging through Ruthie's collections. In her twilight years she sent me searching high and low for letters from her lifelong piano teacher, Nadia Boulanger. It was a daily ritual. In her last years, Ruthie would sit at her desk and re-read her favorite letters every day. She would read favorite passages to me with great care. Things like, "How big is

59 Annette Dieudonné (1896–1991) at age 13 was among NB's first pupils. She went on to teach solfège, harmony, and counterpoint and to excel as a pianist, organist, musicologist, and composer. A close professional associate and lifelong friend of NB's, Annette's career included positions at the Conservatoire de Paris, the American Conservatory at Fontainebleau, and École normale de musique. Upon NB's death in 1979, Dieudonné was executor of her estate. Marcelle de Manziarly (1899–1989), a French pianist, music educator, conductor, and composer, was another NB student who became a personal friend. See http://archives-nadiaboulanger.cnsmd-lyon.fr/page20.html.

> our shrinked world? I am here and you are there, and that makes all the difference," or "Read all what is not written and believe me to be, as ever, yours, N.B." She told stories, like when in 1962 she drove Nadia Boulanger to the Kennedy White House in her Volkswagen bug, or how after the Second World War she sent care packages to Paris with soap, sugar, Tootsie Fudge, spices, or canned meats.[60]

Gabby's adult work as an accomplished conceptual artist causes us to step back and think deeply about the world we live in. Gabby absorbed views on life and art from Ruth, and Robbins's own views on life and art had taken a great leap in understanding over six decades earlier, when Nadia Boulanger befriended her and became her mentor.

On the fifth anniversary of Robbins's death, describing the influence of these letters from her great-aunt's mentor, Gabby wrote about a few days she spent in Robbins's cottage:

> I have become especially fixated on a trip where Ruthie drove Boulanger through the night, from the South of France up to Paris. Forty km from the city, the sun was about to rise. Boulanger decided they should stop and watch the sunrise from inside of Chartres Cathedral. Over the years, they return to this morning in their letters. The cathedral filling with light and people. Buying fresh milk and bread from a farmer as they headed back to Paris through backroads.
>
> It is especially lucky that for the month of May the person who lives in the little cottage where Ruthie lived

60 From Gabby Miller website www.gabby-miller.com, September, 2021.

> and died has been out of the house. I was allowed to stay there, poring over the letters, making strange little videos at dawn. The house is a small cathedral to me.
>
> It is hard to believe that it has already been five years since our warm and hysterically funny Roofus Robbins died on December 10, 2005. I was in Vietnam that day and am here again now. It has been nice spending a bit of time this morning reading through emails from 2005, taking a look at silly pictures, drawings, and letters, and trying to remember again how to live like Ruthie: lick the ice cream bowl clean; whisper jokes under your breath; chuckle easily; listen to music carefully and every day; save everything; and give old pantyhose and paper clips as useful Christmas gifts.[61]

Like other family members, I knew Ruth Robbins from childhood—Ruthie, as our cohort of siblings and cousins called her. Until she moved to Belmont, Massachusetts, in 1958, my aunt Ruth lived at my grandparents' house in Highland Park, Illinois, on the shores of Lake Michigan.

She was a well-loved but enigmatic presence in our family. Ruth was a quiet one. She seldom talked about herself. When she did, it was with humorous self-deprecation. We knew she gave piano lessons, traveled to France, and escorted "Mademoiselle Boulanger" on tours of the United States. We had no idea, however, of the important role she played in Nadia Boulanger's life, or how Boulanger had influenced her life, or the deep values my aunt Ruth held, nor indeed the full extent of her humor until we delved into this remarkable four-decade exchange of letters.

61 From Gabby Miller website www.gabby-miller.com, September, 2021.

These letters reveal Robbins's generous character, moral rigor, pragmatism, and wit. She sought clarity from Boulanger about pursuing music in a time of war. Her mentor's responses touch on war, civilization, death, hope, morality, beauty, loss, and love in a clear articulation of the morals and values of one of the great characters on the twentieth-century stage: Nadia Boulanger.

Encountering Nadia Boulanger

In the autumn of 1940, at age fifty-three, Boulanger fled her summer home in Gargenville, France, and headed south to Uzerche. She had taught semester engagements at the Longy School of Music, in Cambridge, Massachusetts, in 1938 and 1939, so she called upon former student Melville Smith, the Longy director, to rush her a three-year full-time contract needed to secure her visa. The fall term had already begun when she obtained her exit visa from Vichy, France. It was not until November that Ruth Robbins first met Boulanger.[62]

By the end of that academic year, Boulanger already felt an affinity for Robbins, for they corresponded in August 1941 about sharing a house together with a second student for the 1941–1942 school year. The honest expression of information, opinion, and feeling in these first letters—August 13, 18, and 20, 1941—set the tone for a correspondence that was to end with Robbins's last letter to Boulanger six weeks before Boulanger's death.

The letters Boulanger wrote to Robbins were stored in the wooden box in her Berkeley cottage, where she read them with her

---

62 Longy was one of four independent degree-granting music schools in the Boston region in the twentieth century, along with the New England Conservatory of Music, Berklee College of Music, and Boston Conservatory. Since 1937, Longy has been located in a stone mansion across the Cambridge Common from Harvard and Radcliffe. A close relationship with those colleges developed, and many of their most talented music students crossed the Cambridge Common to study with Longy's performance faculty.

grandnieces. Robbins's letters to Boulanger were among the vast collection from people important in her life, preserved by Annette Dieudonné. Robbins's estate donated Boulanger's original letters from the wooden box to the Nadia and Lili Boulanger International Center.[63] All the originals that have been found—Robbins's to Boulanger and Boulanger's to Robbins—now share a home in Paris, a fitting final phase of a correspondence that arose from their lengthy separations from each other.

In her last months, asked about the preferred disposition of her mortal remains, my aunt Ruth laughed and said, "That's not my problem!" Yet I think she would be pleased that her immortal remains—words written lovingly over a lifetime—now rest safely in Paris beside the words written by her mentor, protected for posterity by the Nadia and Lili Boulanger International Center.

In her own family, mild-spoken Ruth Robbins did not stand out like her strong-minded siblings. Yet her character and personality can be best understood through the lens of her family background. She lived her life in response to an extraordinarily dynamic home environment that did not fit her. She was born in the wrong nest. She longed for validation of spiritual and aesthetic interests that were not in the Robbins family vocabulary.

Ruth Robbins in 1943

Encountering Nadia Boulanger transformed Ruth Robbins's life, filling an emotional gap. Ruth wanted to learn to live

63 Centre international Nadia et Lili Boulanger, http://www.cnlb.fr.

in beauty—musical, artistic, and moral. She found a guide brilliant at teaching how to connect passion to beauty and to the highest of moral goals—that is, to protect and preserve the fruits of civilization and pass them on to future generations. Who was this unknown, calm-spoken Midwesterner? Why did she and Nadia Boulanger develop a deep lifelong bond?

FAMILY

Ruth Robbins was the middle of five children born to Percy Arthur Robbins (1874–1938) and Sophie Snowell Robbins (1876–1969). Percy was a Victorian renaissance man with multiple skills and wide interests. He was educated at the Chicago Manual Training School, founded in 1883 by the Commercial Club of Chicago, with prominent industrialist George Pullman and retail giant Marshall Field on the board of trustees. The school combined carpentry, drawing, and machine shop with mathematics, science, and language. Practical shop skills, they believed, improved perception, observation, practical judgment, visual accuracy, and manual dexterity and taught the power of doing things instead of merely talking or writing about them.

This view of life as a sequence of material actions for practical ends had an impact on Percy. He went to Cornell, where he was a star halfback and stroked the crew, graduating with a degree in electrical engineering in 1898. Finding scant opportunity in the depressed economy of the time, Percy struck out for South Africa and supported himself upon arrival by playing the violin in restaurants and bars. He networked his way to Kimberley, where by 1902 he was general manager of the De Beers diamond mine. He returned to Chicago to marry his childhood sweetheart, Sophie, and returned with her to South

Africa in 1904. When Sophie became pregnant, she was dispatched to London to deliver her first child, Helen, born in July 1905. The birth was difficult. Sophie developed an infection and fever that left her almost completely deaf. Until portable electronic hearing aids began to appear in the late 1930s, she used an ear trumpet. Communicating with her required shouting into it. Percy did not like to raise his voice, so before long it became Helen's job to shout into the ear trumpet on her father's behalf.

Helen's brother Jim was born two years later in 1907, and they were joined by Ruth in 1910, Pete in 1912, and Jane in 1916.[64] Percy, ever outgoing and entrepreneurial, had left his position in Kimberley in 1906 to manage the development of the new Hollinger gold mines in Timmins, Ontario, Canada. A couple of years later, he struck out to Cobalt, Ontario, where he opened a silver mine for the Timmins brothers, part owners of the Hollinger mines. He then staked claims and opened his gold-mining operation in Kobuk, Alaska. He did well enough to retire with his family to the Claremont Hotel in Berkeley, California, in 1918, in his early forties. Deciding that California was not where he wanted to settle his family, he bought a large Victorian house on the shores of Lake Michigan in Highland Park, Illinois, north of his native Chicago. He soon tore down the old house and built two houses side by side—the main house and a cottage, with ample accommodations for each of his five children. Once settled, he enjoyed playing the violin, drew masterful illustrations, cofounded the Adventurers Club of Chicago, wrote his memoir, and self-published an economic treatise, *The Power of Gold*, before succumbing to cancer at age sixty-three in 1938.

64 "My name is Old English for a skilled swordsman—pierce-eye," Percy asserts in his unpublished autobiography. He nonetheless felt burdened with his unusual given name, so he determined that his children would have only the most common of names; hence Helen, Jim, Ruth, Pete, and Jane.

Sophie, Ruth's mother, was quiet and kind, with a gentle sense of humor. She devoted herself entirely to domestic affairs and family life. Although hard of hearing, she had no problem instructing nursemaids, cooks, or gardeners when the need arose. She could artfully not hear what she did not want to hear and could inject humorous remarks that sometimes surprised. At one family dinner, Ruth's brother Pete sat next to their mother at the table, a tall glass of scotch and ice in his hand. "What are you drinking, Pete?" "It's iced tea, Mother." "Oh, let me have a taste!" He handed the "tea" to her. She took a sip. "It needs more sugar" was Sophie's only comment. Her skills were as subtle and inward as Percy's were bold and outward. She was accepting and non-judgmental, where he was decisive and opinionated.

Ruth's oldest sibling, Helen, identified with her father. Helen's mission in life was to uphold Percy's values, instill them in her children, and judge everybody else against them. As she was the eldest, and perhaps because of her experience amplifying Percy's voice whenever he spoke to Sophie, Helen took upon herself the role of primus inter pares among her siblings.

The second born, Jim, also took after their father. A handsome redhead and avid aviator with a Smilin' Jack mustache, he followed in Percy's footsteps to become a mining engineer. He developed and patented Robbins Mechanical Mole tunneling technology. Since the 1950s, Robbins boring machines have dug major hydroelectric and transportation tunnels around the world, from Niagara Falls to Moscow to Tokyo, including serving both French and English contractors on the fifty-kilometer Chunnel from Folkestone, UK, to Pas-de-Calais, France.

The younger son, Pete, was rebellious, perhaps because he resented constant pressure to excel or because he felt he could not measure up to his older brother. Percy sent preteen Pete to military school in Indiana to straighten him out. Pete, too, became an engineer. He served in the Army Corps of Engineers in Burma during the Second World War under General Joseph "Vinegar Joe" Stilwell, building the Burma Road to enable land shipment of supplies from northeast India to southwest China.

The youngest sibling, Jane, also became an aviator. She served in the Women Airforce Service Pilots (WASP) during the Second World War and was a bush pilot in Alaska after the war. Yet she also inherited Sophie's acceptance and understanding. A highly compassionate person, she shooed spiders and flies outside rather than kill them, and tamed chipmunks, squirrels, and blue jays to eat out of her hand. After her flying days, Jane became a Christian Science practitioner. A lecturer for the Mother Church, she traveled the world spreading the "illness is illusion" spiritualism of Mary Baker Eddy.

Ruth was born right in the middle of this high-octane, adventurous, and strong-willed pack. She was inwardly directed and made little attempt to compete with her siblings. If Ruth inherited her father's artistic and musical sensitivity, she also took after her mother's serenity and quiet humor. Although she knew she valued music and art above all else, she did not know how to escape her family and truly find her way.

Childhood

"On January 21st, 1910, our daughter Ruth was born," wrote Percy Robbins in his unpublished autobiography, "not amid the squalor of a bush hut as some might think because of the location, but in a comfortable home with a trained nurse and a well-qualified doctor in attendance."[65] The location was Cobalt, Ontario, a mining town on the

65 Percy Robbins, "Autobiography of Percy Arthur Robbins" (unpublished typescript, n.d.), 465.

western shore of Lake Timiskaming, some three hundred miles due north of Toronto. Cobalt was a boomtown. Silver had been discovered there in 1903. Ruth's father arrived in late 1907 as general manager of a silver mine owned by financiers he had met in New York City.[66] By 1908, Cobalt was considered the world's largest producer of silver. Today, the population is just over a thousand inhabitants, but the population had reached ten thousand souls by the time Ruth was born.[67]

Soon after Ruth's first birthday, her father moved the family one hundred fifty miles northwest to what is now Timmons, Ontario, where he was general manager in charge of opening the Hollinger Mine to exploit claims for gold-bearing tracts owned by the Timmons brothers, who made their first fortune from silver mining in Cobalt. The mine he opened is still in operation and produced 19.3 million ounces of gold from 1910 to 1968, more than any other single mining operation in Canada.[68] Until she was eight, Ruth lived in this mining town that her father built. As general manager, her father was in charge of everything. He constructed houses for the miners, built them a church and a school, then hired a minister to meet their spiritual needs and teachers to meet their children's educational needs. He also designed and built his family home there.

> Our domestic life was as comfortable as one could desire. The house was modern in every detail, hot and cold water, two bath rooms equipped with modern plumbing, steam heat, electric lights, hardwood floors, plastered walls, Oriental rugs, and all the furniture we needed. Food was

66 Robbins, "Autobiography," 418–420.

67 John Willis, "A Glimpse into the History of Cobalt, Ontario," Canadian Museum of History, last modified August 18, 2015, www.historymuseum.ca/blog/a-glimpse-into-the-history-of-cobalt-ontario/.

68 Operations McEwen Mining, last modified January 2021, www.mcewenmining.com/operations/lexam/.

> the same as we would have had in Toronto or any other city; we kept our own cows and always had a cook and chore-boy to do the house work.[69]

Childhood was rough-and-tumble in northern Ontario. Winter was long and cold, but with low humidity. The children played outdoors even on the coldest of days.

> Most people have a vague notion about winter life in the north, as their ideas are based upon pictures and descriptions of esquimaux, igloos, and the like. We lived in about the same comfort as people do in Chicago, Toronto, Minneapolis, and other cities, but with this advantage: Our winter was always winter. We had days when by comparison the temperature was warmer than usual, but the steady cold lasted for months, and we became adjusted to it in dress and living habits. The air was dry and the cold not nearly so penetrating as one finds it in Chicago and Toronto. We were careful of our extremities, over shoes for the feet, lined gloves for the hands, and caps with ear covers. Frozen noses and cheeks were common, but one experience made people doubly careful, and we learned not to expose ourselves. . . .
>
> Many of us used snow shoes more or less, for although the roads were usually broken, it was a pleasure to cut across country on top of the snow, feeling independent of the roads. Helen and Jim [Ruth's older sister and brother] had their little snow shoes and enjoyed them tremendously: Jim learned to use his snow shoes before he was

69 Robbins, "Autobiography," 465.

> able to walk, the flat webs seeming to help him to balance his heavy body. He had an experience which might have been serious, but which fortunately was not. A member of the mine staff noticed a pair of little snow shoes lying on the snow, and going to pick them up, was surprised to find Jim attached to them. A drift, five or six feet deep, had formed against a ledge on the hillside, and Jim, coming to the edge of the ledge, had lost his balance and toppled head first into the drift, with the result that he was suspended upside down in the snow with only his snow shoes showing.[70]

Ruth's younger brother and sister were born in Timmons, Pete in 1912 and Jane in 1916. The family remained in Timmons until the United States entered World War I in 1917, when Percy decided to return to the United States and retire from working for others. He moved the family to the tower suite at the Claremont Hotel in Berkeley, California. At that time, a trolley line ran from the intersection of Claremont and Ashby Avenues at the foot of the Claremont Hotel property directly down to the ferry slip in Oakland. Percy would commute by trolley and ferry to downtown San Francisco to conduct his business affairs, offer his consulting services to the war effort, investigate gold-mining opportunities in Alaska, and manage his assets. He did indeed find gold in Alaska and opened a large placer mining operation in Candle, Alaska, "on the shores of the Arctic ocean."[71]

Ruth, now eight, and her older sister, Helen, were sent to the Anna Head School for Girls in Berkeley. All the children enjoyed romping through the wide hallways and multiple staircases of the

---

70 Robbins,"Autobiography,"462.
71 *Woodstock (Illinois) Daily Sentinel*, February 15, 1941, 2.

Claremont. A favorite sport was sliding down a spiral-chute fire escape attached to the exterior of the building.[72]

Percy Robbins was nothing if not peripatetic. Even after purchasing a lot in Berkeley near the Claremont overlooking the San Francisco Bay and crafting a wooden model of the house he considered building there, he decided to try out the San Francisco Peninsula for his family. He moved to Palo Alto and enrolled his daughters in the Castilleja School, an all-girls private school. After a year there, he again moved the family for a year to Santa Barbara. Then he made a fourth attempt at finding a satisfactory home for his family in Los Angeles.

Education

Ultimately, Percy decided California was not for him. He would raise his family in Illinois, where he had grown up. His mother resided in Highland Park, near her sisters, so Percy bought a large Victorian house on several acres overlooking Lake Michigan. Ruth, now a young teenager, for the first time lived in proximity to relatives other than her nuclear family. Both grandmothers were nearby, as were her great-aunts and her mother's sisters.

Ruth attended local schools until, at age seventeen, her father sent her off to Pine Manor Junior College, a finishing school in Wellesley, Massachusetts. After four years among family and relatives, she was alone. When the headmistress of Pine Manor sent back a report that Ruth was not applying herself as well as she might, Percy wrote a lengthy response detailing his thoughts about childhood development. The gist of his theory was that each child develops his or her various faculties at different ages and different speeds. To insist that

72 Percy Robbins died in 1938, having completed his autobiography only up to 1915, so information about the family from 1915 onward is from family anecdotes. Readers can decide for themselves if the anecdotes—or, for that matter, Percy's autobiography—include elements of exaggeration.

all children should develop their understanding of mathematics, for instance, in lockstep according to the school's schedule, was to miss the individuality of the students. He clearly thought his children should not be judged by arbitrary standards that might or might not recognize the full breadth of their talents.[73]

Although the powerful influence of her father reached out to her school to touch upon her grade report, nonetheless, for the first time Ruth was away from a household in which Percy was the sun around which all others orbited. Whether or not his attitude toward women was socially acceptable during his own time, it would certainly raise eyebrows today. Relief to have escaped her father's control was no doubt one strand of the mix of emotions she felt leaving home for the first time.

Percy's autobiography reveals a strongly opinionated, judgmental man, firmly assured his views were correct. Ruth's mother, on the other hand, was retiring, perhaps in part due to deafness but certainly also due to her innate personality. On the family stage, she acted in the background, not the foreground.

It is telling that in the course of his almost five-hundred-page autobiography manuscript, Percy Robbins never once states his wife's name, "Sophie." His description of their marriage upon a return from South Africa after an absence of eleven years follows his lengthy recounting of renewed acquaintance with his boyhood chums:

> So the chapter of my boyhood is almost closed; almost but not quite. There were of course girls, and one of these I had corresponded with throughout my time in college After leaving college this correspondence had waned, but had

73 I read a typescript author's copy of this letter some years ago and recorded my memory of it shortly thereafter, but I do not have it in my possession. I hope the letter remains intact somewhere in our distributed family archives, but in any case, I believe this summary to be accurate.

> been renewed from Kimberley, and one important piece of business which I had come home to contract was to get married.
>
> The preliminaries to marriage have been so often depicted in films, and so thoroughly analyzed by writers of novels, that there is nothing left to tell. Suffice it to say that the date was set to coincide with my return to South Africa, and as there was much I wanted to do in the meantime, I did not remain long at home, but returned to the East to investigate more fully the opportunities, and to see what progress was being made by my friends of college days.[74]

After a trip of several weeks away from Chicago to visit friends and survey opportunities, Percy returns for the actual marriage ceremony:

> Of my visit home there is not much more to be told. The usual paganistic rites were performed September the fourteenth, 1904, at Christ Reformed Episcopal Church, Twenty-fourth Street and Michigan Avenue, in the City of Chicago, County of Cook, State of Illinois. The formulae were recited by the Right Reverend Bishop Charles Edward Cheney, with all due solemnity, and we were thenceforth man and wife.[75]

Today it is hard to imagine someone writing about their marriage without providing any background about his bride or her family, not even supplying her name. Percy's reluctance to touch upon anything "feminine" or even emotional—except contempt for those who

74 Robbins, "Autobiography," 360.
75 Robbins, "Autobiography," 364.

wronged him—could perhaps be attributed to Victorian reticence about such matters. He clearly prided himself in being a "manly" man, and there is little doubt that his need to dominate shaped his marriage and family life. His opinions and attitudes certainly had a large impact on his five children. Of the five, four modeled themselves on him. Helen, the oldest, was domineering and judgmental just like her father. The two sons, Jim and Pete, both became mining engineers and led lives of risk and adventure. His youngest child, Jane, joined the Women Airforce Service Pilots during World War II and then was a bush pilot in Alaska. Only Ruth, the middle child, took a different course in life.

When Ruth left her family for the first time in her life and found herself on the East Coast in an environment that was completely new to her, she surely felt relief from the all-male-all-the-time blitzkrieg with which her father ran his family.

Pine Manor was founded in 1911 as a postgraduate environment for graduates of Dana Hall School, an all-girls prep school that was a feeder school for Wellesley College. Many Dana Hall students did not have the natural intelligence or competitive spirit needed to succeed at intellectually rigorous Wellesley or even to be admitted there. Pine Manor offered an alternative environment for prep school graduates of social standing. Rather than preparing young women to be academic leaders on a competitive level with graduates of the best men's colleges, Pine Manor espoused values of sophisticated femininity, comportment, social grace, and musical and artistic aesthetics, a perfect combination of attributes to be the supportive wife of a successful man.

Ruth had been raised in a northern Ontario mining camp, had attended excellent schools in California and Illinois, and had no reason to accept unquestionably the Pine Manor set of values. Rather, I imagine, she was fascinated with and curious about this completely new environment. Her whole life had been in northern Ontario, California, and the Midwest. She had the background and experience to put finishing school values into the perspective of the much larger world she had known. In fact, Pine Manor may well have been a catalyst to set Ruth on the path of true emotional and intellectual independence. She had to filter all the new information through a strong mind and strong personality—she had to be strong just to survive in her family—and felt perfectly comfortable forming her own opinions. She could put the other women in perspective as well. How would they have done on snowshoes in twenty-below winters? How did they compare with her California classmates at Anna Head or Castilleja—often offspring of entrepreneurial types such as her father? Ruth had plenty of life experience not to be cowed by East Coast social snobbery.

Moreover, it seems likely Ruth had little interest in defining herself in terms of a husband. If she appreciated her mother's gentle and humorous nature, at the same time she saw clearly how completely Sophie was dominated by Percy. If she loved her mother—and I am sure she did—she must have felt some distance from and distaste for male arrogance. "Please, God, don't let me be dominated by a man as my mother was," she may well have thought.

Thus I imagine she did indeed filter the Pine Manor experience, casting aside what seemed too weak or too feminine for her taste but gravitating especially to the refinement of art and music appreciation. As it turned out, art and music were to define her life.

Upon completing Pine Manor, Ruth returned to Highland Park and her nuclear family. She had no choice, or rather no choice that appealed to her. She certainly was not interested in finding a husband, a choice that in that day would have meant giving up her personal aspirations and her identity as an independent woman; after all, her parents did not provide a model for a relationship between equals that might have worked for her. She was not interested in becoming a secretary or otherwise pursuing a career as an employee of a business.

Indeed, Ruth did not need to pursue a career to support herself after graduating from Pine Manor. She was welcome to return home. Percy razed the original Victorian house on his Highland Park lakefront lot and built a totally modern house, designed for him by local architect Hans Benkert to accommodate his entire adult family. This was "Grandma's house," which we visited on weekends during my childhood in the 1950s. At one end of the ground floor was a suite for Ruth with a baby grand piano; across the hall was a suite for her brother Pete, where he kept his war medals and his Army-issue .45; upstairs were suites originally for Helen and Jim (later occupied by Jim and his three children after his wife Murnie died); and in a little cottage next door resided Jane. Ruth's brother Jim moved out when he married at age twenty-five in 1932. Sister Helen moved out when she married in 1935 at age thirty. Jane moved out at age thirty-four in 1950. Pete kept his suite as a home base as he wandered the globe pursuing a variety of engineering projects. However, the Highland Park house remained the primary residence of Ruth until she purchased her home in Belmont, Massachusetts, in 1958, at age forty-eight.

The Percy Robbins Family Preparing for Annual Trip to Home Under Arctic Circle

One Son Already on Way North with Supplies for Home at Gold Mine Site: James, Visiting Here, to Leave This Month.

THE Percy A. Robbins family of Highland Park contributes materially to the business of Alaskan homesteading. Months before the pilgrimage of prairie families set out last fall to establish new homes and new farms, two prefabricated houses stood serenely in the midst of vast stretches of tundra moss just ten miles south of the arctic circle. The most impressive residences in the little settlement of Candle, they are monuments to the pioneering instincts of the Robbins family.

Mr. Robbins, a former president of the Adventurers' Club, owns a gold mine near Candle. He and his two sons, both mining engineers, spend their summers supervising its operation, and the women go along to keep them company. Some of the women go along, that is. Mrs. Robbins has never seen the family domain in the far north, nor has her oldest daughter, Helen. Last summer they preferred to stay at home and work on wedding plans. When the rest of the clan returned in the late fall Helen Robbins was married to William Whipple Miller. Now she is too busy keeping house in an apartment on the near north side even to think about housekeeping problems in Alaska.

Last year the family colony all but starved when their food supplies, not to mention the houses, were delayed by ice floes. Supplies for this season are already on the way north with the younger son, Peter, and the domestic details will be quite simple. The settlers eat canned goods and game, plus the rare fresh supplies delivered by plane.

Before the month is out, James Robbins and his young wife will be on their way, too. Having spent the winter in Seattle, where their third child was born in January, they are now visiting both their families on the north shore. They are still undecided whether to take their children along (the oldest is 4) or leave them with their grandmothers. Last year the whole family went, but they feel that the new baby might be a trifle young to appreciate such an adventure.

When they leave Highland Park they are leaving spring behind.

Ruth Robbins, who was packing her camping togs for the journey this time last year, is currently in Paris and will not be coming home for another month. She went over in January to study music and French. The youngest child, Jane, will be returning from school at Pine Manor about the same time.

A newspaper clipping dated 1936 in my mother's hand gives a snapshot of the Robbins family life in Highland Park.[76] Most family members traipsed up to Alaska to tend to Percy's gold-dredging operation, taking pride in their ability to "rough it." Ruth had made the expedition in 1935, the previous year. In January 1936, however, she went to France to study French and music for several months. This clipping is the only information I have about this trip, but I can imagine her father deciding that after graduation from Pine Manor, his second daughter would benefit from the cultural broadening of a few months in Paris. She was in her mid-twenties. No doubt she continued her search for a role that was not defined by her family. Thus, four years before she met Nadia Boulanger, Ruth was already on a quest to find an identity related to French musical aesthetics, about as far as imaginable from the rough mining town in northern Ontario where she spent her first years.

Responsibility and Freedom

Percy died of cancer in 1938, creating a vacuum in the family dynamics. Without a dominant paterfamilias, lines of responsibility were redrawn. Helen and Jim had married, Pete was a nomad engineer with no interest in taking responsibility for others, Jane was four years younger than Ruth. Thus, by process of elimination, much household responsibility fell to Ruth, including caring for their mother, Sophie. This burden further tied her to Highland Park, even as she wanted to find a life of her own. Ruth's dedication to her mother's welfare, tinged with occasional sighs, was something Nadia Boulanger could fully understand. From the day her father died in 1900 until her mother Raissa's death

76 I did not find this article in any of the major Chicago papers with online archives. It was likely in one of the small suburban weeklies, such as the *Winnetka Talk* or the *Highland Park News*.

in 1935, Boulanger carried full responsibility for her mother. She knew what Ruth was experiencing.

Years later, at the time of the marriage of Ruth's niece Barbara Robbins to Jon Lindbergh in 1956, his mother, Anne Morrow Lindbergh, who had already met brother Jim and sister Jane, wrote in her diary, "I was surprised to find another sister, Ruth, not as striking as Jane; does she keep house for Jim?"[77] In fact, Anne Morrow Lindbergh's first impression of Ruth had elements of truth. Ruth was not striking either in personality or in looks. Her social strategy was to be retiring and observe rather than to strive to impress or entertain others. It took time to get to know her intelligence and depth. She did not do first impressions well.

Nonetheless, in 1940, sixteen years before the Lindbergh diary entry, when Nadia Boulanger first met Ruth, Boulanger was struck by Ruth's character and personality, to the extent that they formed a lifelong bond. The difference between these two first impressions had much to do with context. When Anne Morrow Lindbergh met Ruth, Ruth was a background figure in a family of high-energy extroverts. Ruth's brother Jim—inventor, mining engineer, and aviator—had a personality that could stand up to anyone, famed aviator Charles Lindbergh included. Her sister Jane was strikingly attractive, intelligent, verbal, perceptive, and an experienced aviator not at all cowed by Air Corps colonels or their wives. Understandably, compared to her siblings, Ruth was hardly noticed by Anne Morrow Lindbergh.

When Boulanger met Ruth in 1940, however, no family member was within a thousand miles. She was one of some twenty students in a music theory class. In a classroom situation—slower paced and more thoughtful than a wedding reception—Ruth's emotional intelligence,

---

77 Anne Morrow Lindbergh, *Against Wind and Tide: Letters & Journals, 1947–1986* (New York: Pantheon Books, 2012), 99.

sensitivity, and humor no doubt stood out. At thirty, she was the oldest person in a class of late teenagers and young twenty year olds. She was not socially pretentious, egotistical, spoiled, pampered, or otherwise impaired by characteristics no doubt frequently encountered by Boulanger. She was articulate and thoughtful. Although she did not have the brilliant musical talent of many of her classmates, she had a depth of character, a sense of humor, and a perceptiveness that caused Boulanger to take notice.

Ruth Robbins was a self-contained individual. Although she was not brilliant or exceptionally talented, she had a quietly confident emotional maturity and great compassion for others. Nadia Boulanger had plenty of brilliant people in her life. In November 1940—in emotional crisis herself—having fled the Nazi invaders and left her life behind her, her need for compassionate companionship rather than brilliance was no doubt great.

At that moment of need, she found Ruth Robbins in her music theory class. Ruth's innocence of worldly affairs, calm demeanor, mature years, self-deprecating humor, lack of pretense, and honesty stood out. Ruth must have appeared to Boulanger to represent a simpler, more peaceful mode of existence. Emotionally, Ruth provided Boulanger an oasis of peace in a world of turmoil.

Ruth gained much from her decades-long bond with such an outstanding mentor, but she also gave much back. It was a two-way relationship.

ADVANCED THEORY DIVISION			Mlle. Boulanger
Student	Subject	First Semester	Second Semester
Allenbrook, Douglas	½ Comp.	B	Drafted – U. S. Army
Aiken, Louise	Adv. Th.	B+	1st Award in Advanced Theory
Ames, Richard	Comp.	A	3rd Award in Advanced Theory; 3rd Award in Counterpoint
Cirel, Tulie	Comp.	B	3rd Award in Advanced Harmony; Honorable Mention in Counterpoint
Crecraft, Jane	Fugue	C+	Cancelled 3/1/43
Culbertson, Ruth	Adv. Th.	A-	
Fillmore, Albert	Comp.	A-	2nd Award in Composition
Hoffmann, Newton	Adv. Th.	A-	2nd Award in Counterpoint; " " " Harmony
Johnstone, Winifred	Adv. Th.	B-	
Lavoie, Claude	Comp.	B+	3rd Award in Advanced Theory; 3rd Award in Counterpoint
Martin, Charlotte	Fugue	B	Left School April 1st
Papineau-Couture Jean	Comp.	A-	1st Award in Composition
Pellerin, Germaine	Fugue	B	1st Award in Counterpoint
Rhoden, Natalia	Comp.	B	Cancelled 3/1/43
Robbins, Ruth	Piano Music.	B B	2nd Award in Advanced Theory; 1st Award in Counterpoint
Shapero, Harold	Comp.	A	
Trainer, Foster	Fugue	C+	
Whiemant, Alexine	Teach.	A-	
Ziembo, Marie	Comp.	A-	3rd Award in Composition; 3rd Award in Counterpoint
2nd Semester Only:			
Fuelin, Theodore	Comp.		
Speis, Claude	Comp.		

In addition to Ruth Robbins, Nadia Boulanger's 1943 Advanced Theory Division students included Douglas Allanbrook (B in Composition fall semester; drafted by the Army spring semester); Jean Papineau-Couture (A in Composition); Harold Shapero (A in Composition); and Claudio "Claude" Spies. What an experience to learn music theory with this amazing array of first-rate talents. Robbins was no doubt pleased with her awards in Advanced Theory and Counterpoint. Another student, Winifred Johnstone, became an important supporter of Boulanger after World War II, serving effectively as her American volunteer coordinator/manager. [Longy School of Music Archives]

Idil Biret playing on the Bosphorus Bridge joining Europe and Asia. [Idil Biret Archive] YouTube video: www.youtube.com/watch?v=r8SvyfZWOFY

Nadia Boulanger with Marian Baring-Gould and Marian Sachs; "the two Marians" were tutored at home so Boulanger could have the company of children when she was a guest of Georgette and Arthur Sachs. [Ruth Robbins Archives]

And this
matters of values, of education, of tradition, of thought, of art
is so great, that we have only to stop for a minute to think
of history, to have the answer. With high intellectual standards, you
can ask any sacrifice. With lower standards spiritually or intel-
lectually, you meet selfishness, weakness, & despair. There must
be men to fight, making the gift of their best years, of their life
to save what the one who cannot fight, as women must defend
of the not less precious treasury. Done to escape is awful, done
to develop is what has to be, if one fights not only against, but
also for — what is more than life — & what gives its real mean
to Victory.

"And this problem of values, of education, of tradition, of thought, of art is so great that we have only to stop for a minute to think of history, to have the answer.... There must be men to fight, making the gift of their best years, of their life to save what the one who cannot fight, or women must defend of the not less precious treasury. Done to escape is awful, done to develop is what has to be, if one fights not only against, but also for—what is more than life—and what gives its real meaning to Victory."

The Longy School of Music in Cambridge, Massachusetts, where Nadia Boulanger and Ruth Robbins met in November 1940. The institution merged with Bard College to become the Longy School of Music of Bard College in 2012. The two second-floor windows on the left illuminated Boulanger's music theory classroom with soft afternoon light as she lectured and demonstrated to students gathered around the grand piano. [Ruth Robbins Archives]

Boulanger's Bond with Robbins

Boulanger was at a low point when she arrived in the United States. She felt worried and guilty about those left behind. She saw everything she believed in—spiritual faith, humanitarianism, music, beloved musicians—under threat. Four months after her arrival, in a March 18, 1941, letter to Doda Conrad, she wrote,[78]

> I drag with me the shame of having left (and though I couldn't have done otherwise, that doesn't change anything at all). I carry around my old incurable wounds, whose healing would make me despair: they are all that remains to me of a past that was so sweet, so dear and so beautiful, that, if I were allowed to choose [whether or not to heal], my decision would be without hesitation.

After this brief poetic wallow in misery, Boulanger sets her sights on regaining beauty:

78 Doda Conrad (1905–1997) was a Polish-born American bass operatic singer. He studied with NB in the late 1930s.

> Nevertheless other duties call, and we have to find again our enthusiasm and our energy. . . . We will set ourselves to work, and we will run up against obstacles that we will end up, if not vanquishing, at least diminishing; we will be touched to the bottom of our souls by the music of a poor man, as miserable as we are, in fact, and however sad and miserable he was (after all, just like us), because it was given to him to encounter God, and to make us encounter Him, everything—even our most profound and legitimate distress—will take on a different color. And between friendship and art, we will quickly find again the real meaning of life, its beauty and our love for it.

According to Jeanice Brooks,

> [This letter] ties her [Boulanger's] musical work to her sense of loss, viewed not as trauma to be overcome or forgotten but as pain that can be transformed by music into a renewal of life. The epigraph that had always accompanied invitations to the Mass in memory of Lili Boulanger—"I offer to God all my sufferings so that they may fall again upon you as joy"—seems to encapsulate Boulanger's understanding of the musical work, and her own work in interpreting it.[79]

When Boulanger arrived in the United States and first met Robbins, she was in crisis. Her sense of loss was overwhelming, and she needed to find her direction again. This period also may have been

---

79 Brooks, *Musical Work*, 256.

a turning point in Boulanger's view of her own role and the roles of all who fought with her against the tide of hatred and fear that came with war. She could only agonize over the fate of those left behind, but with fellow exiles like Conrad and Igor Stravinsky, and with the support of her American students and benefactors, she could fight the war on the side of humanism. As the reality of her exile sank in, she realized she and her tribe of humanists were, in fact, engaged in a life-and-death battle for the spirit of civilization.

In 1942, Robbins wrote to Boulanger asking how her study of music could compare with becoming a nurse or working in a factory:

> So many times I wonder if it is not just selfishness that makes me return to Cambridge to have another year of music as full and rich as last year. I love it so, but realize that I have contributed nothing and probably will contribute very little along that line, and would probably be much more useful as a worker in an airplane factory or as a nurse.

In her response, Boulanger ties Robbins's study of music to addressing the greatest problem of their era—the threat to civilization.

> This problem of values, of education, of tradition, of thought, of art is so great, that we have only to stop for a minute to think of history, to have the answer. . . . There must be men to fight, making the gift of their best years, of their life to save what the one who cannot fight, or women must defend of the not less precious treasury. Done to escape is awful, done to develop is what has to be, if one fights not only against, but also for—what is more than life—and what gives its real meaning to Victory.

To fight for "what is more than life—and what gives its real meaning to Victory" is an aesthete's battle cry, with musicians as foot soldiers in a war to preserve beauty and truth. Is the battle metaphor in her description of music a new phenomenon? This is a great question for musicologists to answer. Knocked flat by the German invasion of France in 1940, by 1942 she had clearly rebounded. She channeled anxiety and despair into a new aesthetic militancy and determination to fight the good fight.

There was a wealth of young talent in Boulanger's advanced music theory classes of 1940–1943 at the Longy School. Nineteen-year-old composer and piano prodigy Douglas Allanbrook (1921–2003) had started writing serious music at thirteen and went on to become an illustrious composer. Twenty-four-year-old Canadian talent Jean Papineau-Couture (1916–2000) had a stellar career in music education and composition and, through Nadia Boulanger, became an ardent follower and associate of Stravinsky. Twenty-one-year-old Harvard student Harold Shapero (1920–2013) had just completed his Nine-Minute Overture, a work that caught the ear of Aaron Copland and won the Rome Prize in 1941. Seventeen-year-old Claudio Spies (1925–2020), his secondary school education in Chile completed, came to study at Longy and the New England Conservatory on his way to becoming a close friend and supporter of Igor Stravinsky and a distinguished professor of music at Harvard, Vassar, Swarthmore, Princeton, and Juilliard.

For Boulanger, engaging with these young students must have been a balm that helped assuage the trauma of leaving France. This was not a class in performance or technique; rather, it was a lecture, with the students grouped around the grand piano in Boulanger's airy classroom on the second floor of the Longy School. She opined from the piano bench, using the keyboard to demonstrate. If Robbins lacked the precocity and talent of many of her classmates, her maturity, intelligence, and quiet logic would have served her well in this class. She earned the third award in counterpoint and the second award in advanced theory. In her grade report at the end of the 1942–1943 school year, Boulanger rated Robbins low in musical talent but high in "Application: effort, faithfulness in preparation." In Robbins, she found a student who was earnest, hardworking, intelligent, and good-humored, even if not overly talented.

Boulanger took to Robbins from the beginning. The earliest letter we have from Boulanger to Robbins, dated August 13, 1941, nine months after Boulanger's arrival at Longy, discusses sharing a house. Robbins had been generous, making a scholarship contribution on behalf of Boulanger's students, which was split fifty-fifty between Léo Préger and a scholarship fund for American composers.[80] Clearly from the beginning there was a level of trust and communication between Robbins and Boulanger.

By May 1942, Robbins was exploding with love for her newfound mentor, who opened doors to truth and beauty.

> There is no way for me to describe to you what this year's work has meant to me (and music is only a small part of it), but it has created quite a problem. All my life I have dreamed of having such an experience and of working with someone in whom I had absolute confidence, and now that I have had it, and am having it, I do not know what to dream about anymore! I often wonder why I, of all the millions of people on this earth, should be one of those fortunate few to have been let out of the mist and shown where I am and why, and where I must go, and to be helped

80 See letter dated August 13, 1941.

> along the way. It is such a wonderful discovery. In order to thank you in a tangible way, I am enclosing a check which I hope will make it possible for someone else to study with you who might not otherwise have the opportunity.

The fifty-three-year-old Boulanger certainly appreciated the wealth of talent in her Longy classes, yet she had the strongest appreciation for perhaps the least talented. Long experienced with working with younger people, and with her highly sensitive perceptiveness, she could easily see Robbins's character, and she liked it. It was much the same character Winnaretta Singer, Princesse Edmond de Polignac saw in Boulanger herself when they first met in 1932. As described by Sylvia Kahan in her biography of Polignac, the princess was struck by Boulanger, who "presented herself so simply and modestly, yet whose quiet fervor for the music that she loved communicated itself so powerfully."[81] Did Nadia Boulanger see something of her younger self in Robbins? When she first met Polignac, Boulanger's faith and fervor had not yet been tested by the cultural and social destruction she witnessed in the run-up to the Second World War and the Nazi invasion of France. Robbins may have reminded her of her own innocence.

If so, Robbins's modest ambition to improve herself while contributing to a better world as well as her quiet wit and firmness of purpose likely rekindled in Boulanger an earlier and more optimistic version of herself. In midcrisis—while reorienting her life and redefining her values—she may have found in Robbins an innocence and a faith in the future similar to what had once been her own.

For her part, Robbins was immensely struck by the wisdom and vision of her new mentor. She had "absolute confidence" in Boulanger.

---

81 Sylvia Kahan, *Music's Modern Muse: A Life of Winnaretta Singer, Princesse de Polignac* (Rochester, NY: University of Rochester Press, 2009), 295–296.

Such trust and adoration were no doubt welcomed by Boulanger in her time of duress.

In fact, Boulanger clearly says as much. In an August 1942 letter, she writes to Robbins: "for old as I am, the only hope and consolation is found in you, the young ones, and your affection and your confidence are great comfort."

In October 1943, an exhausted Boulanger decided to take a long-needed rest from her overbooked teaching schedule at Longy and in Baltimore to spend a few months at the Montecito estate of Arthur and Georgette Sachs in California. She promptly wrote to Robbins to come immediately: "Go tomorrow to the ticket office."

This relationship was of great emotional value to both parties. Boulanger benefited from the companionship and enthusiastic assistance of a modest, honest, good-humored admirer with whom she got along easily. Robbins was enraptured by Boulanger's world of refinement, elegance, and moral clarity. With Boulanger's affection and support, Robbins was welcomed into her inner circle, both in the United States and, after World War II, in France. After their travels together in the United States in 1962, Boulanger wrote to Robbins, "How strange it will be to go on without you—and how sad—but these weeks will always remain with me. Such a gift of one self is a blessing, and it has given to all these journeys a character of confidence, of rest, of intimacy quite unique."[82] Robbins's upbeat manner inspired confidence in Boulanger, her relaxed manner allowed Boulanger to rest, and her directness made intimacy easy.

Their affection for each other remained strong until Boulanger's death in 1979. Robbins carried her memories of Boulanger in her heart until her death in 2005 at age ninety-five. Robbins's last years were in a

82 See letter dated May 7, 1962.

cottage on a family compound overlooking the San Francisco Bay. Her beloved grandnieces, Nathalie and Gabby Miller, lived across the lawn. To amuse them, Robbins would often read passages from Boulanger's letters. Wonderful turns of phrase emerged, as Gabby wrote, "Things like, 'How big is our shrinked world? I am here and you are there, and that makes all the difference,' or 'Read all what is not written and believe me to be, as ever, your, N.B.'" What is fascinating about these phrases is not just unusual grammar. They also convey a sense of the grand and universal heights from which Nadia Boulanger viewed the world.

One anecdote already alluded to had a profound effect on Gabby. Perhaps it captures in narrative form something important to Boulanger and to Robbins as well. As Robbins told her grandniece, on one of her summer visits to France in the early 1960s, she was driving Boulanger from the south, through the night, back to Paris for an important engagement the next day. Intent on making it to Paris, Robbins was surprised when Boulanger told her to turn off the main road to visit Chartres Cathedral. Before dawn, they approached the west portal and entered the cathedral, passing under the magnificent tympanum of the left door featuring Christ floating above on a cloud supported by two angels. Once inside, one can only imagine what was in their minds. Surely they were mostly silent, perhaps with quiet whispers between them. Boulanger must have felt great emotional comfort to be within the embrace of the magnificent cathedral. I imagine her running through her mind passages from Stravinsky's Mass and Bach's Mass in B Minor, feeling the aptness of the music to the ritualized space of the church. No doubt she cast her eyes on the artifacts she loved, and she took in the vaulted heights, expanses, and mysterious qualities that made one feel God's presence. As dawn grew, she may have noted how light gifted by God illuminated the stained-glass art of man, creating within the viewer a sense of connection and holiness.

Church and religious ritual had never been a part of Ruth's life. Yet Boulanger opened a door to beauty and gave Robbins a sense of purpose and value she had never had. Robbins repeated the story of this visit to her grandnieces and others. It made a good story; the experience had made a deep impression on her. Was this story important to Robbins because it encapsulated a truth she had learned from Boulanger? Boulanger had plenty of drive, clear purpose, and important engagements, but all to one end—to create and experience beauty. Robbins, that morning, may have looked up at the growing colors of the filtered dawn and felt deep gratitude for Nadia Boulanger's greatest gift to her: how to put beauty at the center of life.

Entryway to 36, rue Ballu, where Boulanger grew up and resided her entire life. Here she gave private lessons and welcomed students and colleagues to her "Wednesday Afternoons." This intersection of rue Ballu and rue de Vingtmille has been renamed Place Lili Boulanger, and a plaque (inset) now commemorates the two outstanding musicians. [Images: Wikimedia Commons]

Moral Leadership

Nadia Boulanger influenced others profoundly. She had charisma. While the Greek root of "charisma" refers to a state of grace or favor that draws others into one's orbit, the word, even in modern usage, offers no clue as to how the mechanics of charisma work. Nadia Boulanger displayed a range of personal and psychological characteristics that help explain her charismatic effect on others.

Important among these may have been a heightened sense of perception. A highly sensitive person or someone with a high sensory processing sensitivity (SPS, as the neuroscientists describe it) reacts somatically to nuances that may go unnoticed by others.[83] People with high SPS experience the environment with physical sensation. If one uses music as an example, they may physically feel jarred by discordant tones, feel soothed by expected tones, or feel delighted by unexpected but right tones.

With music or art, this can mean experiencing the sublime beauty of a passage or scene in the musculature of the body. Although unproven, high SPS theory applied to social relations may mean hyper-awareness of others, sensing in body language or tone of voice what another person does not express. High SPS would help explain how Boulanger knew with such certainty what was musically right or wrong. She could, one might say, feel it in her bones. It would also help explain why she was able to build loyal long-term relationships. As a friend, teacher, or leader, she was present and understanding.

A different angle on Boulanger's character can be drawn from considering Carl Jung's four personality variables: sensation, thinking,

---

83 Corina Greven et al., "Sensory Processing Sensitivity in the Context of Environmental Sensitivity: A Critical Review and Development of Research Agenda," *Neuroscience & Biobehavioral Reviews 98* (January 2019): 287–305.

feeling, and intuition. "The essential function of sensation is to establish that something exists, thinking tells us what it means, feeling what its value is, and intuition surmises whence it comes and whither it goes."[84] Boulanger was undoubtedly deeply endowed with the fourth of Jung's functions: a high intuitive, someone who sees patterns and relationships behind things, who can see the past in the present, and in the present see the future. High intuitive function is what enabled her to see the future of her protégés as she put them on the right path, for example, or experience a keen need to champion spiritual beauty in a battle against the tide of poor taste. Her desire to pour energy into supporting and guiding Stravinsky in the creation of his Mass arose because she knew it would be a work that would stand in time. High intuitive function would account for much of the urgency and passion in Boulanger's life and work.

A third trait to note is Boulanger's spirituality. She experienced tragedy and took on great family responsibility at a young age. For emotional support, she relied on spirituality, especially as experienced in the rituals of the church—a conviction not just of the existence of God but of his presence and interactiveness in all aspects of life. This carried over into her understanding and appreciation of music. She had faith in higher meaning accessed through spiritual experiences, and the greatness of great works of music was their ability to create such experience, especially for those who learned how to listen.

Such faith helps explain how she was able to rise above personal circumstance and devote her life to creating an ideal realm of communal spirituality through music. While Boulanger was devoted to Catholic ritual, I find it unlikely that she thought too finely about theology. Without considering how many angels can dance on the head of a pin or how to explain transubstantiation, she could simply

84 Jung, C. G., *The Essential Jung*, comp. Anthony Storr (Princeton: Princeton University Press, 1983), 144.

experience the comfort of the Mass or feel connected to those she had lost with her annual ritual of memorial services for her mother and sister.

Not only highly sensitive, highly intuitive, and highly spiritual but also highly educated and highly cultured, Boulanger grew into her leadership role not merely due to strategy and tactics—although with her vast knowledge of the musical world she was born into and had navigated all her life, she certainly knew how to achieve her ends—but because she filled a void in early and mid-twentieth-century culture.

She had passion, perception, and expertise. Many people sensed—with dread—that the decadence, Dadaism, and desire to "épater la bourgeoisie" flourishing in France during the fin de siècle and pre–World War I eras were far from the sublime heights of civilization. Who could they turn to? Who could articulate their concern with conviction and passion? Who could correct the course of cultural decay?

Nadia Boulanger addressed these concerns on a small scale with her circle of students. It was a natural progression for her classicist influence to grow in harmonic counterpoint to the cultural chaos of the first half of the twentieth century. And it was just as natural for her influence to wane during the self-satisfied 1950s and 1960s when civilization no longer seemed at risk.

Another reason for Boulanger's impact is that the aesthetic beliefs she espoused were deeply established in philosophical traditions. During a time of moral uncertainty and social unrest, her views were highly attractive to the educated and cultured. To contextualize Boulanger's beliefs, consider the conflict between a traditional noble view of aesthetics as the appreciation of truth and beauty versus the view of philosopher John Locke that art and poetry are "quite irresponsible and not troubled with truth or reality."[85]

85 John Locke, *An Essay concerning Human Understanding*, 1689, in *Works*, II, 11, 3, cited in C. M. Bowra, *The Romantic Imagination* (New York: Oxford University Press, 1961), 3.

For Boulanger, the creation of music is a sacred act aiming to bring out the highest, most spiritual part of human nature. Such connection between art, emotion, and morality is described as early as the fourth century BCE. "Catharsis" in Aristotle's *Poetics* is "the purgation or cleansing of the emotions of pity and fear." Moreover, like Aristotle, Boulanger saw the importance of structure, of following the rules, in the creation of great art:

> When Aristotle prescribes that a tragedy must have a beginning, a middle, and an end, he is again being faithful to one of the principles of his general philosophy. A tragedy, like every other product of art or nature, has its own unity as an individual thing. . . .
>
> The action of a play must be complete (*telelios*), just as the life of the good and happy man in the Ethics must be complete.[86]

Aristotle's vision of art influencing human emotion and morality is by no means unique, or even uniquely European. The connection between music and ethics was a basic tenet of Confucius, as well: "My young friends, why do you not study the *Odes*? The *Odes* can stimulate your emotions, broaden your observation, enlarge your fellowship, and express your grievances."[87] The *Odes*, or *Book of Songs*, a collection of folk lyrics related to early agrarianism, celebrates the rhythms of life with simple cadences and images.

When in the fifth century BCE Confucius asks, "Why do you not study the *Odes*?" he venerates a far older oral tradition—chanted or sung

86 Renford Bambrough, *The Philosophy of Aristotle* (New York: Mentor Books, 1963), 410–411.
87 Wing-tsit Chan, ed., "Analects 17:9," in *A Source Book in Chinese Philosophy*, (Princeton: Princeton University Press, 1963), 47.

verse passed down, generation to generation, since before the dawn of Chinese written history—collected and recorded during the time of Confucius to become a foundation stone of the Confucian canon.

Music and ritual, as represented by the tradition of the *Odes*, were essential to the development of morality. "If a man is not humane (*jen*), what has he to do with ceremonies (*li*)? If he is not humane, what has he to do with music?"[88] Music and ritual were foundational to humaneness or benevolence to fellow humans, a cardinal Confucian virtue. The words "let a man be stimulated by poetry, established by the rules of propriety, and perfected by music" may have been uttered by Confucius 2,500 years earlier, but they are not far from describing the role Nadia Boulanger saw for music in the twentieth century.[89]

Interestingly, another early Chinese philosopher, Zhuangzi (fourth century BCE), expressed something similar to Boulanger's belief that the work itself embodies an ideal that musicians can only attempt to attain: "Chao Wen was a famous lute player, but the best music he could play was only a pale and partial imitation of ideal music."

The Way—truth beyond words—is an ideal path of existence in harmony with the universe. However, later in the same passage, Zhuangzi says, "The torch of chaos and doubt—this is what the sage steers by." The sage accepts things as they are, even if to people seeking established values, things appear chaotic, doubtful, and needing explanation.[90] While Confucianism focused on maintaining and developing humaneness via ritual and respect for tradition, Taoism was a disruptive philosophy that encouraged questioning all established beliefs, practices, and standards. Safe to say, Boulanger was more Confucian in outlook than Taoist.

88 Chan, "Analects, 3:3" 24.

89 Chan, "Analects, 8:8"33.

90 'Zhuangzi quotes are from *Chuang Tzu: Basic Writings*, trans.Burton Watson (New York: Columbia University Press, 1964), 37.

In 1938, Boulanger wrote to Stravinsky that "the work of art, to a certain degree, is an image of God,"[91] referring to the sublime experience of music. A first-century CE Greek treatise, *Peri hypsous*, or *On the Sublime*, argues that sublimity, evoked by the highest level of rhetoric, is not due merely to technique or style but "is the echo of greatness of spirit." The treatise, once commonly attributed to the third-century rhetorician Longinus, holds that the sublime "is a thing of the spirit, a spark that leaps from the soul of the writer to the soul of his reader."

The author cites both Genesis and Zeus to emphasize the enlightened spark of artistic creation: "God said, 'Let there be light,' and there was light"; and "Father Zeus, kill us if thou wilt, but kill us in the light." He held that sublimity is a quality or feeling distinct from mere emotion, for not all emotion is noble or true. The sublime, he holds, arises from five sources: great thoughts, noble feeling, lofty figures, diction, and arrangement. The first two are a gift from heaven, or genius, while the latter three are arts that can be learned.[92] The *Peri hypsous* view of art and genius is at the heart of Boulanger's commitment to Stravinsky. He had mastered the art and he had native genius—a spark from heaven.

The relationship between art and "divine breath" is key to Sir Philip Sidney's *The Defense of Poesy*, written in the late sixteenth century.

> Only the poet, . . . lifted up with the vigor of his own invention, doth grow in effect another nature, in making things either better than Nature bringeth forth, or, quite anew, forms such as never were in Nature. . . .The heavenly Maker . . . who, having made man to His own likeness, set

91 Brooks, *Musical Work*, 251.

92 Alex Preminger, ed., *Encyclopedia of Poetry and Poetics* (Princeton: Princeton University Press, 1965), 819.

> him beyond and over all the works of that second nature: which in nothing he showeth so much as in Poetry, when with the force of divine breath he bringeth things forth far surpassing her doings.[93]

As with *Peri hypsous*, the combination of art and genius brings forth experiences that surpass nature, transcending the material world.

This noble view of art was summarily discarded by the mechanistic thinking of Locke in the seventeenth century. His metaphysics of material cause and effect was at the base of both the scientific revolution and the Industrial Revolution. What more proof could one ask of Lockean validity? Art, music, and poetry were brutally cast aside. Locke considered poetry mere wit or cleverness "to combine ideas and thereby to make up pleasant pictures and agreeable views in the fancy." In Locke's view, such cleverness "is quite irresponsible and not troubled with truth or reality."[94]

The industrial and scientific revolutions undermined traditional faiths and at the same time gave rise to the "dark Satanic Mills" that poet William Blake, in 1810, questioned could ever be blessed with the divine.[95] The Romantics saw the moral and imaginative sterility of the Lockean universe and, in reaction, celebrated the spiritual power of the individual imagination to rise above and beyond Locke's reality-grinding machine. Keats's close to his 1819 *Ode on a Grecian Urn* ("Beauty is truth, truth beauty,—that is all / Ye know on earth, and all ye need to know") could crudely be considered a middle finger

---

93 Philip Sidney, "The Defense of Poesy," in *Classic Writings on Poetry*, ed. William Harmon (New York: Columbia University Press, 2003), 138–139.

94 Locke, *Essay concerning Human Understanding*, 3.

95 "And did the Countenance Divine, / Shine forth upon our clouded hills? / And was Jerusalem builded here, / Among these dark Satanic Mills?" From William Blake's "Jerusalem."

extended toward Locke, as if saying, "You idiot! You missed everything important."

The Romantics piled it on, enthusiastically and ecstatically weaving imaginative webs throughout the nineteenth century. At the same time, freed both of the restraints of traditional faith and of the Lockean trap of mechanical productivity, new unconstrained schools of thought and practice arose. Decadents expressed sickness at the world, delight in perversion, and belief in the freedom to make their own rules. Poet Charles Baudelaire celebrated the perverse in *Les fleurs du mal*, published in 1857. He begins the preface ("To the Reader") with,

> If rape, poison, dagger and fire,
> Have still not embroidered their pleasant designs
> On the banal canvas of our pitiable destinies,
> It's because our soul, alas, is not bold enough!

And concludes it with:

> It's Boredom!—eye brimming with an involuntary tear
> He dreams of gallows while smoking his hookah.
> You know him, reader, this delicate monster,
> Hypocritical reader, my likeness, my brother![96]

Writer Oscar Wilde so brilliantly and openly flaunted his disregard for convention in the 1890s that he was convicted of gross indecency with men and spent two years imprisoned in Reading Gaol for his crime. In the early years of the twentieth century, the anti-art

---

96 Si le viol, le poison, le poignard, l'incendie, / N'ont pas encore brodé de leurs plaisants dessins / Le canevas banal de nos piteux destins, / C'est que notre âme, hélas ! n'est pas assez hardie. . . .
C'est l'Ennui!—l'œil chargé d'un pleur involontaire, / Il rêve d'échafauds en fumant son houka. / Tu le connais, lecteur, ce monstre délicat, / Hypocrite lecteur,—mon semblable,—mon frère!

movement of Marcel Duchamp metastasized into Dadaism, a wild, no-holds-barred nihilist movement that questioned whether there was such a thing as meaning after all. The Dada Manifesto, introduced by poet and author Hugo Ball in 1916, makes a mockery of language itself:

> How does one achieve eternal bliss? By saying dada. How does one become famous? By saying dada. With a noble gesture and delicate propriety. Till one goes crazy. Till one loses consciousness. How can one get rid of everything that smacks of journalism, worms, everything nice and right, blinkered, moralistic, europeanised, enervated? By saying dada. Dada is the world soul, dada is the pawnshop.[97]

Ball and other Dadaists believed society was in a terrible state, disliked philosophies that claimed ultimate truth, and held that meaninglessness is a guiding principle of life.

People of good faith, people who believed in humanism and the perfectibility of man—already disturbed by the rise of decadence, meaninglessness, and nihilism—were shocked when the First World War laid waste to remaining hopes. The Great War, seemingly a product of the same Lockean logic as the Industrial Revolution, decimated Nadia Boulanger's generation of Frenchmen as she entered her thirties.

Hope that the end of the Great War would bring political peace and international understanding decayed quickly during the 1920s. A current of doubt and despair was in the air. The horrors of the Great War had spawned a new wave of decadence, with an epicenter in Weimar Berlin. In his last novel, *Metropolis*, Philip Kerr, who displays a deep understanding of Weimar Germany in his fiction, quotes George Grosz, one of the Dada movement's leading artists:

97 "Dada Manifesto (1916, Hugo Ball)," https://en.wikisource.org/wiki/Dada_Manifesto_(1916,_Hugo_Ball).

> My drawings expressed my hate and my despair. I sketched drunks, puking men, men shaking their fists at the moon. I drew a man, his face filled with horror, washing blood from his hands. . . . I drew a cross section of a tenement house: through one window could be seen a man beating up his wife; through another two people making love; from a third hung a man, his body covered with flies. I drew soldiers without noses, war cripples with crab-like steel arms; I drew a skeleton dressed as a recruit having a medical for medical duty. I also wrote poetry.[98]

In the 1930s, National Socialism grew into a hateful and increasingly menacing movement. Self-deluded statesmen strutted the European stage as international tensions heightened. Then France was invaded. "Can no one save us from this insanity?" was no doubt a question on the minds of many when Nadia Boulanger fled France. The highest values of European civilization were under mortal threat. Would the nihilism of the Dadaists and the tribalism of the Nazis overcome the quest for truth and beauty that had defined the highest achievements of Western civilization?

Nadia Boulanger, to her core, knew this could never be allowed to happen. The death of Enlightenment truth and beauty would be a catastrophe beyond measure and comprehension. In this sense, she had no choice. Her die was cast. She had to put all her energy and all her devotion into the struggle against chaos and depravity.

98 Philip Kerr, *Metropolis* (New York: G.P. Putnam's Sons, 2019), 366–367.

Boulanger's Tribe of Torchbearers

If a tribe can be described as a people linked by social ties with a common culture, a common dialect, and a commonly recognized leader, then when she met Ruth Robbins in 1940, Nadia Boulanger was a well-established tribal leader. Her tribal culture was based on belief in the transformative, spiritual power of music. The tribe's dialect originated at the Conservatoire de Paris, where Boulanger was educated, and was nurtured and perfected in her Wednesday salons. It spread internationally through her lectures and performances as well as her work at the American Conservatory at Fontainebleau, the Longy School of Music, and a variety of American universities.

Widely diverse in nationality, social status, and gender orientation, the Boulanger tribe (often ironically referred to by her students as "La Boulangerie") attracted a number of notably strong-minded, independent, highly competent women.[99] Take Annette Dieudonné (1896–1991), for instance. An early student who became a lifelong collaborator and supporter, she occupied Boulanger's Paris apartment during the Second World War. In her role as Paris Conservatory librarian, as the Germans approached Paris, she buried the Conservatory's valuable manuscripts in the countryside to protect them from bombs or confiscation. She was awarded the Légion d'honneur in recognition of her bravery.

Cécile Armagnac (1913–1997) began as a student of Boulanger's in 1935. During World War II, she served in the *ambulancières* (women's medical corps) and was awarded a Croix de Guerre for her heroism. Independently wealthy, she chose not the easy life available to her at the Armagnac estate but rather to engage with her tribe to preserve

---

99 NB had strong male supporters as well, including Walter Damrosch, Prince Pierre of Monaco (1895–1964), Igor Stravinsky, and Leonard Bernstein.

a culture threatened by international chaos. She served as a founder and *secrétaire générale* (general secretary) of the Nadia et Lili Boulanger foundation.

Or take American sewing machine heiress Winnaretta Singer, Princesse Edmond de Polignac (1865–1943). Twenty-two years Boulanger's senior, she was impressed by "the simple and modest young Boulanger with a fervor for music." The princess dedicated her heart and purse to leadership in the arts and public service. From 1894 until her husband's death in 1901, the de Polignac salon hosted the first performances of Debussy, Fauré, and Ravel, among others. After her husband's death, she honored his memory with numerous commissions, including for Stravinsky's *Renard*, Erik Satie's *Socrate*, Darius Milhaud's *Les malheurs d'Orphée*, Francis Poulenc's Concerto for Two Pianos, and Kurt Weill's Symphony no. 2. After she met Nadia Boulanger in 1932, she became a strong supporter of students, composers, and performances related to the Boulanger circle.[100]

One could continue to list independent, competent women in Nadia Boulanger's orbit—Marcelle de Manziarly, Louise Talma, and Winifred Johnstone come to mind—but the point is that Nadia Boulanger was their commonly recognized leader. Why? What drew such strong personalities to her, and how did she ignite their passion?

Recent literature on Boulanger understandably focuses largely on her musical career. Music is what animated her. Kimberly Francis convincingly demonstrates the depth and breadth of Boulanger's impact on taste, theory, and performance of twentieth-century classical music in her incisive study of Boulanger's influence, *Teaching Stravinsky*. Francis leaves little doubt Boulanger was the dominant strategist and tactician in the neoclassical arena. Jeanice Brooks highlights Boulanger's strongly felt belief that fidelity to the work itself is

100 Kahan, *Music's Modern Muse,* 295–296.

the principal goal of music. Fidelity to "works that stand for time"—those with enduring value, representing the highest culture of their time—creates a communal ritual. Performers, audience, and the work itself participate together in an evanescent unity of spiritual experience. Boulanger wrote to Stravinsky in 1938 that "the work of art, to a certain degree, is an image of God." [101]

Nadia Boulanger shaped, inspired, and prodded twentieth-century musical taste, theory, and performance in a direction she knew to be correct. Music could and should bring out the better angels of human nature. She was a torch carrier who acted on her belief that the aim of music was to enable an experience of the beauty of the soul. She poured seemingly limitless creative and productive energy into her musical projects, building cultural capital in her field of music. This passion was central to her character.

However, as with many extraordinarily talented people, Nadia Boulanger's personality was complex. Her correspondence with Ruth Robbins highlights her complexity. I am drawn to the mystery of the affectionate relationship Boulanger had with my aunt, precisely because Robbins's value to Boulanger was clearly unrelated to cultural capital. Robbins was of mediocre talent as a musician. She was not wealthy, well-known, or well-connected. When the fifty-three-year-old Boulanger met her in 1940, Robbins was a naïve thirty-year-old striving to find her own identity separate from her family. Despite lack of sophistication or musical talent, Robbins struck a chord in Boulanger's heart. Why and how did that happen? What value did Boulanger find in her relationship with this unworldly Midwesterner? And from Ruth's perspective, what was it about Boulanger that caused her to feel awed, inspired, and enlightened?

101 Brooks, *Musical Work*, 251.

No expert in music or music history, I have drawn upon a background in aesthetics, literary theory, psychology, and philosophy—both Western and Eastern—to consider the dynamic between mentor and mentee revealed in these letters. Viewed through a broad lens, these letters offer their insights into Nadia Boulanger's personal thoughts and beliefs, as well as the cultural currents of the times. The aesthetic tradition she championed is an important part of what she imparts to Robbins in these letters, but they also reveal much about who she was as a person.

Applied to Boulanger and her followers, a torch metaphor is apt. The flame—an evanescent experience of the highest spiritual beauty—survives only if its bearers do what is necessary. Without bearers, the flame ceases to exist.

This was Boulanger's role, one she inspired others to take on. Her ardor and faith may have peaked during the Second World War, but Nadia Boulanger lived to be ninety-two. During the last four decades of her life, shared in her correspondence with Robbins, she experienced betrayal,[102] death, shifting musical taste, and the gradual diminishment of her influence and capacities. In her letters, we witness a losing struggle to retain the tremendous momentum of her first fifty years. But she never lost her faith that carrying forward the torch of civilization is the highest calling in life.

102 In an ugly spat, Louise Talma (1906–1996), a former student enjoying considerable career success, accused NB of anti-Semitism. The accusation does not seem consistent with other accounts of NB's personality. See Francis, *Teaching Stravinsky*, 129–131.

The Letters

Note: The contents of 227 handwritten exchanges—the entire correspondence that remains—are published here, including letters, cards, and brief notes. Not every letter has survived, so there are lacunae. I have placed the few undated missives where they seem to fit in the sequence and have quietly made minor grammatical corrections to ensure readability.

For ease of reference, the letters are numbered by year and by sequence within the year, so, for example, **Letter 42-15** refers to the fifteenth letter exchanged in 1942. Thus, the reader can follow the exchange chronologically.

APPLICATION FOR ADMISSION

THE LONGY SCHOOL OF MUSIC
Incorporated

One Follen Street
Cambridge, Massachusetts

Name of Applicant Ruth Robbins

REGISTRATION BLANK

Ruth Robbins took a course under Nadia Boulanger during the 1940–1941 academic year as evidenced by the first surviving letter in the joint archives, dated August 13, 1941. In May 1941, she applied to study with Boulanger in the fall semester "Seminar in Composition including one private lesson weekly for 6 weeks." [Longy School of Music Archives]

1941

Letter 41-1

13 August 1941
c/o Mrs. Arthur Sachs[103]
Rayben Farm[104]
Hope Ranch Park
Santa Barbara

Dear Ruth,

Everything is in order: we have the house (how afraid one is to speak of the future!). There might be a little complication, for I may be obliged to share a part of the house with you in the daytime. But I will try to arrange it otherwise. If that were to happen, we would

103 This letter addresses living arrangements in Cambridge, Massachusetts, where NB was to return to teach at the Longy School of Music for the 1941–1942 school year. RR had been one of her Longy students the previous year. Arthur and Georgette Sachs frequently hosted NB during the summers at their Santa Barbara estate and at their Lake Tahoe retreat. When NB fled the Nazi invasion in 1940, she went from northern France first to the villa in Uzerche owned by Georgette's parents before escaping to Madrid and Lisbon.

104 Rayben Farm was part of the Sachses' Santa Barbara estate. See Walsh, *Stravinsky,* 147.

of course make a financial arrangement, so that I share also the expenses.

I have anyhow retained the house for September 15 unless you prefer September 8. Let me know.

The renting is 125 dollars a month, no taxes. The heating is 125 dollars about, for the year. About blankets and linen am expecting details. But am so happy it seems settled.

As for your check, I decided to add it to the money sent to a young French composer named Leo Préger[105] for the 1/2 plus 1/2 to build a scholarship for a group of American composers. Shall let you know who will get it.

But I already thank you deeply. I cannot possibly do all what ought to be done, and your help means a great deal to me. Shall see you in Chicago on the 4th of September. Could you take to Cambridge some music, a little, it would help me greatly!

As ever yours, N.B.

I suspect you ought to bring linen and blankets.

Letter 41-2

18 August 1941

Dear Mademoiselle,

I have discussed the house situation with Julie and her mother, and we all feel that it is rather complex and quite expensive. If Julie and I had the house alone, the cost of living plus the tuition at school

---

105 This letter indicates NB was providing Léo Préger (1907–1965) financial support as early as 1941, as she adds RR's donation to what had already been given to him. In a December 5, 1955, *Harvard Crimson* review of Préger's "Mass for Three Men's Voices," Stephen Addiss noted, "Préger's style is stark, powerful, and extremely difficult."

and lessons with Miss Whisnant would be more than the Cirals[106] feel they can afford, and I feel is very expensive. If we shared the house with you, we would of course be very restricted in our practicing, and, from the Cirals' point of view, in our social life. They feel that it is very important to be perfectly free to come and go and to entertain, and that would be very difficult if you were teaching there.

Julie said that she hoped they were not deciding too hastily as she realizes it would be a valuable and fine experience, but that she is afraid that she could not do her best under those conditions, and for that reason and the others I have given, feels that it is an unsatisfactory arrangement. She is quite upset as she feels she is making it impossible for me to take advantage of such an opportunity, but I told her that I had the same things to consider as she, and that I would never be happy with an arrangement for two that would be satisfactory for only one.

However, I am greatly disappointed. From the financial point of view, although it is expensive, I feel that it is an investment I would be perfectly willing to make for such an opportunity. I wish I could manage it alone, but I could not possibly, so that is out. From the social point of view—well, I haven't any, so what is very important to Julie means very little to me. I know I am at fault there, but that is the way I am.

But more fundamentally than that, the very situation in which Julie feels she could not work, would be the one thing in the world that would force me to break through my limitations and cause me to function as I should. It would probably be very painful, but I think I could stand that if I felt I would be forever different after such an experience. If I could not work, knowing that you would be hearing

106 Alexine Whisnant was a teacher associated with the Longy School of Music who gave RR private lessons. In RR's October 2, 1942, letter to NB, she mentions that Whisnant had introduced them. "T. Ciral," also a student of NB's, has two compositions in Harvard's Loeb Music Library, Isham Memorial Library.

everything, it would be better to find it out right away, and stop trying to be a musician. It seems to me that a few months of acute discomfort along that line would be a great relief, after years of being on the outside and just looking in at real things. I do not know if I am making myself clear at all. Words are so inadequate. People do not understand why I am willing to give up (from their point of view) freedom and independence, and I cannot explain that when one is searching for something solid to stand on, he does not count the cost.

Goodness, I did not mean to start along this line! I merely wanted to explain why I am so disappointed about not having the house, and that I could not ask Julie to take it merely to oblige me. But it is so easy to write to you about such things, and since I started, I could not stop.

If I keep telling you that I feel you understand so deeply, it is because I am not used to it, and it overwhelms me.

I am so very sorry to have involved you in sharing a house and then not been able to go through with it. If there is any satisfactory adjustment that can be made, please let me know.

We are still in the midst of clearing out this house, and the day that I <u>must</u> leave is still vague. I will let you know, and will be very happy to relieve you of some of your music when I leave for Boston.

Much Love, Ruth R.

P.S. I have asked Julie or Mrs. Ciral to write you as I feel they could explain much better than I of their point of view.

Letter 41-3

20 August 1941
Rayben Farm
Hope Ranch Park
Santa Barbara

Dear Ruth,

Needless to say that your letter at first troubled me deeply, but . . . do not worry. I shall keep it, in order not to harm Mrs. Forbes who had been so nice about it. The fact that I was to teach a few hours a week had only relieved you from a third of the expenses, but . . . it is quite all right. Had I known we were undecided, perhaps this would be easier. But anyhow, the matter is now settled, decisions made, and you have no more to think about the house. Do not feel I am worried. It is my fault and I ought by now to avoid such things. Perhaps it is much better so—shall see you in Chicago on my way to Cambridge. If you leave before my arrival, do not inquire about the music; shall take it with me on the train.

Am not less happy to have you this winter in Cambridge, even if not so near. It means very much to me.

Hastily, affectionately yours, N. Boulanger

Letter 41-4

8 September 1941
Rayben Farm
Hope Ranch Park
Santa Barbara

Dear Ruth,

You are very thoughtful and kind, and I thank you deeply. But as I said, I took other dispositions, and do not think it can be managed now. For I shall give more lessons than I sought in the little house; it would not work for you anymore.

It is perfectly true that it did worry me when, having rented the house for you, I heard it was no more to work as planned. But, considering at once the situation, I realized that you were right that something had to be done, and finally, I found a solution.

So, have no more this question on your mind. Either I had been in your way, or you in mine. Now it is in order, and I deeply hope you are to find a nice apartment for you both.

Am sorry to have to delay my departure, but the doctor is right, and I hope, in following his advice, to have a fruitful winter amongst you who bring so much light in my life. It is so wonderful, and now more than ever, to be with young people, with their hopes and their future.

So affectionately, N. Boulanger

Letter 41-5

21 September 1941
Rayben Farm
Hope Ranch Park
Santa Barbara

Dear Ruth,

Your trouble I fully understand. Let know to Mr. Smith[107] that for the private lessons you prefer to wait for my arrival. I will replace the missed one, of course. It is much wiser than to change direction now.

Glad you had an apartment. Hope to see you soon, very likely on the 13th.

You understand I am sure how worried I am to be away—but there was nothing to do.

With affection and most good wishes,

Nadia Boulanger

107 Melville Smith, a former student of NB's, was director of the Longy School from 1941 to 1962.

1942

Letter 42-1

May 1942
Wednesday night

Dear Mademoiselle,

For weeks I have had a feeling in my bones that you would once again become the victim of my pen. I have tried my best to refrain from writing this letter, but I am bursting with something, and if I do not get it out of my system, I shall probably turn into a camel and grow humps on my back which will be the result of unsaid things. As you are responsible for what I feel, you will have to take the consequences, and anyhow, when I get a pen and paper in my hand, I go sort of mad, so I refuse to accept the responsibility for anything that may come out.

There is no way for me to describe to you what this year's work has meant to me (and music is only a small part of it), but it has created quite a problem. All my life I have dreamed of having such an experience and of working with someone in whom I had absolute confidence, and now that I have had it, and am having it, I do not know what to dream about anymore! I often wonder why I, of all the millions of people on this earth, should be one of those fortunate few to have been let out of the mist and shown where I am and why, and where I must go, and to be helped along the way. It is such a wonderful discovery. In order to thank you in a tangible way, I am enclosing a check which I hope will make it possible for someone else to study with you who might not otherwise have the opportunity.

That takes care of one hump.

The other is not so easy to write about, as it is caused by the constant pricking of my conscience ever since last summer when I backed out of an agreement and left you stranded with a heavy financial obligation. Were it not that that is part of the reason for the check and that I could not tell you less than the whole reason, I would not mention it. Whenever I have made decisions that I have later regretted, they invariably have been the ones in which I did not consider how I really felt, as the basis for the decision. There should be two checks, one for each hump, but I am obliged to kill two birds with one stone in order to be certain of having another year's work myself. That I would not give up for anything.

Please accept this scholarship fund as a gesture of gratitude for what you have done, and of remorse for what I have done. With so much love, Ruth

Letter 42-2

1 June 1942
Featherhill Ranch[108]
Montecito
Santa Barbara, California

Dear Ruth,

Cross thoughts! I was to write, cannot you bring your car? On the other hand, I hate not to have our expedition together. Well, perhaps we could. How long in the car does it take?

Half joke, but anyhow keep for the present your reservation, even if you do not employ it, I may need it for Suz. Fortier.

Other point: are you full of courage? Yes, always. So, you have better to know that for a time, indefinite, I must stay in Boston. Important questions to settle. So, we have to be ready for cooking. As much as you hate it—no more than myself. And according with the fact that nothing happens as planned. We may finish on the top of a mountain, or on an island.

Am sorry not having written when so painful an anniversary came. You were in my heart—and she—and your brother and the children.[109] Why I did not; I cannot forgive myself. So happy to see you soon, my dear (am arriving on the 15th and leaving on the 19th with you and Father Fortier).

I am, as ever, devotedly yours.

---

108 Featherhill Ranch was the main Sachs residence in Santa Barbara. Renowned architectural photographer Maynard Parker's photos of the estate are in the Huntington Library collection of Parker's work (https://www.huntington.org/).

109 RR's sister-in-law Murnie died, leaving RR's brother Jim Robbins a widower with three young children.

[Postscript]:

Of course shall see Dick and give him what to him will be a long lesson!

Can you bring him some time on the 16th or 17th or 18th? If you get the car, wire me Saturday or Sunday at the [name obscured] or on Monday here, where I will be back, for it might change my own plans.

Again, yours, Nadia Boulanger

Letter 42-3

9 July 1942

Dear Ruth,

Can you come at 10:45? Ask to Mrs. Friedman[110] 567 Ash St. Winnetka to come at 8:45. Drive me at 12 at Mrs. Shortall's 339 Barry Ave.?[111]

We have a saying: Who says no word, consents (agrees). So . . . till Saturday, I hope!

Yours, N.B.

Please, Miss Whisnant address—summer one, campus.

---

110 An unidentified student of NB's.

111 Wife of Harrington Shortall (1895–1984), a music composer and educator. According to *Guide to the Harrington Shortall Papers* (University of Chicago Library), "Shortall studied under Nadia Boulanger, and went on to compose a diverse body of musical work. As an educator, Shortall taught at the Chicago Theological Seminary, and Rosary College. Shortall's papers contain a collection of material related to Nadia Boulanger, including correspondence."

Letter 42-4

[1942][112]

[TELEGRAM]

ARRIVE MONDAY MORNING SEVEN O'CLOCK TEN AFFECTIONATELY = NADIA BOULANGER.

Letter 42-5

[1942][113]

St. Clara Convent [114]

Sinsinawa, Wisconsin

Dear Ruth,

Will you thank your mother and say I shall be delighted to come tomorrow after the lecture if really it does not disturb your

112 This undated telegram likely refers to NB's mid-July 1942 arrival in Chicago from California.

113 This undated note, written on St. Clara Convent stationery after NB's arrival there, refers to plans for a visit to RR's family home in Highland Park, a four-hour drive east.

114 St. Clara Convent was founded in the nineteenth century for the sole purpose of training teachers. The convent is associated with St. Clara Academy and Edgewood College, Roman Catholic educational institutions with a faculty drawn exclusively from the order of St. Clara's Dominican Sisters. An 1890 poster notes St. Clara Academy provides "Vocal music class and private lessons; Instrumental music—piano, organ, harp, guitar and violin; Painting in portraits and landscapes; Bookkeeping, stenography, typewriting, and elocution; Latin, French, German, and Italian," all subjects appropriate to Catholic schools. St. Clara Convent had strong musical ties to Paris and Rome. Sr. Amanda Cortaux, an 1879 graduate of the Paris Conservatory, taught piano there in the 1920s. Sr. Mary Edward Blackwell, the first woman to earn an advanced degree in music at the American Conservatory of Music in Chicago, was awarded a scholarship to study with Ottorino Respighi and Igor Stravinsky in 1933; from 1936 to 1938, she studied with NB in France; in 1939, she became the chair of the music department. NB taught choir, composition, and piano at Edgewood College, and gave evening concert lectures, open to the public, during the summers of 1941–1944 (http://music.edgewood.edu/history). NB spent six weeks during the summer with her former students Sisters Ignatia and Edward at the St. Clara Convent in Sinsinawa, Wisconsin. Sinsinawa was a four- or five-hour drive from RR's family home in Highland Park, Illinois. NB would arrange lessons with Chicago-area students before and after her St. Clara sojourns. RR made these arrangements for her and provided transportation from Chicago to Sinsinawa and back. On a few occasions, NB stayed or provided lessons at RR's Highland Park family residence on the shores of Lake Michigan.

mother.[115] Were it to be, you could perhaps find a place to give the lessons Saturday morning. From 9 to 12 Mrs. Friedman please phone to her and say I can manage three hours—and 12 to 1 or 1:15 better for you. Shall give the other appointments Friday afternoon.

Am going back Saturday at 3:30 with so many thanks and deep affection, N.B.

Letter 42-6

[Summer 1942][116]

[Greeting card text]

And after these things
I heard a great voice
of much people in heaven,
saying, Alleluia; Salvation,
and glory, and honor.
—Book of Revelation

[Handwritten note]

Dear Ruth,

Let me say how happy you are here, and how I wish you what you deserve to such an extent. May the Lord bring you the knowledge of His light.

As ever, devotedly yours, Nadia Boulanger

---

115 NB accepts an invitation to the family home in Highland Park, Illinois, where RR lived with her mother and her widowed brother Jim's and his three children.
116 Undated card welcomes RR on a visit to St. Clara's Convent.

Letter 42-7

24 July 1942
St. Clara Convent
Sinsinawa Wisconsin

Dear Ruth,

Shall be in Chicago at Mrs. Shortall's Monday morning. Shall see you at 9:30, Mrs. Friedman at 10:30. Could see Olga at 8:30—if so, please send me a wire here.

How happy to have one hour more with you before my round trip to East, North, and back, before to be on my way to Nevada on the 1st of August!!

Most affectionately, N.B.

Letter 42-8

5 August 1942

Dear Mademoiselle,

Time is skipping by so fast that I had not realized until today that I must let my landlady know in a week whether or not I am to retain my apartment for another year.[117] If you could let me know as soon as possible what you decide about the little house, I will appreciate it very much.

Let me reassure you that no matter under what condition, to be with you would be a great privilege, and nothing would make

117 RR is discussing sharing a house with NB for the 1942–1943 academic year.

me happier. HOWEVER, unless such an arrangement will be to your advantage, I do not want it. Please do not hesitate to tell me if a better arrangement for you turns up, or a better person to share the house, or just invent any old excuse, if you like (for example, "Mary Jones can cook. You can't. Goodbye!") or just say "no" without any explanation if you feel so inclined. I will admit that I will be disappointed if the answer is no, but then I needed to be disappointed when I could not have the moon, so I am accustomed to it. It is just that I want you to be sure it will be an arrangement that you feel is worth something to you, and will not hesitate to decide against it if not. From my point of view, being with you is like finally reaching home after hunting for it all my life; but I already feel that, and it will be the same no matter what you decide.

Mother was so touched by your gift, and she asked me to thank you and to say you should not have done it. And I must admit that I have a very guilty conscience because I voted for the chocolates, which tasted much better than a shawl. However, Mother had some of the candy and loved it, and anyhow, I was perfectly honest, only slightly influenced.

Thank you for everything. The piano lessons were wonderful, and I feel that everything is much clearer, and I am much more certain about what I am striving for and how to go after it. I never did get to the point of discussing with you my piano work for next year, but I guess when I see you again will be time enough.

I hope you are having a wonderful vacation and are enjoying Lake Tahoe as much as I did. It is such a beautiful place that I am afraid you will never leave!

So much love, Ruth

LETTER 42-9

[UNDATED][118]
GLENBROOK, LAKE TAHOE[119]
NEVADA

Dear Ruth,

Your letter touches me more than I can say. Let me first thank you for it. As ever, Mr. Hayes is silent, and I sent immediately a telegramme to know if the house is still available and what answer he can give to my different questions. If there is no answer by Friday, keep your apartment. What else can be done? In spite of the extreme kindness of Mrs. Smith and W., I am rather worried, for I do not see how living in Boston will work out.[120] Being in Cambridge was also a feeling of trees, of sun I did like so much—and everything could have worked out so nicely!

Well, we have to wait. I do not know why, for it is the interest of the Bowers to rent the house. It may have been wrong not to look for something else in Cambridge, but . . . what can we do now? You in the middle of this world, and I, at the end!

Strange, in such a time, to find time for such questions. But, that is just life. The mind knowing that our whole civilization is in mortal danger. That only each of our will can still help to save it, in being really ready to die for the values in which we ought to believe, and here, one of these foolish (and rather honest) human beings, weeping for the loss of a little dream. But I do, without forgetting

118 This undated letter was written in response to Letter 42-8.

119 Arthur Sachs's summer home.

120 "W." refers to Winifred Hope Johnstone. Winifred Johnstone, a trained secretary, handled much of Boulanger's correspondence, arranged schedules, received and disbursed money, and did what was needed to see to Boulanger's comfort, in effect acting as Boulanger's American agent. Offered a place to reside by Winifred Johnstone, NB is concerned about the location of the Smith-Johnstone residence at 122 Bay State Road in Boston, a commute of several miles from the Longy School in Cambridge.

for a minute that there is no more time to waste, and that we must really be alive, if we are not to help (to give our consent) to complex and primitive destructive and accumulated strengths to destroy what centuries have, at the price of a great labour and great honour, created.

Dear Ruth, thanking you again—for old as I am, the only hope and consolation is found in you, the young ones, and your affection and your confidence are great comfort.

As ever, N.B.

[POSTSCRIPT]

Would you please ask Mrs. Friedman to let me know how much time she likes to have on the 11th of September (shall be in Chicago the 11th and 12th morning).

Olga Sandor, does she want time?

And D. Billingsley?

And Maurine Parzybok?[121]

Knowing that, I could more easily settle the day, for I have some appointments to arrange.

Do you forgive me?

121 Olga Sandor, accomplished pianist, vocalist, and composer, was a friend of RR's sister Jane. D. Billingsley is unidentified. Maurine Parzybok, a contralto soloist who performed with the Chicago Symphony, was on the faculty of the Northwestern University summer music school, and appeared in oratorios in many communities in the Midwest. She performed the role of Queen Dido in a University of Chicago production of Henry Purcell's *Dido and Aeneas*. Alton Illinois, "Four Chicagoans Messiah Soloists," *Evening Telegraph*, November 17, 1945, 2.

Letter 42-10

12 August 1942

[Telegram]

Impossible get necessary information from Hayes. Have sent telegram. If no news by Friday keep your apartment. Letter follows. Affection = Nadia Boulanger.

Letter 42-11

20 August 1942
Glenbrook, Lake Tahoe
Nevada

Dear Ruth,

When the telegramme arrived, it said Rosamand's house was already rented. Well . . . that forced the decision—it had been nice, but may be settled in another way later.

Do not think I do not appreciate Mrs. Smith's offer, but Boston is complicated, and our arrangement was so pleasant.

When one considers life today, one feels no right to stop at any personal wish, but only to weep. But it is the strange, mysterious power of life: here tragedy and nearby life going on! However, something is totally different. Never yet had the world entire been in question, and we begin to realize that from these years we have to understand problems which had been forgotten, neglected—and . . . we pay, what a terrible price.

It will be good to see you soon! The need for the ones who are dear to us has such an acuity—one is so sad! Either than to hope, I know, when we will really hope, we will have found the way!

As ever yours, N.B.

Letter 42-12

31 August 1942

Dear Ruth,

Shall only be in Cambridge the 29th, to give you eventually time—but . . . as far as Philipp, Cortot, Dubois[122] are concerned, I think Cambridge is a good climate.

You do not know how happy I shall be to see you again.

Do not bother about Mrs. Friedman—shall send her a note, and know how to reach Miss Parzybok.

Hastily, most affectionately yours, Nadia Boulanger

Here until the 12th. After with Mrs. A. Sachs 475 Riven Rock Road, Montecito, Santa Barbara, Cal.

---

122 Three influential French composers and pianists: Isidor Philipp (1863–1958), a pianist, composer, and pedagogue of Jewish Hungarian descent; Alfred Cortot (1877–1962), a Swiss-French pianist and conductor; and Théodore Dubois (1837–1924), a composer, organist, and music teacher. The names reference a lesson plan NB had for RR.

Letter 42-13

4 September 1942

Dear Mademoiselle,

I am so sorry that you will be late arriving in Cambridge, and I hope it is not illness that is detaining you. You will have to be in A-1 condition to knock ideas into this thick skull, so be sure to get a good rest if possible.

Cortot and Dubois have found that the climate here has improved considerably since my nieces and nephews left,[123] and who in h-ll is PHILIPP????

I am happy to have more time to get ready, but if I had from now to Christmas, it would be the same. I still would not be ready.

So many times I wonder if it is not just selfishness that makes me return to Cambridge to have another year of music as full and rich as last year. I love it so, but realize that I have contributed nothing and probably will contribute very little along that line, and would probably be much more useful as a worker in an airplane factory or as a nurse.

But I keep seeing past the war, and know that no matter how bitter and furious a struggle it is now, it cannot go on forever. When it is over, there will be plenty of work to do in the search and establishing of better values, and if I have not learned to believe in myself in the meantime, I will be just as useless then as I always have been. If it were only development in music that would be gained from another year's study, I might really hesitate, no matter how much it means to me. But already, in one year, you have helped me so much to find my own convictions, and to have the courage of my own convictions, that I cannot even imagine what another year

123 She means being able to practice Cortot and Dubois unencumbered by visiting nieces and nephews.

will bring forth. There has always been a great chasm between my imagination and everyday life, but you have flung a bridge across, and all I have to do is take the necessary steps to cross it. So in the face of every doubt and criticism, I can only look forward to the coming year with great joy.

So much love, Ruth

Letter 42-14

[Undated][124]
c/o Mrs. A. Sachs
475 Riven Rock Rd.
Montecito, Santa Barbara, California

Dear Ruth,

Let me only say a word: all these people stopping to accomplish normal duties often chose the easy way—one walks, the others follow—and, no more need to think, to struggle, to hope. You are a part of a mechanism. If this part is needed, well, no question, one must be this part. If people are missing, well, no question, one must go. But, as that is never the case, in any country, except for people having special training, special power, one has overcrowd[ing] at one place, and emptiness at the other.

And this problem of values, of education, of tradition, of thought, of art is so great, that we have only to stop for a minute to think of history, to have the answer. With high intellectual standards, you can ask any sacrifice. With lower standards spiritually

124 This undated letter was sent in response to Letter 42-13 after NB started her 1942 sojourn at the Sachs ranch in Montecito.

or intellectually, you meet selfishness, weakness, and despair. There must be men to fight, making the gift of their best years, of their life to save what the one who cannot fight, or women must defend of the not less precious treasury. Done to escape is awful, done to develop is what has to be, if one fights not only against, but also for—what is more than life—and what gives its real meaning to Victory.

So, do not feel troubled. What you prepare yourself to do and to give will be more than badly needed. If missing, everything will fall in pieces. Shall see you on the 29th and am so happy for it in advance.

As ever, so affectionately yours, N.B.

Letter 42-15

2 October 1942

Dear Mademoiselle,

I have been thinking about our conversation about Miss Whisnant[125] ever since I left you this afternoon, and feel that in this case it would be much better to say too much than too little. I would feel very, very badly if she were to be deprived of any work with you on my account. It was entirely through her and the work I had with her that I was able to come to you at all, and to think that the result of that might be that I would come between her and her study with you, upsets me tremendously. And I seem to have quite a gift for making trouble between people, so I have to be very careful

125 Alexine Whisnant, RR's private piano teacher, who introduced her to NB in 1940.

what I do and say. And yet I have to make decisions according to what I feel deeply, no matter how unreasonable that may be. I have studied music with Miss W. for seven years, and I have never during those years felt satisfied with her teaching of piano technique. The reason I kept studying with her was because I valued her teaching of ear-training and musicianship so highly. At first the technical end did not bother me, as I had so much to learn from other points of view. But for several years now I have realized that I was not getting anywhere technically, and became so discouraged that I was ready to give up on music altogether if you had not given an encouraging opinion about my music when you did. Since then, I have been waiting for an opportunity to discontinue my work with Miss W. without hurting her, as I know how easily she is hurt.

I realize it is a very awkward situation for you, and would understand perfectly if you decided not to give me piano lessons, even though I would be terribly disappointed. But if I were to go on with Miss W., it would be for personal reasons, and not for musical reasons, and that I cannot do.

On one hand she gives her pupils an invaluable musical experience, but on the other hand squeezes all the joy and vitality out of it by not yielding to the natural course of development in her pupils. It is so hard to say exactly what it is that goes wrong, and if it were only I who felt it, I would say nothing, but so many of her pupils have said the same things.

Perhaps I have said too much, but as you seem to be able to help her more than anyone, I think that it might be helpful for you to know how I and some of the others feel. She has so much to give, and I should like so much to be able to really help her for what she has given me.

By the way, her piano is still in the same house, only it had to be moved into another boarder's room when her room was rented.

If I can do anymore to help you get settled, do let me know. Only we must invent excuses for me to disappear at mealtimes as I do not want to impose on Mrs. Smith. It is such a temptation!

So much love,

Ruth Robbins

Ruth Robbins (standing far right under awning; second from left in front of trees) in Francis Poulenc's 1953 Composition Class at Fontainbleau [Ruth Robbins Archives]

1943

LETTER 43-1

3 JANUARY 1943

[INSIDE GREETING]

C'est l'ange du jour (This is today's angel)

[WRITTEN IN BOULANGER'S HAND]

Nothing is obtained without pain, and life is perpetual work. — Education cannot be conferred; it is obtained by work, and is communicated. —It is by reading that a man shapes himself and not by reciting hand-books. And it is also by working, modestly—

Charles Péguy[126]

Dear Ruth,

Thank you so much for the lovely vase—and for the beautiful letter. You do not know what warmth brings to the heart such confidence.

Many many wishes—and all my deep affection,

N.B.

Letter 43-2

3 July 1943
Dominican Sisters Convent
Edgewood College
1000 Edgewood Avenue
Madison, Wisconsin
3 July 1943

Dear Ruth,

"Les bons comptes font les bons amis."[127]

Therefore here is a check! And accurate!! Will you be good enough to unorder this bedroom that I am not to employ? But do that only around the 12th.

Until Thursday—so affectionately,

N.B.

---

126 Charles Péguy was a poet, essayist, and editor who espoused socialism and French nationalism. He was a reluctant agnostic who, toward the end of his life, became a believing but not practicing Roman Catholic. He was killed in action defending France at age 41. NB no doubt was familiar with his works in her youth—he was well known and highly influential in the years before his death. His death in defense of France must have been for NB a touchstone for the destruction of intelligence and culture wrought by war.

127 "Good accounts make good friends;" that is, if you want to keep good friends, pay up and clear accounts promptly.

Letter 43-3

6 October 1943
Featherhill Ranch
Montecito
Santa Barbara, California

Dear Ruth, Go tomorrow to the ticket office, probably more hospitable now than in July. Retain a bed for Los Angeles, and let me know when you are to arrive.

Will be here until Christmas, anyhow. Such a long stop would, it seems to me, a mistake. And moreover, it is sad not to see you for so long.

Seriously, I think it is the right decision—we return then together—and you settle at the D, I hope[128] (I promise not to take advantage of your being here).

Of course, you could wait for me in Chicago, but it is such a delay. If you have a bicycle, bring it, or I may find one for you. The Bostonian may love the West!

Hoping so much you will give me the joy of measuring your progress. I shall watch the arriving mail with impatience.

Am so ashamed not yet to have thanked you for who will have the 60 dollars. Life becomes so hard for the youngster who has little to spend. Shall I let you know who?

With sincere regards to your mother, and love to you, dear Ruth.

And love to you,

As ever, N.B.

128 "The D" is a shorthand reference to an accommodation near the Sachses' Montecito ranch, likely the neighboring Baring-Gould ranch where Robbins stayed.

TEACHER'S REPORT FOR ACADEMIC STUDY

Student Robbins, Ruth Teacher Mlle. Boulanger Subject musicalship (Composition) Date FEB 1 1943

Elementary + Adv.

	VERY POOR (E)	POOR (D)	LOW AVERAGE (C-)	HIGH AVERAGE (C+)	GOOD (B)	SUPERIOR (A)
ESTIMATED INTELLIGENCE: Aptitude for learning, ability to grasp ideas and follow instructions.					+	
ESTIMATED MUSICAL TALENT*: Inborn capacity insofar as shown by subject in question.				+		
APPLICATION: effort, faithfulness in preparation; desire to accomplish required tasks.						+
ACHIEVEMENT: progress based on expected achievement according to requirements of course.					+	

*Omit if subject is purely academic, i.e. language, English.

FACTORS WHICH HINDER PROGRESS late start

FACTORS WHICH AID PROGRESS extraordinary application

ESTIMATED MARK: E D C- C+ B A

B

Nadia Boulanger gave Ruth Robbins high marks for effort and faithfulness in preparation on her February 1, 1943, "Teacher's Report for Academic Study." [Longy School of Music Archives]

November 7, 1943

Dear Mr. Smith,

Mlle. Boulanger tells me that the Noble House of Smith is blessed with a brand new heir! How wonderful! I'm sure he is a fine boy, and you must be very happy. Please extend my best wishes and congratulations to Mrs. Smith.

My plans about continuing my work with Mlle. Boulanger were very uncertain until almost three weeks ago, and that is why I had not written the school before that time. And since I arrived, I have been so busy getting organized that this is the first opportunity I've had to write.

I've already had two lessons with Mlle. starting on October 30th. I don't quite know what to do about paying the tuition. Should I wait for a bill from the school, or shall I send a check for one semester's work? If you will let me know what to do, I shall tend to the matter at once. I am sorry not to have let you know sooner about my plans but it could not be helped.

Please remember me to Mrs. Buckingham.

Sincerely,

Ruth Robbins

c/o Baring-Gould
Romero Canyon Rd.
Santa Barbara, Cal

On November 7, 1943, Ruth Robbins wrote to school director Melville Smith to ask if she should pay Longy for lessons from Nadia Boulanger while at the Sachses' Santa Barbara estate. He replied on November 18, "We are disappointed that Mlle. Boulanger will be unable to return here this year but I am sure it is best for her. I have written to her saying that any pupils . . . in California will have no connection with the School."
[Longy School of Music Archives]

November 18, 1943

Dear Miss Robbins,

Thank you so much for your kind letter. Little Nathaniel and Mrs. Smith are doing very well and we were glad to have your news.

We are disappointed that Mlle. Boulanger will be unable to return here this year but I am sure it is best for her. I have written to her saying that any pupils she decides to take in California will have no connection with the School and I would advise you to make any financial arrangements with Mlle. Boulanger personally. I hope your work this winter will be successful and I know you will enjoy being out there.

With kindest wishes,
Very sincerely yours,

Melville Smith
Director

Miss Ruth Robbins
c/o Baring-Gould
Romero Canyon Rd.
Santa Barbara, California

MS/egb

1944

LETTER 44-1

4 JULY 1944
c/o DOMINICAN SISTERS
EDGEWOOD COLLEGE
1000 EDGEWOOD AVENUE
MADISON, WISCONSIN

Dear Ruth, The package arrived safely. And its contents saved my life, for mosticos[129] are aggressive! Thank you so much.

It sounds queer no more to call on you—bringing so much so discreetly. Life is absurd! And where will we meet again? Well, on the 5th I hope. I shall arrive on this Saturday at 5:20 p.m. Leave at 9:15 for Bloomington, be back on the 9th. Hoping to lunch with you this Wednesday. Then leave, 10th, 11th, 12th according to what reservations I can get, for San Bernardino. Hope you can keep a little free time during those few hours.

---

129 NB's charming Franglais for "mosquitoes" ("moustiques" in French).

Am thinking of you all. Of all which gives such a new cause to your life. Hope to be part of it, from afar if not in fact, for you realize, I am sure, how involved I am in what concerns you, and your family.

It has been good to have you this year. May it not be the last.

Understanding your thoughts on this grave 4th of July,[130] and your pride for all that is accomplished daily all over the world, I am in profound affection.

Yours, N.B.

Letter 44-2

11 July 1944
Edgewood College
Madison, Wisconsin

Dear Ruth, Our conversations about the whole situation were in my mind to be entirely personal. You were however wise to recall it to me.

Have wept in reading your letter.

Thank you for the beautiful little stone. So delicate in color. And quite different. Found some bright shining black here. And that, without forgetting for a minute what the world goes through! Is it not strange.

The 5th shall arrive at 1:21. The 9th early morning. Do not forget our lunch!

Am with you, you know, with complete understanding. And hope, do really hope, that the future will not separate our roads.

In profound affection, yours, N.B.

---

130 The D-Day invasion on June 6–7 had opened up intense fighting in northern France.

Letter 44-3

16 July 1944

Dear Mademoiselle,

I hope you are having some of the wonderful cool and refreshing weather that we are having here. Today has been perfect—breezes from the lake all day, and the lake and sky vying with each other to see which could produce the brightest blue. The sky had the advantage of white clouds, but the lake had white waves and sailboats, so in the end, it was an even draw. And to top all that, I have heard such beautiful music on the radio! Serkin played Beethoven's Emperor Concerto with the NY Philharmonic. He plays with such a rhythm that the piece goes from beginning to end in one continuous unbroken line, and all expression is subservient to his steady pulsation. To me his playing is always pure music with no striving for grand effects or expression, and consequently more moving than any other pianist I have heard. I am literally transported by the sweep of his rhythm!

Later I heard Mozart's Concerto in C Major for the flute and harp, and I will not try to describe the beauty of that heavenly music. And just now I heard (recorded) Brahms' Piano Concerto in B♭ Major played by Horowitz and Toscanini. So you see, I am completely saturated with beauty by now. The only thing that could have been an improvement would be to have seen you. But that would have been too perfect. What is the difference between the pronunciation of "penser" and "panser"? I have been trying to read Stravinsky's Poétique Musicale, but it is so difficult that after all this time, I am only on page six. I know it is not exactly the right book to choose to start learning a language with, but I am wild to know what is in it. The only thing I am afraid of is that I will not live long enough to find out.

We do not know yet when to expect my brother and the children, but we think perhaps Jane has started or is about to start with the two girls.

I am hoping that they will arrive before you start west so you can meet them, but I am afraid it will take them quite a while to get here. I wish you knew my sisters' children—especially Susie who is just five. She can (she tells me) play "Mary Had a Little Lamb" on the recorder with one hand while playing "Jesus Loves Me" on the piano with the other. I have not heard this feat yet, but I have heard her play each instrument separately. She has a good ear and has picked out quite a number of pieces on the piano. She also likes to gather rocks and arrange them in boxes. She "arranged" half a dozen boxes for her mother's birthday last week. You would have a wonderful time with her.

I shall see you the 5th at 1:21 and will keep my time free for anything that comes along. I had a nice letter from Marian S. yesterday.

It is late. Love, Ruth

LETTER 44-4

28 JULY 1944

Dear Mademoiselle,

It does not seem possible that I will see you a week from tomorrow at 1:21 p.m. at the station. The time has gone so fast. There have been so many people calling or here for lunches or dinners that I have been quite tied up with them and have not accomplished anything much except in the line of preparing meals and washing dishes. I have worked fairly consistently at French, but my friend is leaving this weekend, and I doubt that I will work very hard by myself. I had hoped to finish all the harmony examples up to the chapter on altered chords before your return to California. Perhaps if I work hard this next week I shall.

We have finally heard that my family in Alaska will definitely start home on August 2. I doubt that they will arrive before you leave, but there is a bare possibility that they will do so.

A letter today from my other brother says he is definitely going into combat service. We think he is in China now as a replacement, and he said he is very nervous about taking men he does not know into combat against men he does know are very good fighters.

I heard a good many concerts at Ravinia Park[131] last week. I heard Serkin[132] twice. The first time he played the Schumann Concerto in A Minor and the second time Beethoven's Emperor Concerto. When I wrote you last, I thought I had been perhaps too eloquent in my praise of his playing, but after last week I decided I had not said enough. This week Efrem Kurtz[133] is conducting. He conducted Stravinsky's Norwegian Moods, Circus Polka, and the Russian Dance from Petruschka so sloppily and clumsily and heavily that it was terrible and sounded like bad sight-reading. I am so glad I have the records! I decided to skip the rest of the concerts this week and wait until Defauw[134] comes next week.

---

131 Ravinia is an outdoor summertime music venue north of Chicago.

132 Pianist Rudolf Serkin (1903–1991), one of the great Beethoven interpreters of the twentieth century.

133 Efrem Kurtz (1900–1995), a Russian-born American conductor most highly regarded for his interpretations of Russian music, was music director of the Kansas City Orchestra from 1943 to 1948. *New York Times,* obituaries, June 2, 1995.

134 Désiré Defauw (1885–1960), Belgian conductor.

Sister Ignatia[135] promised (under dire threats by me) to let me know when your concert would be. A special delivery letter from her arrived today letting me know, but I will not be able to attend it as I will have to be here Sunday.

Thursday is my smallest niece's fourth birthday, and as I have promised her to be there for her party, I do not see how I could manage as it is about a five or six hour trip for me. I am so disappointed!

It will be so good to see you soon. If you do not hear from me again before that, you can expect me to be at the station (Union, I guess) to meet the train.

Love, Ruth

P.S. Do not forget! I still owe you money.

Letter 44-5

22 August 1944
Arrowhead Woods
Lake Arrowhead
Calif.

Dear Ruth,

Sorry not yet having answered.

1. Will you send the gloves to Mrs. Shortall?

2. Will you send me three boxes of your air mail self-sticking?

3. Will you send me two hundred cards for my catalogue (books) more or less this size?

---

135 Dominican Sister Ignatia of Edgewood College in Sinsinawa, Wisconsin, where NB taught the summers of 1941–1944.

4. Shall send check when that is added.

Here is the lunch bell. And very hasty "au revoir."

Have so much to say. Think of you so much, the children, your brother, you.

Well, you know I am really with you.

N.B.

Love to Jane, too.

Letter 44-6

25 August 1944
Arrowhead Woods
Lake Arrowhead California

Dear Ruth,

Your letter[136] is just the one I could dream to receive from you—understanding, feeling each nuance of what makes life so complex, in these highly significant days! Enjoy, one cannot, for the sacrifices are too terrible—and however, such a light in the darkness—But once the hope [is] seen, arises a new, still unknown fear arrives: now, it is no more an awful nightmare one is going through: who is still alive—what will be hear: Killed by the Germans, dead through suffering—gone because it was the time marked by God.

And, in spite of the tremendous relief and hope, one is sad, and . . . one feels more heavily the remorse to have let them go through this agony, without being at their side, sharing the burden,

136 Unfortunately, this letter from RR has not been preserved.

the danger, and the expectancy of those very days. But . . . what friends I would have lost had I not come here for so many years. Friends so close to me, so necessary to my inner life, and having given so much of their heart, as I gave thence so much of mine.

Well, life is not simple, and to come to a con— [FIRST PART OF LETTER ENDS HERE]

. . . Have been interrupted for several days. Must send this at once if you ever are to receive it. You are amongst the ones I do love and respect, and it is not easy to imagine myself without knowing you, my dear.

Hope the children are arrived. And as well as possible. They are young, strong. And if they keep the memory of their mother and remember only how lovely she was, this memory will protect them. You can do so much to guide them.

Shall be happy to see your counterpoint exercise, and hear your thoughts about it.

Am with you, so affectionately, understanding what you face now, to settle the children. But it is a joy to be as useful and helpful.

Yours, N.B.

Dear Ruth,

Your letter is just the one I could dream to receive from you – understanding, feeling each nuance of what makes life so complex, in these highly signi-ficant days! Enjoy, one can't, for the sacrifices are too terrible – and however, such a light in the darkness – But, once the hope seen, arises a new, still unknown fear: now, it is no more an awful nightmare one is going through: who is still alive – what will be hear: Killed by the Germans, dead through suffering – gone because it was the time marked by God –

The first paragraph of Boulanger's letter of 25 August 1944.

LETTER 44-7

10 SEPTEMBER 1944
ARROWHEAD WOODS
LAKE ARROWHEAD
CALIFORNIA
TOMORROW S.B. FEATHERHILL RANCH

Dear Ruth,

It is good to have news of you. I understand and can see that waiting is the only thing to do, for the present. Never did I speak of your work, for it was obvious that decisions for the children had to be taken first.

But as it remains indefinite, I admire you for going for your harmony and counterpoint to Mr. Shortall.[137] If you ask him in my home, or if you want me to write him, he will do it. And it will work quite well, I feel sure.

For the organ I do not advise you to consider it now. Were you to wish it, however, you can ask Barrett Spaeh,[138] who has the best tradition.

For the piano, do not you think Olga Sandor would be quite qualified? Let me know if for some reason it is not easy, being so close. But she would guide you quite well. We leave tomorrow morning and it is needless to say the state of the house and of the minds.

We are also rather tense. Mrs. Sachs and I are expecting and fearing the news to come.

Here is the bell for dinner. Good night, my dear. It is sad not to have you to say "I arrive," but the Lord knows, and we hope.

As ever yours, so affectionately,

N.B.

---

137 Harrington Shortall (1895–1984), Chicago-based music composer and educator.

138 Barrett Spaeh was the head of the Northwestern University organ department, and organist and choirmaster of Chicago's Fourth Presbyterian Church.

Letter 44-8

17 September 1944
Featherhill Ranch
Santa Barbara

Dear Ruth,

Beaten, flatly beaten! For such a good one, with its "cook slowly," never did I imagine! When it was phoned, it first sounded as if you had found gloves from Mrs. Shortall. And not understanding clearly, I was to wire: go ahead, as many as obtainable. We were there serious, for I consulted Mrs. Sachs—she came to the conclusion "there is no point for gloves." And not 57 for size. We decided to wait for enlightenment through the eyes! And certainly you succeeded. The Coutures,[139] the Sachs, and more than any of them, I had a very good time.

Before reading the telegramme, came looking through the box. The ingenious, thoughtful, amused, and amusing box. Everything in it is as beautiful as the books I shall read with such interest. The illustrated one is already appreciated by the eyes—then bath, mail, ranging, counting, fishing. What cannot be accomplished with its contents?

Really, you are too kind. And I do thank you very very much. This said, how sad you are not here! Never speak of it, because understanding where you have to be. And in many ways, want to be.

---

139 Jean Papineau-Couture (1916–2000), Canadian composer and academic, and his wife Isabelle. He was a student of NB's at Longy and later in Paris. "In June 1944 . . . he received another grant which enabled him to resume studies with Nadia Boulanger in Madison, Wisc., and at Lake Arrowhead, Cal. A United States patron, Arthur Sachs, invited Papineau-Couture and his wife, Isabelle, to spend the winter at his ranch in Santa Barbara along with a few other privileged visitors, including five of Nadia Boulanger's pupils. There they were joined on occasion by Stravinsky and his wife, Vera" (https://www.thecanadianencyclopedia.ca/en/article/jean-papineau-couture-emc) .

However, the loss remains the same. In friendship. In study. I do miss you exceedingly. Wonder when, or where we can meet another year. And regret so deeply not to guide you in your work. Try to find comfort in the thought of the quality of help which Mrs. Shortall will give you. But . . . selfishness prevails! Speaking very loud.

Everybody sends you regards, affection, greets you. I add to the chorus the solo voice, being the one who knows the best! That is not pretension, but only the certitude of one who does fully appreciate you and loves you with a faithful and solid and deep feeling.

Yours, N.B.

Have no more received "my" newspaper![140] Would you send it here in c/o Couture?

LETTER 44-9

19 OCTOBER 1944
FEATHERHILL RANCH
MONTECITO
SANTA BARBARA, CALIFORNIA

Dear Ruth,

How good and interesting is your letter! I see you with the children, and if something could console me of your absence, this would. It means so much, and does so much. But . . . it is sad. Even if I refuse such a selfish thought—who knows—perhaps it is not so forever. That would seem too hard.

Life brings us directions that we cannot unacknowledge

140 NB clarifies what she means by, "my, newspaper" in her next letter (October 19) to be *La Victoire*.

and . . . we are not always able to see it, but there are reasons for the happenings. Yes, I feel really badly about your absence. In the mean time I am so really happy for the children. And I try to forget myself to look only at them.

What a good idea for the fountain pen. If you could find two, still better.

Would you rent your car to the Coutures? If so, how much? (They are not in Canada, but here??) Would you rent your bicycle? How much?

And on this note of business, I leave you to work piano. Saturday am going to Los Angeles and San Francisco. Mr. Stravinsky and I are playing together at Mills College. And my hand is not willing!

La Victoire[141] here to Couture—Sorry to have been so vague!!

With love from everyone, and especially from the one who loves you so profoundly, N.B.

141 *La Victoire* was a French-English bilingual newspaper published in New York City during the Second World War.

Letter 44-10

25 October 1944

[Published review, hand-copied by Ruth]

San Francisco, California
Concert at Mills College
Oct. 25, 1944
Stravinsky Recital at Mills College
by Alfred Frankenstein[142]

Three new works of Igor Stravinsky[143] were introduced to Bay Region audiences Wednesday night at Mills College when the Russian composer gave a lecture-recital with the assistance of Nadia Boulanger. "Composing, Performing and Listening" was the title of Stravinsky's talk. In essence it was another exposition of the principles of definitiveness, specificality, clarity, and scientific self-consciousness that run through Stravinsky's writing and compositions of the past 20 years. This was, one suspects, one of the famous series of lectures Stravinsky prepared for Harvard some years ago, lectures which, through an incredible lapse, have never been published in English and have gone out of print in the French edition. In view of the immense size and enthusiasm of Wednesday's audience, Mills could clearly do worse than engage Stravinsky for the whole course.

It was interesting to hear Stravinsky do the talking while Miss Boulanger sat silently by to assist only in the playing. She has one of

142 Alfred Victor Frankenstein (1906–1981) was an art and music critic, author, and professional musician. The longtime art and music critic for the *San Francisco Chronicle*, he taught at Mills College, UC Berkeley, and Stanford University and was noted for his wit and his lack of tolerance for pretension. Paul J. Karlstrom, "Alfred Victor Frankenstein, 1906–1981," *Archives of American Art Journal* 21, no. 2 (1981): 23.

143 The three pieces were Sonata for Two Pianos, *Scherzo à la russe*, and *Circus Polka*. Walsh, *Stravinsky*, 161–162.

the most formidable musical intellects of the century, and one of the most articulate and influential theorists of this era, but Wednesday night she was content to provide profound and fluent performances at the first piano while the composer played the second piano with his customarily mordant virtuosity.

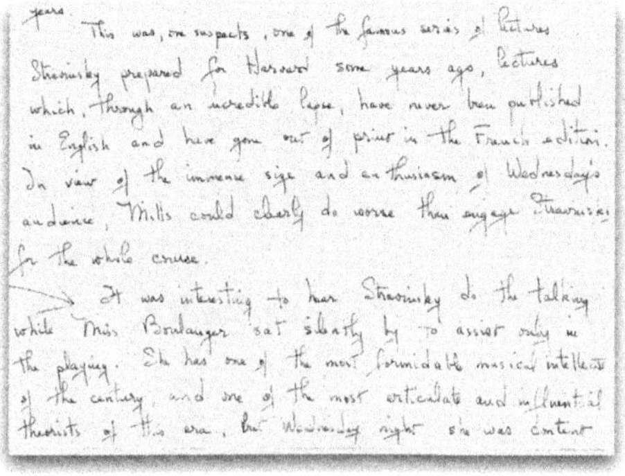
years
This was, one suspects, one of the famous series of lectures Stravinsky prepared for Harvard some years ago, lectures which, through an incredible lapse, have never been published in English and have gone out of print in the French edition. In view of the immense size and enthusiasm of Wednesday's audience, Mills could clearly do worse than engage Stravinski for the whole course.

It was interesting to hear Stravinsky do the talking while Miss Boulanger sat silently by to assist only in the playing. She has one of the most formidable musical intellects of the century, and one of the most articulate and influential theorists of this era, but Wednesday night she was content

Ruth Robbins copied Alfred Frankenstein's review by hand (no faxes, copiers, or digital scanners in 1944!) so she could send the original clipping from the San Francisco Chronicle *to Nadia Boulanger. [Ruth Robbins Archives]*

The biggest of the three works they played was a sonata for two pianos that is fresh off Stravinsky's work table. On first hearing it seemed remarkably simple, and characterized by a kind of unpretentious elegance. One had expected a more fiery work like the Stravinsky two-piano concerto, but it was quite apparent that Stravinsky knows the difference between the two forms.

At all events, the purling counterpoint of the sonata challenged the intellect and soothed the ear in a most original and delightful fashion.

The program also contained two-piano versions of the Scherzo à la russe and the Circus Polka. Both of these are vigorously tuneful pieces, the scherzo all open, airy, and full of reminiscence of the Bellini period in Russian music, the polka richly dissonant and witty and closer to Petrouchka than any other recent work of Stravinsky's. The polka was written for Ringling's[144] elephants some years ago, and according to New Yorkers they didn't like it much; Ringling's

144 Ringling Bros. World's Greatest Shows is a circus founded in Baraboo, Wisconsin, in 1884 by five Ringling brothers.

bandmaster, acting as spokesman for the pachyderms, said he felt Stravinsky didn't have rhythm. Some elephants of the public are like that, too; like elephants, they never forget.

Letter 44-11

[Oct. or Nov. 1944][145]
Featherhill Ranch
Montecito
Santa Barbara, California

Dear Ruth,

Another day is coming, which finds us all, and I especially, missing you badly. And the wishes I am sending do not console me a minute for the loss. On the contrary! However, it is with the deepest feeling that what you deserve, plus what is given by God, will become yours. What this year is for you must bring a great inner joy. Help the children struck by such a sorrow to build their life harmoniously; peace is of a meaning which overcomes everything else. But . . . how could the ones who love you, and attach importance to your own development not regret to be deprived of participating in it. And, of course, I do, profoundly. Realizing what you gain in another field, it is easy for me to enjoy your joys. Knowing you are guided, it is also easy to understand the growing of your musicianship. But . . . but we were so happy to have you here. You are always such a helpful, comforting, and joyful friend. The future, what will it bring? Where will we all be, when . . . everything

145 Written after RR's departure from Montecito in 1944.

is still so vague that we had better not think too far ahead, and only be ready for what the Lord will send us. The news from home comes now a little more often, and it brings as much profound happiness as anxiety. Through Mr. Sachs' daughter, who is in Paris, we heard that Annette . . . [146]

Letter 44-12

7 November 1944

Dear Ruth,

The car . . . that is easy. But the sigh which shows the selling of it is really meaningful. And to lose the last hope to see you again . . . well, that is sad. Let me think that something will happen. And believe me to be in profound affection.

Yours, N.B.

Letter 44-13 [postscript]

7 Nov. 1944
Featherhill Ranch
Santa Barbara, Cal.

Well, perhaps the summer with Dick but . . . summer is so indefinite, and far, as near as it is and as fast as it will come.

Let us plan so, as it sounds less discouraging, anyhow. And indeed love the idea!

146 Letter cuts off here; end is missing.

Letter 44-14

28 December 1944

Dear Ruth, we miss you all so much, and I, of course, more than anyone. But it is right, and good, to help the children who have been deprived of the presence we need the most, and your heart must know a great joy in being so near their heart.

Must leave you—but never do, for we all speak of you, practically every day. Mrs. S. is in despair for not having sent you the planned present, but . . . it is all my fault. Could not yet find what I wished her to give you.

May the year to come bring you what you so highly deserve—be the peace of God yours.

With all my love, dear Ruth.

Your old friend, N.B.

Say to your brother my profound sympathy and all that I am wishing him and his children.

[margins]

What beautiful envelope, cards, paper—you did paint them yourself, did you not? Seldom have I seen such a nice result!

1945

LETTER 45-1

[JANUARY 1945][147]
FEATHERHILL RANCH
MONTECITO
SANTA BARBARA, CALIFORNIA

Dear Ruth,

Smile would I, were I not moved, really moved by all such a present brings. Thought, kindness, intelligence, lightness, gift of smile—and much more—all so beautifully, so thoughtfully planned. Well, you cannot realize with what a profound feeling I am looking at three objects chosen with such care. You are a darling, and a friend as (that I know) one very seldom has!

Thank you, thank you! Will look at the sky, bubbling with delight, and dress protectively, making holes, sticking on two sides, or reconciling separate parts of my teapot—still solid owed to

147 A thank-you note for RR's 1944 Christmas package to NB.

you—filing cards in alphabetical order, pinching, solidifying turning pages, clipping here and there. Well busy and helped owed to your ingenuity.

Really, you are an angel, but a missing one, and it was really sad to have another Christmas without you. It was a moving Christmas, though, for we were all so close, with Father Fortier, his sisters (so touching), Sister Ignatia, Dick, the Coutures, Rico Lebrun (so wonderful a painter and a man he is), and also Zo and Miss Whisnant.[148]

But how tense an account of the news—knowing the price of such tragic events—and there were a lot of prayers. We went to the midnight mass at the convent, a night of dream, so calm and light, and we were grateful.

Letter 45-2

January 1945
Featherhill Ranch
Montecito
Santa Barbara, California

Dear Ruth,

Will you accept all my wishes, and know that I put a condition: we have to read the score once together. Do not wait too long,

148 "Dick" and "Father Fortier" are unidentified; "the Coutures" are Jean Papineau-Couture and his wife, Isabelle; Federico "Rico" Lebrun (1900–1964) was an Italian American artist who won back-to-back Guggenheim Fellowships in 1937 and 1938 followed by numerous prizes and awards from the Art Institute of Chicago, the Metropolitan Museum of Art, the Los Angeles County Museum of Art, and the Pennsylvania Academy of the Fine Arts; composer Alonzo "Zo" Elliott (1891–1964) studied with NB (see Wikipedia entries for "Rico Lebrun" and "Zo Elliott"). For Miss Whisnant, see footnote 127.

for . . . like to be still there to answer the call. We miss you badly, needless to say so.

For your dear ones, prayers and wishes.

And for you, with the fondest love, Your devoted N.B.

Letter 45-3

16 March 1945

Dear Mademoiselle,

It is such a great joy to finally have real spring weather after a long, snowy winter that I cannot resist the temptation to neglect everything and spend as much time as possible out-of-doors. I have started at least half a dozen letters to you in the last two weeks, but each time I have decided to go out to do a little clearing or digging or some other outside work first, and one thing would always lead to another, and before I knew it, your letter would fall by the wayside. It has not been for any lack of desire on my part. I think of you so often, and would give anything to be with you. What I miss more than anything at this time of the year is reading one of Bach's Passions with you. Easter won't be the same without that.

Miss Whisnant has kept me pretty well posted as to the recent activities at Featherhill Ranch. Needless to say, I have followed her accounts with great interest, to say nothing of jealousy. She tells me that you and the children are learning Latin. No doubt that that will be the official language of the music lessons from now on. Must I learn to speak Latin in order to have more work with you, or will you accept me on the old ignorant terms?

My work with Mr. Shortall is progressing slowly but surely. I never seem to work proficiently, but I feel that this year I have had time to digest much of the knowledge I gained from you, and will be better prepared to absorb and profit by whatever ideas and criticisms you present the next time I see you.

I do not believe I have a bit of news to tell you! My brother is in Alaska now and should return some time in April. My other brother is in India, and has now been assigned to constructive and interesting work for the first time since he has been in the army. He has certainly not been in love with the army for any reason whatsoever in the past, so we are all happy that he has finally met Dr. Seagrave, the famous "Burma Surgeon" and says he is a fine man.[149]

Mr. Shortall lent me his score of Mozart's Idomeneo, which I have been reading with great interest. I did not know that such a work existed. It is so beautiful! How I would like to hear you read it!

Lotte Lehmann[150] gave two very beautiful concerts here in the last two weeks. The first was all Schubert and the second all Brahms. Next week she is to give a Schumann recital. She is a superb artist and sings with such ease and good taste that it is the greatest pleasure to hear her.

It seems so strange and appalling that a nation that has given the world such superb gifts as the music and musicians of Germany

---

149 RR's older brother, Jim, was opening a gold mine in Alaska. Her colorful younger brother, Pete, served in the Army Corps of Engineers under General Joseph "Vinegar Joe" Stilwell, building the Burma Road to enable movement of material by truck from northeast India to Nationalist Chinese troops in Chongqing. The "Burma Surgeon," Dr. Gordon Seagrave (1896–1965), born in Burma, was the son of American Baptist missionaries. Educated at Denison University and Johns Hopkins University, he returned to Burma to practice medicine and surgery on the Chinese border of Burma for nearly twenty years. He joined the United States Army Medical Corps in 1942, worked with Stilwell, and served with the Chinese New Sixth Army through the Burma Campaign in the Second World War.

150 Lotte Lehmann (1888–1976), the great opera diva of the early twentieth century, "performed in every major opera house in Europe and the United States and under every major conductor in her stage career, which extended from 1910 to 1945 . . . . In her lieder singing career, which continued until 1951, she excelled in songs by Schubert, Schumann, Brahms, Wolf, and Strauss and never failed to pack recital halls." Alden Whitman, "Lotte Lehmann Dies at 88; Diva and Lieder Specialist," *New York Times*, August 27, 1976.

should be able to even approach the horror and ruthlessness of this war. I do not believe that Germany's strength can even be permanently suppressed or annihilated, so that the only salvation for her and the rest of the world is to re-educate the people, and re-awaken and cause to grow their great gifts as writers, musicians, etc. To me, the real meaning of Easter is to show us that it is possible for the greatest accomplishment to be the result of what appears to be an utterly hopeless and despairing situation.

We are celebrating Mother's birthday tomorrow, so I must go to bed earlier than usual in order to have enough energy to cope with seven nieces and nephews all at once and for all day. I expect that by this time tomorrow night I will be a complete wreck.

I am eagerly waiting to hear what your plans for the summer will be when you know them. As I said before, I think of you always, but I wanted you to know that I am thinking of you especially this time.

With all my love, Ruth

P.S. The second gold fountain pen was not satisfactorily repaired, so it has been sent back to the factory.

P.S. 2 Please give my love to the Sachses.

LETTER 45-4

12 MAY 1945
FEATHERHILL RANCH
MONTECITO, SANTA BARBARA, CALIFORNIA

Dear Ruth,

Things have moved so fast that . . . at least I hope you agree, I have made reservations for you, a roomette, on the 18th or 19th for Boston. Keep yours one day or two more, for S.B.

But it does no longer sound as if I can be there this summer. Shall explain later, want you only to know that we are on the edge of big changes. Try to go at least for a trip to Europe. Better to be east to plan for it. We would stay a few days on Bay State Road,[151] and after at Cape Cod. Say you love it, for I am so in need of seeing you again that I would feel most distressed if a change of place would deprive me of what has such a significance to me!

If the person to whom I have asked to make the reservation could not take care of it, I would wire you at once.

Needing two roomettes—one for you, one for me.

One lower section for Father Fortier.

You would be good enough to do it, yes? Am so impatient to see you soon, but so sad to leave the Marians,[152] the Sachses, and the Stravinskys. So goes life—always go on and on. Have not yet adapted and am most happy—a joy being given for the loss—but joy does not erase sorrow.

As ever yours, N.B.

---

151 The Winifred Johnstone residence. Winifred Hope Johnstone first met NB in Boston in 1937, and soon became a friend and ardent supporter in effect providing NB an American office to look after her complicated arrangements there. Spycket, *Nadia Boulanger*, 98–99.

152 The Sachses' daughter Marian and their neighbor's child, Marian Baring-Gould. The Sachses arranged for the two children to study with a tutor on the estate so NB could be around children.

Letter 45-5

[Undated, written after VE Day][153]
Featherhill Ranch
Montecito
Santa Barbara, California

Dear Ruth,

The beautiful plant is near me on the table, as is, on the terrace, the rose tree you gave me last year—and they are as the witness, so gay and colorful, the pink and the white and the yellow, of your presence amongst us. Am sorry for having not sent a sign of all these feelings for Easter. But I am terribly upset about the conditions at home, where people need so badly our help—and we are doing packages. But if I write or not, you are always in my mind, you know it, I feel sure. And the hope of seeing you soon helps me to dream in silence, that you are to be here one day for which I wait so eagerly!

Why would you not come here for the summer? The little house is ready and quite nice. I mean from June 15, for instance, to October, when, whatever will be my further plans, I am to go to Boston for a month. Perhaps stay there, perhaps go to France. Even possibly come back for one month or two, waiting for a passage. In fact, everything is still vague, except the summer, for which I feel rather settled and the concerts in Boston during the fall.

You have probably heard of the terrible tragedy, the death of Alexei Poutiatine wounded in Italy. Marie has an extraordinary courage, but you can imagine her distress![154] It is so terrible that the same grief is felt in so many houses all over the world.

153 This undated letter was likely written in May 1945.

154 Marie Poutiatine was a student and friend of NB's. Her son Alexis Poutiatine, mortally wounded in combat in Italy, died on March 17, 1945, and is buried in the Florence American cemetery (https://www.honorstates.org/profiles/52062/).

Do write, dear Ruth. One needs so profoundly the ones one really loves, always—and now, more than ever.

Forgive this hasty ending, but the mailman is here.

Oh how I wish you could come!

In deep profound affection yours, N.B.

LETTER 45-6

DECEMBER 25, 1945

[TELEGRAM]

DO MISS YOU PROFOUNDLY NOT FOR TOO LONG HOWEVER FOR EXPECT IMPATIENTLY NEXT MEETING SAILING NOW 31ST WISHES TO ALL YOU GRATITUDE AND LOVE = NADIA BOULANGER.

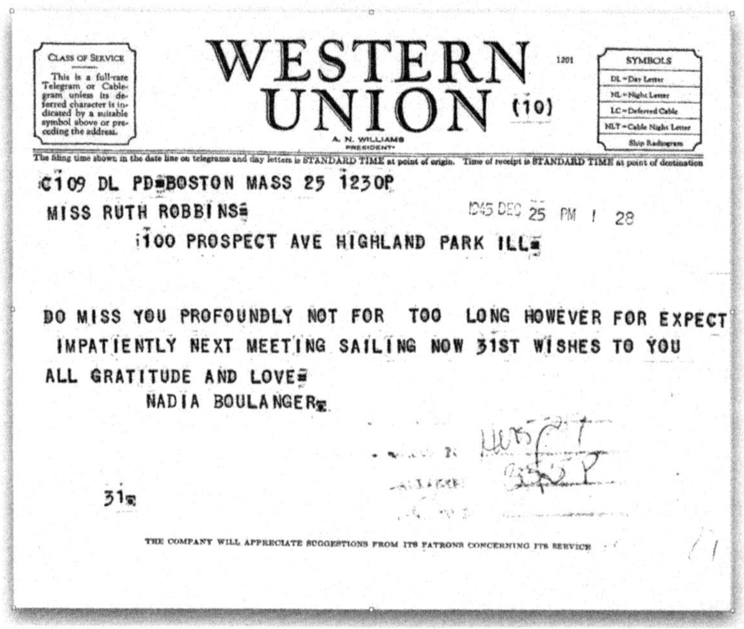

CLASS OF SERVICE
This is a full-rate Telegram or Cablegram unless its deferred character is indicated by a suitable symbol above or preceding the address.

WESTERN UNION (10)

1201

A. N. WILLIAMS
PRESIDENT

SYMBOLS
DL=Day Letter
NL=Night Letter
LC=Deferred Cable
NLT=Cable Night Letter
Ship Radiogram

The filing time shown in the date line on telegrams and day letters is STANDARD TIME at point of origin. Time of receipt is STANDARD TIME at point of destination

C109 DL PD=BOSTON MASS 25 1230P

MISS RUTH ROBBINS= 1945 DEC 25 PM 1 28

100 PROSPECT AVE HIGHLAND PARK ILL=

DO MISS YOU PROFOUNDLY NOT FOR TOO LONG HOWEVER FOR EXPECT IMPATIENTLY NEXT MEETING SAILING NOW 31ST WISHES TO YOU ALL GRATITUDE AND LOVE=
NADIA BOULANGER=

31=

THE COMPANY WILL APPRECIATE SUGGESTIONS FROM ITS PATRONS CONCERNING ITS SERVICE

1946

Letter 46-1

[Spring 1946][155]

Dear Ruth,

Were you thanked for one of the loveliest, most touching presents I have ever received? Such love in the care in which it all was presented—you cannot imagine what it meant and means. Thank you so much, so very much.

Really, you ought to come this summer. Such events. Menuhin, all the original works, Jean Françaix's little opera.[156] You would have

155 Earliest extant letter to RR after NB's return to France. RR had sent NB a package of gifts, no doubt with a humorous note about each gift, as was her wont.

156 Jean René Désiré Françaix (1912–1997) was a French neoclassical composer, pianist, and orchestrator. NB considered him one of her best students. Perhaps she refers to a performance of *Invocation à la volupté,* a piece for baritone and orchestra completed in 1945 (http://data.bnf.fr/16537767/jean_francaix_invocation_a_la_volupte/).

to take care of food and room, but the rest we could arrange. A kind of scholarship—after all, it will not happen another time!

Try to laugh, but in fact am very sad. The news about Sister Eunice is distressing! We all walk this last day, the first of surreal life, but . . . we are too small to understand it all.

Before I forget, if I can be of any help, call me. Writing, phoning to people. I would so much like to help.

Winifred must have written about Alexis Poutiatine's death. Marie is as she always is . . . but . . . how great is her distress in spite of her extraordinary faith.

Dear Ruth, Let me know what I can do. I so do wish you may come!!

As ever, thank you and . . . be well!

Your devoted, N.B.

All that you sent was amazing, lovely, useful, needed, and welcomed!

Letter 46-2

23 March 1946

Dearest Teacher (?!)

It does not seem possible that over three months have gone by since I left you in Boston in the midst of mountains of books, music, clothing, etc., all over the place. Various reports have it that you are again in the midst of mountains of books, music, clothing, etc. . . . and have not even room to put both feet on the floor at the same time.

Well, you have always been enthusiastic about mountains, but you must be rather tired!

A nice letter from Annette Dieudonné came some time ago with news of you and thanking me for the bed jacket and socks that Suzanne gave her. I am ashamed that I did not write immediately and tell her, but that is just one of the many things I have not done.

I have not heard from anyone for several weeks so have not much in the way of news. I have been seeing Sr. Ignatia quite regularly once [NOTE IN MARGINS: "She is much better now"] a week, and we bolster each other up with dictation, etc. Outside of that, I am working alone, which goes very well as I have no feeling of not knowing what should be done or how to do it. The only problem is to find time to do all I should.

Ever since I came home, I have avidly read any reports I can find about conditions in France. But reports have been so contradictory that it is hard to get a clear picture. At first the reports stated that the food situation was really desperate, so I have been sending boxes to various people with food that was not very inspiring but the most nourishing I could think of. But in the last week there have been several reports saying that bad conditions have been exaggerated a great deal and that it is possible to get good meals in almost any restaurant.

In a few weeks I expect to go to my camp for most of the summer. In fact, I may go up for a week in April.

(I just this minute heard on the Open Radio Quiz that everyone knows that no operas have been written by women, and someone denied it and said that you have written an opera called The Dead City.[157] I must listen to my radio more often and learn more about you!)

Do you still think I should try to go to Paris in the fall? Perhaps now that you have been there for a while, it does not seem such a good

---

157 *La ville morte*, opera, 1910–1913, composed jointly with Raoul Pugno, based on Gabriele D'Annunzio's 1898 play *La città morta*. "My camp" refers to RR's rustic summer cottage in Coboconk, Ontario.

idea to you anymore. I am so eager to know what you think and advise. Now I am listening to a speech on the radio saying that every American must cut down on wheat and meats and have Victory Gardens so we can meet the emergency food relief for starving Europe. So you see how it is!

I would try to tell you how much I miss you, but it would make my letter much too overweight, so I will say that I do, and that it seems as though it will be forever before I will see you again.

All my love, Ruth

Ruth Robbins and Gaby Casadesus at Fontainebleau in 1946 [Ruth Robbins Archives]

Letter 46-3

27 April 1946
36, rue Ballu, Paris IX
Trinité 57-91

Dear Ruth,

Here are the bundles, so wonderfully chosen. How shall I ever thank you? When you are to be here, you will at once understand what we all feel.

When are you arriving? Can hardly wait. It will be so good to see you again. Let me know and do not come too late.

Forgive this queer style; I am so busy! So many wonderful things happen here, behind the mud spoken of. And it gives such a feeling of greatness, this delayed humble acceptance of such long-lasting sacrifices.

Paris is in its spring loveliness, speaking for the future through its past.

You are with us. Annette believes she knows you quite well!

I do love you dearly, and cannot wait much longer.

As ever, N.B.

Letter 46-4

8 June 1946

Dear Ruth,

Just a hasty note to say how profoundly I am happy for you coming. Do not worry too much to bring food. If you are willing to pay you can get many things, even meat sometimes, so people say. Rice is very scarce, and everything is very high.

I do hope you bring your car—transportation is so difficult and slow. One can buy a very nice Simca, transformable (opening) at 800 dollars. For us it is not the time for such an undertaking but perhaps the right thing for you. Three weeks, at least, to obtain it.

Life is strange—so terrifically hard for the majority, with an outside which does not always allow to measure the daily troubles.

Let me know the exact day of your arrival. A room, not too good but friendly, is waiting for you.

No use asking to bring things . . . where to begin, how to stop the list.

Your packages do arrive and are of such help. You will understand when here. With so much love and joy, it will be so good to have you here.

As ever, N.B.

LETTER 46-5

2 SEPTEMBER 1946
36, RUE BALLU, PARIS IX
TRINITÉ 90-17

Dear Ruth,

So happy you will have a nice time. If you can bring, for you, the marvelous paper made in Switzerland—has soft line permitting to write the beats exactly close together. It is the most practicable thing one can find. But . . . if you do not share my enthusiasm, do not feel obliged to buy it!

~~Two pairs of woolen stockings for~~ No, have enough here. Have a gay time. Let me know when Ellzey, Bufkin, Mrs. Cox, Mrs. Todd are to be back, and the others too. It seems strange not to see you here!

With profound affection, N.B.

Many things to all, as we say in French!

1947

LETTER 47-1

23 MARCH 1947

Dear Mademoiselle,

It seems such a long time since I left you in England, but actually, when I look at the calendar, it is just over three weeks. Ever since I left, I have tried to write you, but each attempt was so unsatisfactory that I could not bring myself to mail the letter.

The boat trip home was miserable in spite of my luxurious room and bath as I had to share it with an awful vulgar woman who came in at 3, 4, or even 6 or 7 o'clock in the morning, drunk and sick from too much drinking. I tried to be moved to <u>any</u> other quarters in the boat, but was told that there was not another place available. Needless to say, under those circumstances, I could not bring myself to write anything but the gloomiest kind of letters, so I did not mail any of them.

I had a very nice visit in Boston from Wednesday to Sunday. Winnie rounded up several of your ex-pupils, and they came to tea on Saturday to hear news of you. Shapero, Middleton, Allanbrook, Pinckam, Griselda (Tony could not come), Paul Demarais, Spiess [*sic*], and Leonard Fine.[158] I guess Winnie wrote you the details. They all looked well (although Shapero looked rather pale and tired). After being used to the young men in Paris, I was struck by how much better dressed they are here.

I went with Nora and Winnie to the Boston Symphony and heard Symphony of Psalms[159] for the first time. It was very impressive, but not performed as precisely as I imagine Stravinsky would have done it. Koussevitzky's[160] performance lacked simplicity and was too emotional to my mind. But nevertheless, I was thrilled to hear it after the work on it in Paris. Also, for the first time in my life, I spoke to Koussevitzky afterwards as I knew he would be interested to hear about you. He terrifies me.

Newton Hoffman[161] was in Chicago last week for his father's funeral. I did not see him, but heard that he looks very well.

Returning home seems to be a harder adjustment for me to make each time I do it. Life here is so far removed from that which I have become accustomed to, and instead of arriving anywhere, I am always right back where I started from. It is as though I were two separate persons living two lives, and the one here has nothing whatever to do with the other.

Mother is well, but I think she has aged more this year than ever. Being alone most of the time since last summer was very hard on her, and she says she hopes she will never again spend a winter

158 Students in NB's 1941–1943 music theory classes at Longy School of Music.

159 A choral symphony in three movements composed by Igor Stravinsky in 1930.

160 Serge Koussevitzky commissioned Stravinsky to compose *Symphony of Psalms* in celebration of the 50th anniversary of the Boston Symphony Orchestra.

161 Newton Hoffman (dates unknown) was a composition student of NB's, with five compositions in the Loeb Music Library collection of NB's students' compositions. He was a professor of music at Ball State University in the mid-1960s.

like this last one. She has always had someone (and usually several people) that she has run the house for, and when she has only herself to look after, it takes half the spirit out of her.

I have felt so badly about leaving you stranded without any help that I do not even like to think about it. But I do, all the time, in spite of efforts not to, and keep wondering how you are managing, or even if you are getting along.

By now I imagine the worst of the cold is over, so that probably helps a lot. Please let me know anything I can send you or do for you here. If you need anything in a hurry, I can send it by air-express.

I cannot tell you how happy I am to have had that day in London with you at the rehearsals. Hearing that beautiful music being so skillfully worked out and clarified (and in English too!) was exactly what I would have chosen to do if it had been a choice.

I must leave now to catch a train for Chicago, so will have to stop. I have no car as my brother bought mine, and he is out in California. I will have to try to get one as it is impossible to do things from here without one.

All my love (as always), Ruth

P.S. Please give my love to Annette and Marcelle.[162] I will write them soon.

---

162 Annette Dieudonné and Marcelle de Manziarly. "Toly" in letter 47-2 is a guess at NB's handwriting and has not been identified.

LETTER 47-2

4 APRIL 1947

Dear Ruth,

Just a line, full of love, full of the sadness of your going. What you feel I partly understand, and so goes life! But you will finally fulfill, here or there, your own wishes, and make of your life what you, rightly I think, want.

Everything has been very hectic, many happenings around me—alas, all sad. Toly (?) comes tomorrow, his marriage broken. I did not succeed to prevent this useless hard trip. He made a mistake, I think, and probably this great sorrow prevents a much heavier misfortune.

Home is always home, and I, this crazy, overcrowded human being in it—but there is also much good, and this too is hectic. Lipatti, Jean Françaix, Markevitch[163]—shall let you know later the importance of their doings.

Today, a lot of thanks for all that you did for me. Apologies for what you had to stand. Without knowing it, Marcelle[164] made me feel how badly settled you were. I did not fully realize it. But it was so nice that I still love it.

As ever in profound affection, yours, N.B.

---

163 Romanian pianist Dinu Lipatti (1917–1950) became NB's student in 1934 as a teenager, French composer Jean Françaix (1912–1997) started with NB in 1922 at age ten, and Russian composer/conductor Igor Markevitch (1912–1983) became her student also at age ten, starting shortly after Françaix.

164 Marcelle de Manziarly.

Letter 47-3

5 May 1947
122 Bay State Road
Boston, Massachusetts

What a package! If the house is not shining, transparent, and cheerful, well . . . we are hopeless.

Seriously, you are too kind, dear Ruth, and the labels are priceless. The alarm clock full of memory, making you more present and more absent! More misgiving.

Do come back. Now I have a help and dare say so. Pardon for this hectic message, but now, or never. So, here it is.

With love and deep gratefulness, from the cleaned house, N.B.

Letter 47-4

[Undated][165]

Dear Ruth,

Could you manage with Olga Sandor or Mr. Shortall, at 339 Barry Avenue, Chicago, to borrow Bach's organ work? Especially the three volumes of Chorales, any book of Les Maitres de L'Orgue, the volume of Arte Antiche Torchi, ed. Ricordi, whence for organ,

165 A note written during NB's summer 1947 stay at St. Clara's Convent.

perhaps collections for Peters Edition, with old organist Schum, this period. I could bring them back very soon.[166]

Could you forward this letter to Miss Whisnant?

Until Monday, with so much affection,

N.B.

St. Clara Convent

Sinsinawa, Wisc.

Letter 47-5

18 October 1947

Dear Ruth,

I need (please check)

- sugar (powdered, granulated)
- chocolate
- puddings (state flavor)
- cheese
- powdered milk
- rice
- canned meat (state kind), tongue
- candy
- prepared mixtures (Flako, Tootsie Fudge,[167] pancake flour, muffin mix, cream of wheat and gingerbread mix, flour)

---

166 *Chorales* refers to the collection of Bach's four hundred four-part chorales; *Les Maitres de L'Orgue* is a 10-volume set of organ sheet music; Luigi Torchi (1858–1920), was an Italian musicologist. This request likely refers to his *L'arte musicale in Italia: pubblicazione nazionale delle più importanti opere musicali italiane dal secolo XIV al XVII, tratte da codici, antichi manoscritti ed edizioni primitive, scelte, trascritte in notazione moderna, messa in partitura ed annotate* (1907). "Schum" may be an abbreviation for Robert Schumann, who accumulated a noted collection of Bach's organ works.

167 Flako is a prepared pie crust mix. Tootsie Fudge was for making fudge brownies.

- other foods
- spices, vanilla, cinnamon
- dried fruit

Will you soon come back, dear, dear Ruth? It seems so strange to have you so far away. Do you not feel you must finish Dubois! Your packages arrived safely. The clothing was so helpful. People ask me to thank you very much.

- ~~silk~~ stockings (size large)
- rather heavy thread or cotton
- other clothing
- soap Ivory Flakes
- other household cleansers
- Scotch Tape, glue, paper clips, etc.

Other suggestions:

- sponges for metal cleaning.

Thank you for the suggestions. I do not see why I am checking this little. What you have sent has been so helpful. Forgive my silence. It has been such a busy summer—so hot, too—and still is. I am for two days in Lorraine—how it is like in Paris, I wonder. Here it is unbelievable. Bad for things and for people, but . . . a great year for wines. So, let us take comfort in it. A lot of talk about the international situation. Very likely it is really quite different from what is suggested. You know my ideas about politics. It appears more and more (to me, at least) that if we tried each to do decently our own job, things would soon clear up.

Annie Desprès[168] has had a very great success. First prize, first of all the other students, and she turned 15 on August 1. She was thrilled with the box. Thank you so much for her! Annette just

168 Annie Desprès and "Francois" (next paragraph) are unidentified.

came back from Rome—yes, from Rome, with this heat. But she survived and is most happy to have seen Italy. She made the voyage with a pilgrimage, which means under very hard conditions. But she saw only the good side of everything. Most impressed by the Holy Father.

François has again been in Austria twice. Came back rather concerned. Two of the Fontainebleau boys (V.C. Keneut & Goolery) have seen many things. One in Bucharest, the other in Berlin. Well, open eyes bring very much light. On the other side, amazing personal English reactions. Hard times, but such determination gives strength to wait for a new page! We have all been impressive with such dignity. Your round the world gentleman has done a pretty good job. Endurance, foresee, and complete mastery of himself.

Yesterday, a biting, unbroken Churchill spoke,[169] and for one reason or another, here and there, quality shows in such a way, that you cannot despair of man in spite of all his efforts to succeed to render you skeptical. Admiration finally always prevails—has to.

Do let me know when you land. But remain sure you are never absent.

With all my gratefulness and love, yours, N.B.

---

169 It is unclear which speech NB refers to. Churchill gave his "Iron Curtain" speech in March 1946, and in 1947 he was promoting Pan-Europeanism.

1948

LETTER 48-1

15 FEBRUARY 1948

Still alive, but very sad. Theresa Lumière[170] just died. It is a great blow—alas, expected but not less painful.

Am not coming and fully hope you are arriving with W.[171] Do not postpone. Who knows who is still there afterwards or who can move later on? Do not hesitate.

Shall have a room nearby. Send as soon as you possibly can a note saying you shall be here and will settle this matter. Would you, if you stay longer than W., come back here—or is it too impossible?

Do not hesitate to say so. Am I right to hope you will come?

As always, yours affectionately,

N.B.

170 Unidentified.

171 Winifred Johnstone.

Letter 48-2

[Undated][172]
36, rue Ballu, Paris IX
Trinité 90-17

Dear Ruth,

Just a line: your anticipating arrival was such a joy! I do understand your delay, of course, but the disappointment remains as deep.

Dare hardly hope—so many things may postpone your departure. Feel only, in measuring my deception, how great was my happiness.

With much love, N.B.

Letter 48-3

[1948][173]

So happy you are at last here. Sorry not to see you today, but hope you will dine Saturday, May 1, on rue Ballu.

With much love,

Nadia B.

172 Undated note written in March 1948 shortly after RR's arrival in Paris.

173 Undated note written during RR's 1948 sojourn in France.

LETTER 48-4

[1948][174]

Dear Winifred and Ruth,

Prolongate this unexpected goodbye. Was in a way too difficult.

And I could say nothing. But I wish you to be good, happy, and to bring you great joy. All that you will see is so beautiful! Why can we not divide ourselves, and go and stay? We do, after all, through the memory.

As faithfully as ever to you,

N.B.

LETTER 48-5

[UNDATED][175]

[COPY OF AN ARTICLE, TRANSCRIBED BY TYPEWRITER, ON LETTERHEAD OF WINIFRED JOHNSTONE'S RESIDENCE: 122 BAY STATE ROAD, BOSTON, MASS.]

NADIA BOULANGER

To anyone who has not met Nadia Boulanger, it is difficult to explain her power as a teacher; to anyone who has met her, it is unnecessary. This is because her success is due more to her character than to her methods. Her personality is so compelling, her enthusiasm so irresistible, that the reason for her very wide and lasting influence is immediately obvious. Another reason becomes evident on closer acquaintance—complete disinterestedness.

174 Undated note written during RR's 1948 sojourn in France.
175 Copied from the March–April 1948 issue of *l'Adam International Review.*

When you add to almost terrifying ability utter absence of self-seeking or self-advertisement, you get a force that is going to have a violent effect on people with whom it comes in contact. It is able to concentrate with far greater intensity on its objective than it could if personal ambition were a part of its driving force. I do not deny that many, if not most great men have been ambitious, but not, I think, great teachers, except in so far as they may be said to satisfy ambition vicariously in the success of their pupils. Thus with Nadia Boulanger everything is simplified because all she wants is that better music should be written, and that the best music should be better played. Professionally, nothing else is important to her, and she refuses to be side-tracked by considerations that are irrelevant to her aim. It is in this singleness of purpose, combined with a most unusual detachment from material things, that her power has its source.

Her actual methods of teaching are fairly conventional. Strict counterpoint and fugue—not a hurried reading of a condensed textbook, but a laborious and (to me, at least) painful process of working every species of strict counterpoint and rewriting such exercise until it was correct. Parallel with this, we had to have a sound knowledge of the great masters. We studied chiefly Bach, Mozart, and Beethoven; Chopin, too, was often used as a model, while of more recent composers, Faure and Stravinsky were the most frequently studied. Though we felt that in her view technical competence was of the utmost importance, one was equally clear that it was not an end in itself. It is certain that without craftsmanship, first-class work is impossible, but that at the same time no amount of technical accomplishment is of the least use without talent. I think Nadia Boulanger feels that strict training can sometimes develop a latent gift, and that as many failures are due to lack of it as are caused by an absence of natural facility. What remains most in my mind about her teaching is the fact that she enormously increased my awareness of what was significant in actual sound; this, and the perpetual spur of her own competence as a musician. Her really amazing sight-reading, and the accuracy of her score-reading, away from the piano, was something that one does not easily forget.

Her opinion about the music of well-known composers is very decided. I think her love of Stravinsky's music and her great liking for that of Poulenc, springs (surprisingly enough) from the same thing—a preoccupation with actual sound. Stravinsky shows this in his extreme originality and in his experimental use of sonority, Poulenc in his love of the sensuous beauty of harmony, in the freshness of the sound-quality in his music. In this way Nadia Boulanger, while applying strictly traditional methods in insisting on thorough contrapuntal training, at the same time challenges one's power of original thought in music by setting before one what she admires. Her admiration for Stravinsky shows this spiritual climate which is sympathetic to her. She finds in him alone, or very nearly so (among contemporaries), the quality of aesthetic purity that she so dearly loves. This is further borne out by her dislike of what one might call the "saga" element—music in which the atmosphere is more important than the construction or the quality of the material. A certain type of romantic feeling, the sort that reaches its apotheosis in the Warsaw Concerto, is particularly repugnant to her; because in it sentiment is substituted for aesthetic emotion.

I think that we in England have something in particular to learn from her. We tend to be easily deceived by the grand manner, and the general public still clings to the emotional atmosphere of late Victorian romanticism. We need a teacher of genius to shake us out of certain habits of mind. I can think of no one who could do this more effectively than one who has indicated to so many composers their true path.

Lennox Berkeley (Extrait de l'Adam International Review,[176] March–April 1948)

176 A literary quarterly published in London since 1941. ADAM is an acronym for "arts, drama, architecture, music."

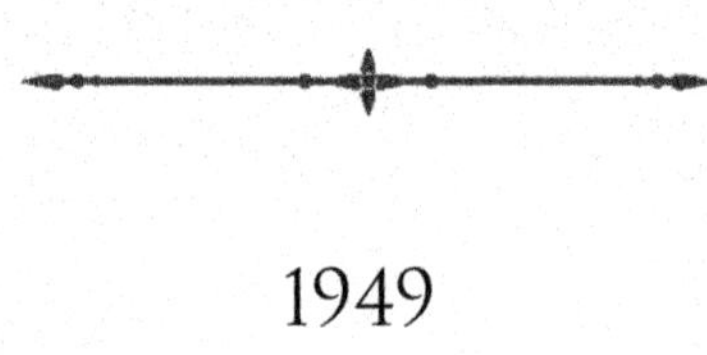

1949

Letter 49-1

23 January 1949
36, rue Ballu, Paris IX
Trinité 90-17

[Written by a friend of Boulanger's]

I hear that today is your birthday, and I send you my best and most affectionate wishes. I hope that this year will bring you back here. It would be such a joy. Poor Mlle B has had "la grippe." She has been in bed for five days; she had very high fever. Now she is better, and the illness is finished, but she feels very tired, and I think that it will need some time before she feels quite normal again. She said that she had never more pleasure than with the lovely Christmas parcel and all the wonderful, useful, and unexpected things in it. She thanks you much, and so do I. I shared with Germaine, which was so beautiful too.

[IN BOULANGER'S HAND] Dear Ruth, Never have I received a more charming, amusing, useful, and touching parcel. Everything so lovely, so well chosen, so nicely presented, so intriguing. Thank you so much. Am awfully ashamed never to write—but, in fact, I am so mad that I hardly manage to fulfill the most important obligations. Too many students, and too many interesting ones! How I do miss you—can hardly express it—but need to hope you will soon be back home.

Interruption—and wonderful news. Annette is appointed professor at the Conservatory. She is very happy—and I, still more. It might render her life easier, and she obtained this nomination with very great success. Nobody knew her before. After the competition, everybody respects and admires her! And this letter is started, for really I have not sent you my wishes which were with [you] but on the 21st I did not write letters—forgive me and feel that you are always with us. Mlle Gonet[177] sends thanks, love. H. wants to see you. She was 86 last Saturday. I think she enjoyed the day!

As ever, I am devotedly yours, N.B.

The car runs very well.

LETTER 49-2

8 MARCH 1949

Dear N.B.,

I keep hearing news of you via Winnie, Marcelle, and yesterday

---

177 Louise (Lou Lou) Gonet (18??–1954), a childhood friend of NB's mother, Raissa, helped care for her from 1930 until Raissa's death in 1935 and remained a close friend of NB's thereafter.

a nice letter from Middleton[178] with all kinds of news about you and all the activities of my ex-classmates. How I envy them! But I should not as I have already had two trips to France since you left us—but perhaps that is worse as otherwise I would not realize what I am missing! Highland Park continues to be the deadest place, culturally speaking (and otherwise, too, unless one is raising a family of children). Last week I "flew the coop" twice—once on an invitation from Thelma Todd[179] to Indianapolis, and once to the University of Illinois. At Indianapolis I had lunch with M and Mme Casadesus[180] at Thelma's home, their concert in the evening—which is always such a treat—and then a party after the concert. Jean played in Chicago a few days earlier—Beethoven's Emperor Concerto—and quite well. On my return Jane had just announced to the family that she was going to Alaska! To pilot a plane for people who were going to hunt polar bears and to take moving pictures. She had to leave at once to get there at a certain date and will be gone about a month. Fortunately, both my brothers were at home, so I did not have to cancel a trip to the University of Illinois for Stravinsky's concert. There was to be a rehearsal in the afternoon before the concert (naturally), so I drove like a madman to get there on time only to discover that the rehearsal had been in the morning! Such a disappointment, but the concert was marvelous. Soulima[181] played

178 Winifred Johnstone, Marcelle de Manziarly, and Robert Middleton. Middleton (1920–2016), a student of NB's, was chair of the music department from 1974 until his retirement in 1985. See "Guide to the Robert E. Middleton Papers, 1939–1954," Vassar College Archives and Special Collections Library, Vassar College Libraries.

179 Thelma Todd is unidentified. She is definitely *not* "the Ice Cream Blonde," a Hollywood actress of the same name who died mysteriously in 1935.

180 Jean Casadesus (1927–1972) and his wife Ivie (d. 2013; née Girard; daughter of painter André Girard). His parents were pianists Robert and Gaby Casadesus, who both taught at Fontainebleau, Robert first, in 1921, and then Gaby who joined him on the faculty in 1939. Jean Casadesus made his debut with the Philadelphia Orchestra conducted by Eugene Ormandy (1899–1985) in 1947 and thereafter enjoyed success as a concert pianist and as a piano teacher, principally at the American Conservatory at Fontainebleau. "Jean Casadesus, Noted Pianist, Dies in an Auto Collision at 44," *New York Times*, January 22, 1972, 32.

181 Soulima Stravinsky (1910–1994), son of Igor Stravinsky, studied with NB. Later, when he was at the department of music of the University of Illinois, RR would travel downstate from Highland Park to take lessons from Soulima.

the concerto extremely well. I had heard it once before and did not like it, but changed my mind completely when I heard it last Thursday. Was thrilled to hear Apollon Musagète[182] for the first time with an orchestra. Thanks to you, I recognized beaucoup even though it has been seven or eight years since you had us read it at Longy. I saw M and Mme Strav. and Soulima for a few minutes after the concert, and of course they were most eager for news from you and wanted me to send their best wishes the next time I wrote. Mr. Kuypers of the music school at the university told my friend Miss Bowers (head of the school's voice dept.) that he hoped he could manage to get you for next year's festival. I have sent you a program so you can see what sort of thing is being done. Unfortunately, I could not stay for any of the interesting concerts to follow Stravinsky's. As yet no prospect of my getting to France in the near future. Now that you are director of Font, I would give anything to be there this summer. I hope you will have a chance to relax and enjoy the [unreadable] and get some rest. How I miss you and want to return! No more room. With so much love.

Love, Ruth

182 Igor Stravinsky's 1928 ballet, *Apollon Musagète,* choreographed by George Balanchine. www.nycballet.com/Ballets/A/Apollo.aspx.

Letter 49-3

11 April 1949
36, rue Ballu, Paris IX
Trinité 90-17

Just a word of affection which still hopes to reach you for Easter. With how many wishes, you can guess so. When will we still be together?

Am here with "your" car, your basket, your guide, your etc., etc., etc., and alone, all your affection.

Hope to come down in better shape than I was in when coming up, but . . . too short.

Read all that is not written and believe me to be, as ever,

Yours,

N.B.

Letter 49-4

19 September 1949
Palais de Fontainebleau
Ecoles d'Art Américaines
Fondation Reconnue d'Utilité Publique
Le Directeur du Conservatoire
Conservatoire de Musique–Ecole des Beaux Arts

Dear Ruth,

Thank you, thank you for the wishes, for the presence your absence keeps here, for the dear lady[183] who carried Annette and I from Paris to Switzerland once more, and to Italy, and now, I hope, back to Paris. She has been so willing, so pleasant, quite worthy of her first owner!

Are leaving in a few minutes, you can see how [unreadable] is my writing. Well, I seem to joke, but in fact, I am sad to part from Miki,[184] and to quit this wonderful landscape. As I write, the tea, the pink town, the mountains, a weather . . . undreamed, undreamed, and so since the 1st of July!

Dear Ruth, rather time to dress, pick up luggage and go, but always hoping to find you standing at the next corner. It will be, it must be, but . . . who knows when. Nevertheless, do not wait too long. A bon entendeur salut.

As ever, devotedly yours, N.B.

---

183 Refers to the Peugeot given to NB by RR.
184 Miki Piré (1893–1973), a friend of Lili Boulanger's and student of Raoul Pugno's. Piré's letters to Lili Boulanger are in the collection of the Bibliothèque nationale de France (http://data.bnf.fr/14846985/miki_pire/).

Letter 49-5

[December 1949][185]
36, rue Ballu
Paris IX

Dear Ruth,

Again another Christmas . . . and you are not here! It is sad, but also so good to feel that for a presence as yours there is no absence.

These very hasty lines bring you wishes, thought, and the deep regret at having been unable to write. Really hopeless—life more hectic than ever.

But let me be your devoted, faithful, loving, N.B.

Letter 49-6

28 December 1949

[Typewritten note from Annette Dieudonné]

36, rue Ballu IX
Trinité 57-91
Le 28 Décembre 1949

Mesdemoiselles,

Mademoiselle Boulanger n'ayant pas eu le temps de faire de carte pour joindre au souvenir qu'elle vous adresse, vous prie de l'excuser. Elle vous l'enverra bientôt. (As Mlle Boulanger hasn't had time to write a card to accompany this remembrance she sends you [of the holiday season], she asks your pardon. She will send it shortly.)

185 Undated note likely written Christmas 1949.

La Secrétaire.

[Handwritten by Annette Dieudonné]

Dear Ruth,

Lots of love. The card follows.

Annette

1950

Letter 50-1

6 January 1950
36, rue Ballu 9^e^
Téléph: Trinité 57-91

Dear Ruth,

Thank you for the image so movingly beautiful. But, how sad I feel for Wendy. Please would you send her my little note? It is nothing, but I need to write her.

Miss you very much. There is so little time, and what is lost cannot be found again. I would love to see you.

All my wishes, my great joy to soon see Suzie and my profound attachment, as ever. And as ever so gratefully, never will I have such a good time traveling in the States. How dear you have been.

Yours, N.B.

Letter 50-2

20 January 1950

[Telegram]

RECEIVED WONDERFUL PACKAGE WARM WISHES = NADIA

Letter 50-3

30 March 1950

Dear Mademoiselle,

I have just returned from another visit to see the marvelous French tapestries that I saw with you in Paris. They are being exhibited here in Chicago until May and then, I believe, will be returned to France and replaced in their original settings. It is not the entire exhibit that was in Paris, but a good portion of it. Aside from the pleasure of the exhibit itself, I have the extra pleasure of associating it with you. Aren't I lucky?

Mother is doing very well. Her shoulder is really healed. She will have to keep it in a sling for about another week, then will be able to begin to use it again. She would do so now, but the doctor wants to prevent future trouble with it, so is making her hold off as long as possible.

If all goes well, I will be sailing in three weeks. I am sorry to miss being in Paris in April as from all I have heard, that is the time to be there. But I am so glad that I will be able to come at all that being a month late does not upset me very much.

M and Mme Casadesus played Mozart's Double Piano Concerto in E♭ last week. It was such a pleasure to hear it that it was disappointing to have it end. And very unfortunately (to my ears anyhow), Rodziński[186] followed it immediately with the Strauss Till Eulenspiegels, which completely wiped out the impression of the delicacy and refinement of the music and the excellent taste of the performance of the Casadesuses. By the time the concert was over (after the intermission, a Beethoven symphony) it was hard to remember that the Mozart had been played at all.

I do not know what is the matter with my pen, but it does not want to write on this paper at all. I hope it will not be too hard for you to make out what I have written.

I think that the De Grasse[187] will arrive on May 1st, so unless you are away at that time, I shall see you then. If there is trouble finding a place for me, I can go to a hotel until something can be arranged.

April 2—I forgot to mail this the other day. You are probably in London now, anyhow, so you would not have received it even if I had mailed it. I sail April 21st, on the De Grasse. Unless there is a delay, I will see you within a month! Winnie must be just about landing in England. My, she must be excited.

With lots of love, Ruth

---

186 Artur Rodziński, Polish conductor; music director of the Los Angeles Philharmonic (1929–1933), the Cleveland Orchestra (1933–1943), the New York Philharmonic (1943–1947), and the Chicago Symphony Orchestra (1947–1948).

187 French ocean liner SS *De Grasse*.

Letter 50-4

1 May 1950
Nice

Dear Ruth,

How long since I wrote you. Your letter is there, so dear, so necessary, but . . . not a second. Am now leaving tomorrow morning. Want just this to reach you, in hoping you are to read what is only implied.

When—now when are you coming?

I know, difficult, problematic, but . . . I do not want to depart without having once more shaken hands with you—so, hurry, hurry!

Am seeing the end of a dream—'tis rather sad. We were in Monaco for the fests given in honor of the accession to the sovereignty of the son of Pierre de Monaco.[188] Do you remember him? And it has been so beautiful, as well in the cathedral as in the Court of the Palace. Had I a little time would I be defeated by myself, for I cannot evocate these ceremonies for you, but . . . no time, and so you must enter into our dream, let your imagination build a fairy tale, and if you let it grow, you will perhaps approach reality.

Another reality expects me now, and if it is somewhat difficult to let go of legend, it will be nice to find again my boys and girls I do so dearly love. "Your" car has assured once more the travel of immeasurable ups and downs the hill, and has been in excellent temper. Feel what a place you always have here, and try to judge by yourself soon.

With so much love, N.B.

188 Prince Rainier of Monaco (1923–2005).

Have I ever thanked you for the marvelous package containing the most useful and lovely things? I hope so but am not too sure.

As ever yours, N.B.

LETTER 50-5

22 SEPTEMBER 1950
LA MOUBRA MONTANA, VALAIS SUISSE

Dear Ruth,

Thank you so much for your wishes. I realize fully what they bring me, and am very touched. If you do miss me, as I write in my mail book, “We leave for Montreal with Ruth,” “We leave for Cauterets[189] with Ruth,” “Ruth is in London,” “Ruth is in Paris,” and . . . you are at the other part of the world.

Came here for a rather necessary rest, intended to stay eight days more, but my dear, poor Lipatti is again very sick. He always is, alas, but in a greater danger. And if I can see him, will return for a few days to Geneva. The struggle for his life is unbelievable, and his resistance miraculous, but . . . how long can an organism stand such a strain? Well, we must all pray. He is one of the greatest artists I have ever known, and an angel. When he is worse, he is worried for all of us, not for himself! Forgive me, you do not know him, but if you have any of his records, you know.

Do write from time to time—days run fast—bring me more often this wonderful affection of yours, which is such a joy and a privilege. Annette arrived yesterday from Rome where she was

---

189 Spa town in the Hautes-Pyrénées.

on pilgrimage. The vision she brings from the Holy Father is so impressive. No words to express it. In our sick, savage, blind world, drunk with her destructive scientific means, it is of utmost need that blessed souls keep open the road of love.

Letter 50-6

Christmas 1950

[Handwritten lyrics]

Je vous essay de ma pensée // I send you my thoughts
Dieu vous envoye bonne journée // God grant you a good day
En ma le cors . . . mandent à vous // In me the horn . . . summons you
Je ne vous ai pas oubli // I have not forgotten you
XV siècle // 15th century

Dear Ruth, How many thanks for this wonderful handkerchief and your dear lines. Here are wishes and hopes and all you may imagine.

Am so distressed by Dinu Lipatti's death[190] that I feel out of reality—but just in his memory, loving more the ones I really love—And you are so profoundly amongst them. N.B.

---

190 Dinu Lipatti died of causes related to Hodgkin's disease on December 2, 1950, at age 33.

Am so distressed by Dinu Lipatti's
death that I feel out of reality —
but just in his memory, loving
more the ones I really love —
And you are so profoundly
amongst them —

Dinu Lipatti's decline and death hit Nadia Boulanger hard. She describes his failing health in her September 22, 1950, letter; expresses her distress at his death in this Christmas 1950 letter; and laments his demise once again in her January 1951 letter.
[Christmas 1950 letter facsimile, Ruth Robbins Archives]

1951

LETTER 51-1

[UNDATED][191]
36, RUE BALLU
PARIS IXE

Dear Ruth,

Will these lines arrive for January 21? How I do hope it. Want so much wishes, thoughts, affection to be with you. It is so hard to no more expect you to come in!

And as life goes and the time shortens, it is harder. You may have heard of Dinu Lipatti's death—a disaster and such a profound, heavy sorrow. As great an artist, as great a soul. One finds it difficult to overcome such a blow!

Remember how dear you are to me and try—but, of course, not easy. Hope you will have a nice birthday party. Let me take place in it, and find here Mlle Gunot's and Annette's affection.

So deeply yours, N.B.

191 This undated letter was sent to RR, prompting RR's response of January 31 (Letter 51-2).

And so many thanks for the ravishing handkerchief. Where have you found such a marvel? Forgive me not having written sooner. This year has not been easy, with this menace and this tragedy.

Letter 51-2

31 January 1951

Dear N.B.,

With all you have to do, I do not see where you found the time to write me birthday letters, and the lovely book with pictures of Vézelay[192] (which I regret I have not seen) came a few days ago in perfect condition. I had decided this year that I have reached the age where I definitely do not want to count birthdays anymore—that is until I reach the age where I will be proud of the number I will have attained—but I changed my mind when your letter arrived (just at the right time, too). Your letters mean so much to me that even though they mark unwanted birthdays, I love them! (The letters, I mean!) I almost do not enjoy the pictures of Vézelay as they make me so homesick for France and travels with you that I do not like to think of it.

We have had a long, cold, and very snowy winter, and the end is by no means in sight. Just two days ago the temperature went down to −24 Fahrenheit, which is colder than I can ever remember in this part of the world. Last week Leonard Bernstein was a guest conductor of the Chicago Symphony, and he made a tremendous

---

192 Vézelay is a commune in north-central France, famous for Vézelay Abbey.

impression on everyone. I heard the Rites of Spring for the first time (since our classes at Longy!) and was terrified! At the same concert Bernstein played the Ravel Concerto in G Major. Very well done. I have just bought Landowska's[193] new recordings of Vol I of Bach's Preludes and Fugues. They are overwhelming, and she is such an artist.

How I wish I could definitely say that I will see you soon, but it is all so uncertain. If I can possibly work things out, I would like to come this summer, but that remains to be seen. Unfortunately, any trip that I might make would be quite limited in time, but that would be better than nothing.

Thank you so much for the book on Vézelay. I love it in spite of what I said about it, and the pictures that show the countryside bring back so strongly my trip with you. And the letters, which I treasure and the lovely little song. If I could tell you how much I miss you, you probably would not believe it, so I will not try.

Love, Ruth

Letter 51-3

1 August 1951

Dear N.B.,

I should write this in French just to show you that I have learned a thing or two, but it is late at night, and my best hours for French are in the morning. Besides, although I finally know where to put the "le" and "lui" and "en" in the sentence and a little bit about

---

193 Wanda Landowska (1879–1959), Polish-French harpsichordist.

the subjunctive tense, I am really very rusty. Do you realize that it will be three years this November since I've heard any French? It makes me sick to think about it! I would give my right arm to have you beating me on the head to correct my pronunciation! Alas and alas! Not a chance this season. We are still trying to find the right person to stay with Mother so I can have a little freedom. It has been like trying to go through a solid rock of resistance, but I have made an issue of it this summer, as I insist that I must be free to carry on my work. If it were a matter of Mother not being able to afford to have someone to look after her, that would be entirely different, but that is not the case, so I am fighting for a chance to carry on a more normal life. We think we have found someone, in which case I plan to teach somewhere this summer and then Fontainebleau next summer! Please take care of yourself, so you will be ready for me. Sister Ignatia has had wonderful news for herself (terrible for me!), but I will not tell you what it is as she will want to tell you herself, and she may not have had time to write you yet. Do not be surprised if a strange young girl seeks you out to speak to you. It will be my niece Barbara's best friend who is traveling in Europe and expects to visit Font. I told her to speak to you and give you my very best regards or else not to come back to Highland Park! I have been concentrating on piano technique lately and accompanying some singers and, thanks to Sr. Ign., I play for someone. However, I still have a long way to go before I will have enough courage to play for someone like Soulima Str.[194] (which I would like to do this winter for an occasional lesson). Being scared is probably incomprehensible to you, but you did not spend the first 35 years of your life trying to be a musician with a complete lack of any kind of technique. There!

194 Soulima Stravinsky, Igor Stravinsky's son.

Now you know! The secret is out! [unreadable] How I miss your wonderful, penetrating understanding of a pupil's problems without having to have them explained to you. It is so easy to learn from you!

All my love, Ruth

I Miss Peugie! I Miss You![195]

Letter 51-4

29 September 1951

École d'art américaines
Fondation reconnue d'utilité publique
Palais de Fontainebleau (S.-&-M.)
Conservatoire de musique
Le Directeur du conservatoire

Miss Ruth Robbins has studied with me for years, and I could not recommend her too highly for the teaching of Solfeggio and harmonic basis. She is born to help, to transfer her knowledge to bring people to love what they understand.

Excellent teacher, Miss R. Robbins is a person of high moral value. She is understanding, and her pupils are indeed well guided and inspired. She knows what mean these elements without which one never becomes a good musician.

Nadia Boulanger

adresse personnelle : 36, rue Ballu, Paris-IXe, Tri. 57-59

---

195 Nickname for the Peugeot RR gave to NB.

Letter 51-5

29 September 1951
Valkenhorst

Dear Ruth,

Poor head, I mean, have I even sent this certificate you asked? I dream I did, but . . . in my doubt, I have sent you another one; if it is a double, choose the one you prefer! Have missed absurdly Sister Ignatia, cannot be consoled. But knowing she is in Florence is as if she were already here. Why is it not so with you!!! Once in Europe, one is already melting in the same pot.

If you know how we did in Venice! The head is the box, the body the *couloir*, salt under the nose—but the heart and the mind full of joy, for The Rake's Progress is a great, dramatic, exquisite, profound work. If we were not copying and writing the whole day long—poor Annette[196] at friends, you know, and Marga Loudon[197] with her eight children—I would send you such a bright letter, full of news, expectancies, temptations, hopes. But—but we leave this very day and must have copied a terrific number of pages, answered still 40 letters, and if possible we will have a short glance on Marga, who must feel we are really queer. Come from Paris to write from morning to morning. If I saw it, what an impression I would get.

Have been very unfaithful to Peugie! In Fontainebleau she waited in the court, later in the garage. But so little signs of friendship were given to her. Will she still welcome me, or remain motionless, hurt, and dignified?

196 Annette Dieudonné supervised preparation of scores for the European opening in Venice.
197 Marga Loudon-Osieck (1903–1979), an accomplished pianist, had a large Netherlands estate, Valkenhorst, where she frequently hosted groups of musicians. See Wenonah Milton Govea, *Nineteenth- and Twentieth-Century Harpists: A Bio-Critical Sourcebook* (London: Greenwood Press, 1995), 26.

Try, really try to come. One day, awake and say, "I am going!" And suddenly it will be quite easy, natural, and done.

Find here these good, strong advices and also my faithful love, N.B.

What is this new number?[198] All habits changed. What a shame. Or do you really live from 60 to 100! It is more than Fontainebleau Palace!

Letter 51-6

8 October 1951

Dear N.B.,

Now that the opening of The Rake's Progress[199] is over, Europe must have calmed down somewhat, and I hope that you are not completely worn to a frazzle! But knowing you, I am afraid you might be, which is a poor way to start your years teaching. I hope that somehow or other you will be able to take things easier for a while (comparatively speaking!). I think of you and miss you so much that I just ache to go to Paris to be with you again. In fact, if I can possibly manage it, I will try to go for three or four months about next March. There is a very big "if" as all plans to have someone be with Mother to look after her have fallen through, but there is no reason for it except that Mother stubbornly refuses to have anyone around, and that means I must stay here. In fact, I had

---

198 NB turned sixty-four on September 16, 1951, and apparently found it hard to believe the years were passing so quickly.

199 Stravinsky's three-act opera *The Rake's Progress* opened in 1951 at Teatro La Fenice in Venice.

to turn down a good job which finally came my way (to teach in a private school in Lenox, Mass.). This situation will go on for years unless I do something drastic. I tried being temperamental, but it did not work, Mother being far worse in that respect! So the only thing that I can think of now is to make a plan to go off, and then go! If it were a financial problem for Mother, that would be different, but she can very well afford help. Anyhow, if I can swing it, could I arrange some lessons with you? You will be amazed to hear that I am being paid for accompanying! But do not be too alarmed! Olga Sandor has been doing a lot of singing for three or four years, and is preparing for a concert soon, and although I will not be the one to play at the concert, I am working with her to check rhythms, etc. You should hear the songs, Debussy-Robbins, Hahn-Robbins, Chaussons-Robbins, and so on. Well, some of them are not too bad.

I have been trying for several weeks to work up enough courage to arrange a few lessons with Soulima Stravinsky, but so far have not mailed the letter. I know it would be wonderful as I have heard from several sources that he is an excellent teacher. Perhaps by the next time you hear from me, I will have had a lesson or two! (Of course, at the rate that I have not been writing you, anything could have happened between letters, I am ashamed to say. I might even have died of old age!)

It is a beautiful October day, and the leaves are rapidly turning red and gold (remember the coloring on our trip to Montreal?), but I wish I were in Paris, just the same.

Please give my love to Marcelle, Annette, and Mlle Gonet,[200] and very especially to you! Ruth

200 Marcelle de Manziarly, Annette Dieudonné, and Louise "Lou Lou" Gonet.

LETTER 51-7

18 OCTOBER 1951

Dear N.B.,

If I was a pauper a few hours ago (before your letter came), now I am a millionaire with such a recommendation! The great danger now is that I will have such a plethora of pupils that I will never be able to get away from them! And aren't you a clever woman! To recommend me to teach solfège! Now I will have to work like the devil to live up to such a reputation! At least I am reading Stravinsky's Poetics of Music. The French copy which you gave me and which I treasure so much is way over my head, but recently I found an English translation. It is a wonderful exposition, and I will have to read it over several times before I absorb it all.

LETTER 51-8

31 OCTOBER 1951

I started this letter over a week ago, but decided to wait until after my lesson with Soulima Stravinsky to finish it. Yes! I have actually started, and am so glad, for as long as I must be here, it will make the difference between another long, drawn out, boring winter and one that will be most interesting and profitable (not financially speaking!). I played terribly—the 1st Beethoven Sonata—and I do not know what he must have thought about my claims of having learned something about music from you! But he is very kind and patient, and I expect will do wonders for my poor brain (which has become a flabby unused muscle in the last three years!). We have another appointment in about two weeks, so I have a second chance.

You are right about my deciding to leave here and then just doing so! I have had the same advice from everyone, including all my family except Mother, of course. It is certainly not an easy thing to do, but it is the only thing to do. So I am really planning a trip to Paris, but cannot say yet whether it will be this spring (about March) or in the fall. It will depend on whether or not I can find a job for next year (school year: September–May). If I do, then I will be able to manage a trip this spring, otherwise I will have to wait. I appreciate so much the little paper you sent as it is rather hard to apply for a teaching position without having graduated from some kind of a professional music school, and one is always asked for references and recommendations. There is a great need here (and particularly in the North Shore of Chicago) for a school or teachers who will teach young children the fundamentals of music. The trouble is with the parents as so many of them are completely illiterate, musically speaking, and have no basis of judging a good or bad teacher, or what it means to develop musicianship. I have one little nine-year-old girl, however, whose mother is 100 percent behind me, and I am having a wonderful time with her.

She is now reading, slowly but surely, Bach Chorales on four staves with C-clefs! She loves to sing, and has already out-stripped me in singing sol-fa syllables (not much of a compliment, I will admit). I would certainly like to see her in the hands of someone without my limitations along that line. It behooves me to work!

Annette was an angel to write me a note. I owe everybody letters, but I will write her one of the first. I also owe Marcelle a letter. I think about all of you so much, and cannot wait for a reunion in Paris! I certainly miss Sr. Ignatia, yet I do not really realize that she will be gone for years, and that our days of giving each other dictation, etc., are over. She is such a fine person, and a wonderful friend.

Well, it is 2:00 a.m. and not being a "Boulanger" or a "Dieudonné," I am collapsing at this hour.

Much, much love, and many thanks for your thoughtfulness, Ruth.

WOMENS'S EDUCATIONAL AND INDUSTRIAL UNION June 1, 1951
264 Boylston Street, Boston 16, Mass.
RE: RUTH ROBBINS

Miss Robbins, who was a student of composition (advanced theory, Harmony, counterpoint) with Mlle. Boulanger at the Longy School of Music during the year 1941-42, is a woman who inspires confidence and who radiates good will and competence. Though my contacts with her were somewhat remote, since the students of Mlle. Boulanger formed a sort of special group within the School which kept more or less to itself, I recall her even after ten years as a person to whom the adjective "worthy" could be rightly applied. Many of the younger students in the group leaned upon her, deriving from her good sense and her placid disposition a certain confidence and comfort.

I understand that Miss Robbins continued her work with Mlle. Boulanger both in California and abroad. I cannot give a thorough appraisal of her musical ability and accomplishment. She started music very late, and was not at all advanced when she studied here. I have never heard her play, nor have I seen her compositions. I think we must accept Mlle. Boulanger's evaluation, if she has given one. It is hard for me to believe the Miss Robbins has become a brilliant musician or an outstanding composer, but I am certainly willing to believe that she has become an excellent teacher of young people, and that she would be able to communicate to them the many techniquesand skills, and some of the inspiration, which she must have received from her teacher.

Furthermore, Miss Robbins sterling character and ideal must, I believe, be a contributing factor. If her musical development has kept pace with the personald factors, she cannot help but be a valuable teacher, and on this suppositional basis, I recommend her highly for your consideration.

Job searching for a piano teaching position in the Boston area, Ruth Robbins asked Melville Smith, the Longy School director, for a letter of recommendation. Note his scrupulous honesty about one of Nadia Boulanger's favorite (even if less talented) students: "It is hard for me to believe [that] Miss Robbins has become a brilliant musician or an outstanding composer, but I am certainly willing to believe that she has become an excellent teacher of young people." [Longy School of Music Archives]

1952

Letter 52-1

[January 1952][201]

Just for the 21st[202] with much love, wishes, and hope!! Cannot write—to sleep! But cannot let the last light die without sending a Happy Birthday to you!

As ever, N.B.

Letter 52-2

21 February 1952

Dear N.B.,

I hardly dare to breathe in case the whole idea pops like a soap bubble, BUT today, nebulously and vaguely but seriously my

201 NB sent birthday wishes to RR yearly; this undated birthday note is from 1952.

202 RR's birthday.

family and I talked about my going to Paris in the fall and taking three of my nieces with me to have a year's study there!!! My sister's two girls who will be 12 and 13 by then and my brother's youngest, Wendy, who is 16. It is one of the things I have dreamed of for so long that the possibility of it becoming real does not register yet. The problem of Mother's care still remains, but she has finally come to see that it really is a problem and is quite willing to make whatever arrangements would be necessary. As I say, it is only an idea at present, and it will all depend on the expenses of the girls' schooling and living. I must get all the information I can along those lines. Wendy will want singing lessons and the younger girls piano, and all of them solfège. Perhaps they could do solfège with Annette? And you could recommend other teachers for piano and singing. It would be wonderful if they could have some work under your supervision. They have all had some work with me off and on for the last few years, but very irregularly as it has not been possible to arrange regular lessons. Besides, a member of the family does not seem to have the same influence on them as an outsider! I have just about worn out the lovely little book of Paris with the nicest and truest colors of any I have seen. It is a gem, and I have an awful feeling that I haven't thanked you for it or the birthday note which I loved receiving. You are an angel to think of me when you have so much to do. Have not yet seen Winnie as I have not been able to plan enough time to go that far. Last weekend had a nice visit with Mr. and Mrs. Jean Casadesus[203] in Indianapolis. They were playing with the symphony, and Thelma Todd had invited them and me for lunch. Have had two more lessons with Soulima, and although I

---

203 "Jean Casadesus . . . .joined the faculty of the American Conservatory at Fontainebleau in 1954 and since 1965 spent half the year at the State University at Binghamton until his untimely death in an auto accident at age 44." *New York Times* obituaries, January 22, 1972.

can see lots of improvement in my playing here and there, I always get so tense when I play for anyone that I fear he must think it hopeless. He is very patient and kind, and I do manage to be a little more at ease each time and keep a little better control. Have started again doing a little accompanying for Olga Sandor. She is singing Debussy's Ariettes Oubliées at present, and although I can only play one out of 50 notes, they are so beautiful that I enjoy the struggle. Well, I must get away and write letters to get information about schools, etc., and also to Marcelle to see what she would think about my coming over and squeezing myself and three nieces in her little apartment, etc. Do you think she will collapse at the idea? I am keeping my fingers crossed, but this time it looks as though something will really work out! I cannot believe it!

Love, Ruth

Letter 52-3

28 February 1952
36, rue Ballu
Paris IXe

Dear Ruth, Read and reread! May the lord help us. Of course I shall do, organize, undertake what you like.

A shadow in the sky: Marcelle? M. de M.? But she cannot even have 1/2 of a person—her apartment is so small. Let us know as soon as you know more, in order to look. It is not easy, and life certainly high. People do not well understand how to handle money which runs with such speed. But children grow and are beautiful. How happy I were if I believed it to be.

Decide soon. If not our hearts will explode.

As ever, N.B.

Letter 52-4

18 April 1952

Dear N.B.,

I meant to write sooner but have been waiting a little so I could tell you something specific, but the more I wait, the more our plans develop in unexpected ways. It now looks as though I will have three nieces with me, after all, but not the same three! Barbara, my brother's older daughter, is thinking seriously of attending the Sorbonne instead of returning to Stanford next year! Not only that, but both Barbara and Wendy (who has just been told of our plans) are trying to persuade friends to join the cavalcade! However, I draw the line on being responsible for more than my family. If any others join the happy throng, they will have to be on their own. Little Susie is already doing her 8th grade work, so she will not attend a regular school. As she has attended the "famous" Winnetka progressive schools all her life, where each child goes ahead at his own rate, my sister thought it might be hard for her to adjust to another system, so she expects her to study French, music, and as she is so used to a variety of activities, art lessons and some sort of gymnastics or dancing. Wendy has to have certain subjects to complete her high school credits. She thinks some of the credits can be in music, but does not know how much of her time can be devoted to it. How the study plans work out, I do not know, but I am planning to sail either the 13th or 20th of August, and I think go straight to Fontainebleau with the girls. They can start French lessons at once, and we will look for a tutor who can work with Barbara and Wendy in whatever will be their most difficult subjects in school so that they will be familiar with the vocabulary, etc. Barbara and Wendy have each had one year of French, so it won't be entirely new. While we have our headquarters in Fontainebleau, Barbara and I could go to Paris and arrange our living accommodations, etc. The mailman just arrived with a big fat letter from Marcelle full of information about schools, etc. It is so wonderful of you and Annette to offer to have the two girls for lessons. I am sure it will work out very well for Susie, and I hope Wendy's curriculum will be such that she too can benefit by such an opportunity. All this is so exciting that I cannot actually believe it!

Had dinner with Rieti and his wife and Rafael Kubelik and Soulima Str. the last time I went down for a lesson.[204] Almost like Paris days! They were down for the first performance of Rieti's new opera at the university. I heard the same concert in Chicago the following week and found it very enjoyable.

I will keep you posted about our plans as they progress.

Much love, Ruth

---

204 Vittorio Rieti (1898–1994), Italian composer, studied under Ottorino Respighi and Alfredo Casella in Rome. He composed music for George Balanchine and Sergei Diaghilev ballets in the 1920s, and after he immigrated to the United States in 1940, he taught at the Peabody Institute in Baltimore, Chicago Musical College, Queens College, and New York College of Music. "Vittorio Rieti, Prolific Composer In Neo-Classical Style, Dies at 96," *New York Times*, February 21, 1994. Rafael Kubelik (1914–1996), a Czech conductor and composer, was music director of the Chicago Symphony Orchestra, Royal Opera House Covent Garden, and Bavarian Radio Symphony Orchestra. Obituaries: Rafael Kubelik, *Independent*, August 12, 1996. In 1950, Soulima Stravinsky was appointed to the piano faculty of the School of Music of the University of Illinois, where he remained until 1978 (https://www.allmusic.com/artist/soulima-stravinsky-mn0001633229/biography). RR would make an eight-hour round-trip drive from the family's Highland Park, Illinois, home to the Urbana-Champaign campus for her lessons with Soulima Stravinsky.

Letter 52-5

17 June 1952

Dear Ruth,

How time can fly slowly!! Here is the paper—here is the assurance that I will do what you decide for the children, with joy. Do arrive fast!

As ever,

N.B.

Letter 52-6

[Undated][205]

Dear Ruth,

Needless to say how I wish you were coming back. When will it be? Do not wait. . . . Find here all my profound affection, my thanks . . . and my hope.

As ever, N.B.

"Your" car is a wonderful friend too. You must have explained how much she was needed, and she understood. May she remain long efficient, in spite of being asked so much! Thank you for that, too, and for all the useful, wonderful, practical objects in daily use.

205 Written after RR's stay in Fontainebleau in the summer of 1952.

1953

Letter 53-1

[Summer 1953][206]

[Telegram addressed to "Robbins 22, rue Barbet de Jouy Paris 44"]

COME THREE FOUR OR FIVE MONDAY WITHOUT FAILURE
WIRE IMMEDIATELY ANSWER = NADIA.

Letter 53-2

[Summer 1953]

[Telegram]

BAYONNE TELEPHONE DE ST. JEAN DE LUZ 0614 12 20 1415.
SEPARATION INCONCEIVABLE COME HERE,
SHALL TRY ARRANGE.
BOULANGER.

206 Although no date appears on these telegrams, they clearly relate to RR's 1953 sojourn in France.

Letter 53-3

28 September 1953

[Copy of a letter from N.B. to R. R. and W. H. J.]

And, so it is. You are gone, my dears—for months, at least. We are all going our path, too often different ones. I am sorry not to have seen you more, but so happy you did this beautiful voyage. As time will go, you will still discover all that your eyes have accumulated. How extraordinary—these poor going men, so fragile—who have changed the face of the world, everywhere spreading what their hands, what their minds can do. Well, well, something to their credit. These fools who also employ their genius one dares not even say to what. And it has to be so, as difficult as it is to accept.

But enough deep, magnificent, and easy commonplace considerations. Do not be too long to return—there is no time to waste. Give love to all the people I have too great care for. Let me thank you for your affection. Do find millionaires for the fund and the school, and realize how dear you are to me.

As ever yours, N.B.

LETTER 53-4[207]

11 OCTOBER 1953
36, RUE BALLU 9E
TÉLÉPH: TRINITÉ 57-91

Dear Ruth,

N.B. has been delighted receiving your letter. She hopes you will be very lucky in all your competitions. Maybe, by finding a name for a new cake or a shaving stick, will you earn a dancing turtle, or a ticket to go to Afghanistan, or goodness knows what! If it could be a summer in France with studies in Fontainebleau, it would be glorious!

Rue Ballu is still rue Ballu, a piece of news which sounds most astounding! Pupils of various nationalities, various ages, sexes, colors, and so forth—so is the conservatoire, but I miss you, and Wendy, and little Susie.

How is Miss Snow? Has she been impressed by my imaginary critters?

Love to you, dear Ruth, from N.B. and I.

Annette

Can no longer say anything to anyone, but . . . still do love you dearly. 3 Fords would be very welcome. 2 sold and another contest brings you in F'eau.

207 (See "[Postcard from Winifred Johnston]" Letter 55-2

Letter 53-5

18 December 1953

Dear N.B.,

How it managed to be this date before my answering your very, very welcome (but brief!) note, I do not know. But, as usual, everything is very hectic right now in my family as they are all planning to go to Colorado for the holidays and to ski for two weeks. So we have been having our Christmas in installments and will have the final one tomorrow night. Well, not exactly, as I am staying here with Mother, so will have a little more with her. As I did nothing last year except write letters home, I sort of have to make up for it this year. Also, as Barbara has only a little time to select things for her trousseau, we are all occupied with that. So far the newspapers have not got hold of the news of her engagement, but it is going to be difficult to keep it quiet as it has leaked out among friends and acquaintances to a considerable extent. Two or three weeks ago, Col. Lindbergh[208] came to have dinner with us. He is such a quiet, unassuming, simple, and "clean-cut" man that we are very happy Barbara will be related to that family. Barbara and Jane have met Mrs. Lindbergh, and both were so impressed with what an exceptionally fine person she is. Jon was very much in the news recently when a member of his mountain-climbing party fell and was fatally injured, and Jon and four others tried desperately to save him, but could not. The newspapers and television concentrated very much on Jon, being the son of the famous flier, and as a result,

208 RR's niece, Barbara Robbins, married Jon Lindbergh, son of the famed aviator, in 1954. In her book *Against Wind and Tide* (New York: Pantheon Books, 2012), Anne Morrow Lindbergh wrote, in a diary entry, of first meeting RR: "Another sister of Jim Robbins (I wasn't prepared for her—Ruth. She is unmarried too, I gather. Does she keep house for Jim? Older & not as attractive as Jane but a nice open, sympathetic face)" (99). RR's siblings Jim and Jane were both aviators and had a natural rapport with the Lindberghs, while RR, typically, remained in the background.

he hates the press more than ever. Col. Lindbergh told us that the press can be very mean, particularly the Chicago press, and advised us to put them all off the scent of the wedding date, if possible, without offending them, if possible!

I sent you a box a few days ago with a few things for you and several others. I could not seem to get into the Christmas spirit soon enough to send it six weeks ago, so had decided to send it via air-mail so it would get to you for Christmas. However, when I found out how expensive it was that way, I changed my mind at the last minute (afterwards I was sorry) and sent it by ordinary mail. So I'm afraid it will have to be considered an early 1954 Christmas box!

Have been concentrating on score-reading. I bought the book you recommended (Wittmark)[209] and found another excellent book: Preparatory Exercises in Score Reading by R.J. Morris and Howard Ferguson (Oxford University Press). I like it better than the Wittmark as it has many more examples and progresses more slowly, but covers the same ground, even more as it includes a section on the necessary transpositions in orchestra score-reading. I must say that I move like molasses in January in that part, but the result is that quartette reading is becoming more fluent. Also, I finally have new reading glasses, which helps a good deal. Have also been concentrating on trying to memorize, and that too is painful! Have been working on one of the Bach Suites, one that I knew by heart about 12 years ago, and it is just as though I have never seen it before! Well, no, that is not quite true, because the music itself I remember easily, but the fingering, hand formation, etc., it is just as though I have never played before. I often wonder if I chose the right career!

209 Not identified. Possibly a publication from M. Witmark & Sons, sheet music publishers.

Susie feels that she is quite adult this year as she is now in high school and is, of course, entirely with children her own age and older. (She would be quite chagrined if she knew I referred to them as "children.") She is doing very well in her studies—I believe she has A's in everything except algebra so far. She is taking third-year French, however she is not doing much with her music, although she did play one of the Bach interventions in a music appreciation class. She was just elected president of her class, so I do not know how much hope to hold out for any practicing.

I miss you so much, and I keep trying to think of ways I can really plan to stay in France. Well, this is not the moment to think about that as I must finish my Christmas preparations.

All my love, Ruth

1954

LETTER 54-1

14 JANUARY 1954
36, RUE BALLU 9^{E}
TÉLÉPH: TRINITÉ 57-91

Happy Birthday, happy birthday!

Dear Ruth,

How sad you are not here. So goes life, but as it goes to its completion as far as I am concerned, I feel it badly. Unfair, indeed, unfair. Well, with hope, obstination,[210] and skill, why would not a solution be found?

Anyhow, here are the warmest of the warmest wishes. And the very deep affection you know is mine for you.

As ever,

N.B.

---

210 She uses the French term for "obstinance."

Letter 54-2

26 March 1954

Dear N.B.,

Now that life is back to normal (?) I can begin to collect my wits and hope to be able to decide definitely about this summer, anyhow. Next fall is still very vague. I had an interview yesterday with the head of a girls' school in Tacoma, Washington, but I do not know if anything will come of that. One of the things they wanted was not only organ playing, but organ teaching! Otherwise I think I could qualify. But to my mind, it would be like being buried alive, especially as I would be expected to live in the school and have other duties besides teaching. I would rather starve in Paris! Anyhow, I have until the end of April to say yes or no to that proposition.

The wedding was really perfect, especially as the press had no inkling of it until yesterday when the license was being registered by the county clerk. Within a few hours the news was in the papers, the telephone rang continuously, photographers appeared, and radio and television broadcasts were in full swing! It was really a miracle that the news did not leak out when they were applying for the license a few hours before the wedding, as the clerk remarked about the similarity of Jon's name and the famous Lindbergh family, and they were invited to be on a television show which was to start in a few minutes and which consisted of couples applying for wedding licenses! Can you imagine!

Only the close relatives and three close friends were present—about 30 people in all. Eleven of them were children: the brothers, sisters and cousins. The L. family made me think of the Bonets:[211] fine, unassuming, natural people, and the children are delightful. If you ever have the chance to meet Mrs. L., I hope you will do so. She is a remarkable woman.

We are about to leave for dinner at my sister's, so I will have to stop. Will write again soon. Please be good and take a restful vacation. Please!

Love, Ruth

211 Family of Narcís Bonet (1933–2019), a Spanish child prodigy and student of NB's, who gave the first public performances of his piano compositions at age thirteen. At fifteen, his first symphony, *La vaca cega* (The blind cow), was commissioned and performed by the Majorca Symphonia. He relocated to Paris to study with NB. In 1952 and 1953, he won first prize in composition at the American Conservatory at Fontainebleau, and later succeeded NB as director of the Conservatory (http://www.narcisbonet.org/bio).

1955

Letter 55-1

17 September 1955
Pontresina[212]

Other land, but same hearts. Here we are, Winifred, Annette, I . . . and not so far, Ruth!

Your wishes arrived yesterday and brought joy. The day ought to be rather serious, but must one believe numbers, provisions they give, or listen to the inner burning?

So, I do not send a taking leave, but an awaiting hope.

Do come back soon, one needs you here.

And believe in my profound affection.

N.B.

Tuesday Hotel Victoria

no more summits and snow, per modi calm waters.

212 NB's birthday was September 16. Pontresina is a charming Swiss resort town seven kilometers from St. Moritz.

LETTER 55-2

24 SEPTEMBER 1955

[POSTCARD FROM WINIFRED JOHNSTONE]
MENAGGIO, 24 SEPT.

I'm ashamed of myself, for neglecting you, but kept meaning to write a letter! Now we have just one more week here, and at least I want to get this off. A jovial N and A[213] in Pontresina in time to celebrate the 16th together, then we all took the bus down . . . the 20th and stay till Oct. 1, when N.B. departs for Holland to judge competitions, and A and J leave . . . later for Paris. I fly back the 6th just before N.B. gets back to 36 [rue Ballu]. We left Thursday . . . in Bellagio, just 12 minutes by boat just across from here. Marvelous holiday!

Love, W.

LETTER 55-3

10 OCTOBER 1955

Dear N.B.,

It was just a little over four months ago that I left you, but it seems like at least four years! I have not anything especially to tell you except how much I miss you and the Wednesday class, the Friday evenings at Mme Vergniaud's,[214] etc., etc. If I knew people who liked to get together once a week or so just for the pleasure of

213 "N A" and refers to NB and Annette Dieudonné. Winifred Johnstone, socially stiff, perhaps felt some jealousy at RR's easy intimacy with Boulanger. In this light, the postcard can be seen as competitive one-upmanship.

214 Hélène Vergniaud was a friend, benefactress—even landlady—to generations of Boulanger's students.

making music together, life would be entirely different. But there is such a commercial point of view about music here; you either have to "make money" with it or "get on the radio" (or television, which is even worse), or it is not worth doing. It is so hard to convince people that it is such a pleasure for its own sake! I guess I feel it more in my own family than anywhere as they are in general decidedly unmusical.

However, Susie has kept up her interest, and although she is not studying music, she takes part in all the musical activities at school. She is in the chorus, glee club, quartette, etc. (all singing groups), and has eight periods a week of this type of work, so you see her nine months of study with you and Annette have borne fruit.

I have heard from a mutual friend of John LaMontaine[215] and mine that he is in Paris studying with you! I am so glad for him that it worked out. Please remember me to him, and tell him that I will be greatly disappointed if I do not see him in Paris.

Now that the children are all in school again, I manage to work at least two hours a day at the piano without bothering anyone or being bothered. Although I did not work much during the summer, I find that in certain ways I have made progress. I have assimilated a lot of the material that I worked on last winter.

I am still trying to decide what to do with myself until I can manage to return to Paris. If I decide to teach, it means I will have to rent a place where I can teach and stay put until next summer. Otherwise, I will have to find some other way to earn money. Life is a problem when your heart is in one place and you are in another!

I hope my birthday letter reached you in time, but I am afraid

---

215 John LaMontaine (1920–2013) was a friend of RR's from Oak Park, Illinois, who had just started studying with NB. He went on to win the 1959 Pulitzer Prize in music for his Piano Concerto no. 1 "In Time of War." See Paul Vitello, "John LaMontaine, Pulitzer-Winning Composer, Dies at 93," *New York Times*, May 14, 2013.

that by the time it was forwarded to wherever you were, it probably was late. If I do not write often, it is not because I have forgotten you! It is because I have so little news.

Last week and this week Lotte Lehmann is at Northwestern University giving a series of lessons to some of the students of the music school. It is rather like the master classes at Fontainebleau, but open to the public as well as the students. She is such an artist that even though her voice is gone, her demonstrations are profoundly moving. She speaks very well and has quite a sense of humor as well as a deep penetration of the nature of the songs and words.

Well, I will stop, as the mailman will soon be here and I do not want to miss him.

Please let me know if there is anything I can send you or do for you here.

Love, Ruth

Letter 55-4

15 October 1955

Dear Ruth,

Everything arrived safely. I laughed and enjoyed, for everything is so well chosen, so useful and ingenious.

Only 8 days I am back. Hoped for some peace—already fall turmoil. Cannot write, only say: Do come, and also Thank You.

J.L.M.[216] is a real musician, and what are his qualities as a man, deep, charming. I really love him as if he had been here long.

Love, love again and always!! Yours, N.B.

216 RR's friend John LaMontaine.

Letter 55-5

Christmas 1955

[Handwritten on a calling card printed with Boulanger's name]

Well . . . You are really
amusing and witty, but . . .
when are you arriving????

Nadia Boulanger

With all my wishes for Christmas
and the New Year.
As ever,
N.B. 1955

1956

LETTER 56-1

21 JANUARY 1956
36, RUE BALLU 9E
TÉLÉPH: TRINITÉ 57-91

Dear Ruth,

Soon your anniversary. Is it not a pity we cannot organize a grand meeting in your honour!

Instead, it sounds rather light—few wishes! But . . . what wishes! So burning, so numerous that they will take you away and . . . maybe bring you here on our call. How wonderful it would be! For we cannot wait much longer. We lose our strength. Have mercy on us! I laugh, but life has been rather sad, as Mme de Manziarly[217] is very ill, and Marcelle so anxious, and overtired. No hope. To my mind a little improvement renders the situation more pathetic.

217 Mother of Marcelle de Marziarly.

Paralyzed, 77 years old. What can be hoped? But we are in the hands of God, and that is all. Annette fell in the dining room as we were preparing Christmas and a fracture was feared, but fortunately she is better.

Christmas was nice, the children all happy. You would hardly recognize the boys. They are really nice and intelligent.

Again, so many wishes and all my very deep affection, dearest Ruth, N.B.

Parcel not yet arrived. . . . What an expectation.

Letter 56-2

12 February 1956

Dear Ruth,

Yes, it arrived! And I do thank you, such a nice, useful package. And the book seems so good. Do not think I forget, but what a winter, such sadnesses everywhere, and a life too busy to accomplish even a little of what had to be done. Poor Marcelle willing to be brave, but as you imagine. And here, and there, and not one day of rest, or in fact, or what is worse, in mind, so . . . well rather tired. But . . . still struggling. Do come, one badly needs you! Do send a word to Mme Louis Vergniaud, 20, rue Eugene Flachat. She has one eye ill for the time being, cannot read and needs some sheen. And what can I do? So many other duties, or obligations or calls from my own heart. You are a dear, and one feels so good in thinking of you, my beloved friend.

As ever, so faithfully, N.B.

What I said is the enclosed. Who knows. But here it is!

Letter 56-3

29 March 1956

Dear N.B.,

I wonder if you will ever have anything to do with me again if I ever get back to Paris. You may not believe it, but I think of you and Marcelle and Annette and Paris and France every day, and just long for the day I will return, but for some reason that I cannot explain, I just haven't been able to write letters.

Every time I start a letter, it just peters out into nothing as I have nothing to say. I am so bogged down with household affairs and nursing mother that I have been unable to concentrate on anything, even reading a book! It is an awful state of mind to be in, and I hope that when Mother is walking again I will pull out of it. As a matter of fact, that will be in about two or three weeks when her second cast will be removed and she can begin to get around without help. In order to try to force myself back into regular study, about three weeks ago I signed up for a correspondence course in counterpoint at the University of Chicago (v. Howard Talby), but I have not even completed the first lesson as yet! The textbooks are Jeppesen and Soderlund,[218] and the first lesson requires a lot of reading about the practices of the early composers of the 14th, 15th, and 16th centuries, and as fast as I read it, I forget it! I often wonder if there is anything inside this old skull!

You cannot imagine what a wonderful surprise it was to receive your cable and letter and the lovely book of pictures of Strasbourg Cathedral, all just in time for my birthday! The letter and cable

---

218 Knud Jeppesen, *Counterpoint: The Polyphonic Vocal Style of the Sixteenth Century*, and Gustave Fredric Soderlund, *Direct Approach to Counterpoint in 16th Century Style.* "Howard Talby" is unidentified.

were worn out in no time, but I took care not to wear out the book! And speaking of cathedrals, I will never forget our all-night drive to Chartres and how cold it was there at 5:00 a.m. in the pitch dark, waiting for the doors to open. And how the place gradually came to life with the dawn and how bustling it was by the time we left. And remember the bread and the nice fresh milk you got from a farmer and we headed back to Paris by backroads? Oh my, oh my! How I wish that were all ahead of me instead of in the past!

You must be all excited about your forthcoming concerts in Monaco. A nice newsy letter from Annette about a month ago told me all about your plans for the concerts for the coronation.[219] Please, when newsreel pictures are being taken, stand right out in front and do not let the prince hide so much as the toe of your shoe! Perhaps some miracle will occur, and I will be able to go to the movies and see you there! Really, you owe it to us poor creatures to whom you have given a taste for such a glorious life only to have it snatched away at midnight, so to speak, like poor little Cinderellas.

Poor Sister Ignatia fell and broke her leg. It just happened a few days ago, and I have not seen her, but I phoned the college to see how she is getting along, and she is all right, but of course will have to wear a cast for some weeks. I guess I will see her next Monday as usual.

Poor Annette! She, who is so busy, takes time to write me nice long letters, and I do not answer them!

Poor Marcelle! After inviting her to my summer place, and then hearing that she will probably come, and then not another word from me must have made her wonder if I had changed my mind! I have not, and am wild to have her come. My only wish is that you

219 Coronation of Grace Kelly (1929–1982) as Princess Grace upon her marriage to Prince Rainier of Monaco.

and Annette were to be there, too. Marcelle's second letter just came, and I will answer it tout de suite!

I must go to the store to buy food for tonight's dinner, and if I leave this to add to it later, it may never be sent (as others before it), so I will take it with me now. How I wish I were to be in Paris in April and to be in Monaco to hear what will probably be the most outstanding concerts of the year. (However, if I were there, I would probably be madly copying and arranging music, and would not see the chestnut trees in blossom at all!)

Please remember me to Mlle Gonet. I enjoyed her card so much.

With all my love, Ruth

P.S. Had a nice visit with Jean Casadesus at Rosary College one day when he came to call on Sr. Ignatia while I was there. He promised to give my best regards to all.

P.S. 2 My friend John LaMontaine[220] (who planned to study with you at Fontainebleau last summer but who had to give it up because of his sister's illness [she died] is now playing the piano parts with the NBC Symphony with Toscanini.

Letter 56-4

1 April 1956

Dear Ruth, The Easter holidays this year are not pleasant. You are not with us, the plants and trees have terribly suffered from the cold, and the wind is really ugly. But when are you coming

220 Composer and pianist John Maynard LaMontaine.

to Paris? We miss you immensely and I thought you intended to arrive in February or March? I miss my neighbor of the Wednesday afternoons and also of the Friday evenings. Eulia also wants you badly though she never writes. Nadia will soon be in Monaco for the great wedding. Do answer, please.

Yours forever!! H.V.[221]

I miss you also. After so many rainy days the river has flooded. It is not funny! I hope also that we shall see you soon.

Best love, Nadia / Dominique[222]

221 This is a joint letter from 'H.V. (Hélène Verignaud), Nadia, and Dominique

222 Perhaps Dominique Merlet (b. 1938), at the time a nineteen-year-old student of NB's who had won three first prizes at the Conservatory (https://www.francemusique.fr/emissions/les-traverses-du-temps/dominique-merlet-pianiste-25796).

Letter 56-5

18 April 1956[223]
Palais de Monaco

Dear Ruth,

Here is my word: I will do it! And it is worth [it]. How well they sang today. But . . . will it be so Thursday? She is more lovely than I could imagine, and thus looks so happy. May it be.

When are you to be here???

Decide—it will work.

As ever, N.B.

---

223 Grace Kelly and Prince Rainier were married in a civil ceremony on April 18, 1956, and in a church ceremony on April 19. NB had been a friend of Rainier's father, Prince Pierre, for years and frequently spent time in the spring at the Palais de Monaco. In this postcard, NB refers to her choral practice on April 18. Her singers performed the cantata *Bist du bei mir*—traditionally attributed to Bach, now recognized as the work of Gottfried Heinrich Stölzel (1690–1749)—as requested by Prince Pierre, but NB replaced the inappropriate funereal text of the original with the words of "Ave Maria."

Original text of cantata:
Bist du bei mir, geh' ich mit Freuden zum Sterben und zu meiner Ruh'.
Ach, wie vergnügt wär so mein Ende, es drückten deine schönen
Hände mir die getreuen Augen zu.

If you are with me, then I will gladly go to my death and to my rest.
Ah, how satisfying will my end be, for your dear,
fair hands will shut my faithful eyes!

Text to Ave Maria:

Ave Maria, Gratia plena, Dominus tecum.	*Hail Mary, full of grace, the Lord is with thee.*
Benedicta tu in mulieribus,	*Blessed art thou among women,*
Et benedictus, fructus ventris tui, Jesus.	*and blessed is the fruit of thy womb, Jesus.*
Sancta Maria, sancta Maria, Maria,	*Holy Mary, Mother of God,*
Ora pro nobis, nobis peccatoribus,	*pray for us sinners,*
Nunc et in hora, in hora mortis nostrae.	*now and in the hour of our death.*
Amen. Amen.	*Amen. Amen.*

LETTER 56-6

[UNDATED][224]
HOTEL VICTORIA MENAGGIO, ITA.

Around the 15th

They did arrive . . . they did! Thank you so much. We leave tomorrow for Samanden,[225] not with the car to gain time and rest, but "they" are coming with us, for our mountain parties. (Probably rain, storm, hurricane, but what do we not face with heroism?)

We all miss you. Do come soon. Do not hesitate. Who does not risk, loses! What fine principles.

As ever, N.B.

224 RR and NB had a lively correspondence during the spring and summer of 1956. Unfortunately, we do not have the letters from RR to NB that prompted letters 56-6, 56-7, 56-8, and 56-9.
225 A Swiss village in the canton of Grisons.

Letter 56-7

23 June 1956
36, rue Ballu 9e
Téléph: Trinité 57-91

What a lovely, lively letter. Dear Ruth, I cannot resist acknowledging it! As you see . . . in a bad shape, and a queer haste. Banal, usual constatation,[226] but strikingly needed. Hope to be alive for Fontainebleau . . . but . . . one week more—a problem. You are so amusing, witty, and there I hear all what you sometimes do not say! And it is so nice and good.

Well, struggle, convince someone that there is not another house as pleasant, as dreamed of—and do come. Waiting is not a sign of prudence. So easy to arrive too late, later! Winifred is here. Hardly see her but is often here. Stupid to let everything devour you! I do no more know how to escape, that is all, and have a grand time, to be honest. If only it did not imply such sacrifices.

Dear Ruth, remember . . . and let me hear you are soon to be here.

As ever, so much affection and for all the ones who do not know I am writing, yours,

N.B.

How beautiful must be your mother's estate! My love to Wendy and Suzy.

226 French for "observation."

Letter 56-8

12 August 1956

Have laughed with your young friend. Laughed in reading your letters so alert. Quickly . . . a word of thanks, of hope, of regret. We miss you so much! So much work that not even the time to give you a full description of such a "superb" activity! You must guess, hear, see and have a picture of a life where no friends are seen, no walks admitted, no dreams elaborated, but . . . nevertheless, and really interesting and nice. The students are so full of good will.

When are you arriving? Through the Pole North, the Pole South, Siberia, or Australia—but arriving. Remember, we may not wait endlessly. And if you arrived and found us gone! What a tragedy! Do not take a risk too serious.

Annette is not here, not Winifred, but Tasha. And she asks me to send you her faithful love. Mine is joined, and very deep affection with it.

As ever, N.B.

From Sept. 8 to 16 Venise: Hotel Bauer Grünewald.

Send news, announce the expected one!!

Letter 56-9

12 August 1956

[From Annette Dieudonné on reverse of Boulanger's letter of 12 August 1956 (56-8)

Dear Ruth,

We miss you very much. And do not forget that I am waiting for you to teach. One has to fill in a sure way my contemporaries in driving the car that I am going to buy when I have paid all the taxes, which are asked from me.[227]

Fontainebleau as ever. Life as ever. But a good deal of optimistic view is necessary not to be a little bit anxious.

With love,

Annette

Letter 56-10

11 September 1956

Dear N.B., This is to wish you a VERY HAPPY birthday, which I am sure it will be, as the letter from Winnie tells me you will be with the Stravinskys and the Sachses in Venice for the premiere of his new cantata.[228]

It is also to tell you that a birthday present is on the way (via

227 Mind-boggling Franglais from Annette Dieudonné. Perhaps she means "After I pay my taxes, I'll buy a car to be sure to fill the transportation needs of my contemporaries, so remember I'm waiting for you to teach me to drive."

228 RR is referring to the European premiere. The original premiere performance of Igor Stravinsky's *Cantata* was on November 11, 1952, by the Los Angeles (Chamber) Symphony Society, to whom Stravinsky dedicated the work. See Eric Walter White, *Stravinsky: The Composer and His Works*, 2nd ed. (Berkeley: University of California Press, 1979).

air-mail) to Venice, but it may not arrive in time as I received it only today. It is something I ordered via Canada and of course it was several days late in arriving. Something else that I ordered well over two months ago has not yet arrived!

Our house is not sold and no prospects at the moment. We thought that giving it to a Jewish agent would be a good thing as Highland Park has become 80% or more Jewish (that is probably an exaggeration, but not much). However, it seems that the newer type of wealthy Jew is not buying property here anymore as the town has become so saturated with the undesirable kind! So now we will switch to a gentile agent and hope for better results.

I am starting a siege with the dentist this week, and as I suspect, there are a number of little repairs to be made. I will be obliged to be here three or four weeks after that. Also, I must take Mother to the dentist, and as she has not seen a dentist for years, that might run into quite a bit of time.

But as I told Marcelle[229] (Alas, I was not able to see her as I did not know she was here until it was too late to make arrangements. I almost went to NY this week just to see her but phoned her, instead, and told her that the money I saved thereby would pay for a new boat fare). As I started to say—as I told M., if I do not sail around Nov. 1, then I really expect to do so soon after Christmas (Wendy may be worried around Christmas time). If the house is sold by then, I can stay as long as I wish, but if not, I am afraid it will have to be a short trip. But I am determined to go this winter.

The last mail today leaves in a few minutes, so I must run.

As always, I miss you enormously!

All my love, Ruth

P.S. Love to Annette, Winnie, the Sachses, the Stravinskys.

---

229 Marcelle de Manziarly.

Letter 56-11

12 December 1956
36, rue Ballu 9e
Téléph: Trinité 57-91

Dear Ruth,

Well, in all the sadness, that is a real joy. You do not know how happy I am. Can say nothing, except that I can hardly wait until middle January. Will be away in April. And for a short time.
So . . . arrive.

Many wishes and a great blow of cheerfulness. Such a long expected arrival!!

Happy Christmas—yes, one must still try to say so, and all my love. Ah yes, so happy.

N.B.

Letter 56-12

Christmas 1956

[Written on a card with Christmas tree decoration]

Dear Ruth,

Will it not bring summer at once? Thank you for everything, and hurry, hurry.

As ever,

N.B.

1957

Letter 57-1

20 January 1957
36, rue Ballu 9e
Téléph: Trinité 57-91

In fact, I do hope ardently you are not to receive this message, being already here.

But . . . as doubts unfortunately persist, have our bunches of wishes. Many lovely phrases of love. How nice if they were abandoned somewhere over there where you are not.

And as ever, so much love and expectation,

Nadia B.

LETTER 57-2

5 FEBRUARY 1957

Dear Ruth,

Only to say my joy, my impatience. Hard to wait. But you will not see Annette who has been ill and must leave for a complete rest. Let us hope it is not too serious.

Am sorry not to go at Orly, but have not been well myself and have to restrict severely my activities. Nevertheless, shall be there. Do see me!

Hope you are to have a nice crossing, and measure how dearly you are expected.

In profound affection, N.B.

LETTER 57-3

14 FEBRUARY 1957
36, RUE BALLU 9E
TÉLÉPH: TRINITÉ 57-91

Only to say at once: with you even if not there. Sorry not to come at Orly, but classes are DUTY, in capital letters.

All my love, and my joy.

As ever yours,

N.B.

Do come to the class to hear me shout! Thursday from 1 to 4. Cannot wait until Friday to see you at the Conservatory. Departure 8.50, rue Ballu. Dinner Saturday at 8.

Letter 57-4

12 May 1957

Dear Ruth,

It is hard to accept it is all over: You are gone, in this period so sad with the slow passing from such a dear friend. Your departure seems in a way still harder. The time goes, we go. And to see depart, even for a voyage, the ones one loves is difficult. Well, we are there to accept, and also to be grateful for the joys granted. So, must not forget how great remains the joy of having seen you, and I do not forget. Am happy to feel you progress, happy to have seen you, even if not enough!

Give my warmest thoughts to dear Jolanda.[230] Have a nice time in the lovely city, and believe me to be so faithfully yours, N.B.

Letter 57-5

29 May 1957

Dear N.B.,

I hope you have not noticed (but am afraid you must have) that as old age approaches I am becoming very profitably absent-minded. I meant to hand you a whole fistful of dollars before I left, but forgot twice, and needless to say, the dollars melted into thin air en route to Boston (where I am now). I do not think it safe to send currency in a letter, so I will instead give Winifred a check for the entire amount I owe you: 64 dollars for eight lessons.

230 Jolanda is unidentified.

Please forgive me!

As I arrived only last night (after a long but surprisingly not uncomfortable voyage) I have not seen anyone I know, so have no news as yet. With all Jolanda had to do on her return to Copenhagen, she took time to take me on all kinds of sight-seeing excursions and to visit the Jersilds and another time the Holenbecks[231] in their fascinating house, and they in turn gave up a whole day to show us the countryside and the beach and to serve two sumptuous meals. What lovely people they are! But that was easy to see when I met Mrs. H. in Paris. I have been so spoiled during my visit with Jolanda that I will probably be impossible from now on!

. . . I may not make it to Copenhagen. Somehow, I seem to find my way back to France quite often, so feel that after not too long a time, I will see you again. Anyhow, next spring, I hope! That is, if you need transportation here and there. My car seems to be in good shape after Toby's care while I was away, so unless it wears in between now and next year, it is at your service (including driver!), old as it is!

It is hard to believe that I was less than three months in Paris, as it was one of the most satisfactory times I have spent there. Time is relative. Much love and thanks, Ruth

---

231 Jersilds and the Holenbecks remain unidentified.

LETTER 57-6

29 JULY 1957

[WRITTEN AT AN ANGLE AT TOP LEFT]

Love, Annette!

[MAIN TEXT OF LETTER]

We are alive. I have laughed as always in reading your peppering letters, dear Ruth. But we are frozen, and so busy. . . . Ridiculous!

So, only a line to say we all miss you—W., A.,[232] and I—that you must come back. Well, let us say with me next June! You do not know how sad it is you are not here.

No details. After all, we are well, pleased to be here, and loving you dearly. So . . . what more.

As ever, N.B.

LETTER 57-7

[OCTOBER 1957][233]

Dear N.B.,

I am too embarrassed to date this letter, so you will just have to guess! The truth is that I keep procrastinating on purpose as I keep hoping that the next letter [I write] will contain news that

---

232 "W" and "A" refer to Winifred Johnstone and Annette Dieudonné.

233 RR left this letter undated on purpose. This apparent response to NB's note of July 29 has a wealth of information about RR's life and interests. Her comment on my ("nephew Jimmy") piano lessons with Ruth Roberg demonstrate RR's optimism, for I truly had no talent, and Roberg soon gave up.

everything is settled, and that I am now living in such and such a place in such and such a town, etc., etc.

But it is not so, and I am still packed up in Highland Park and waiting for something to happen. The only silver lining to my perpetual cloud is that I am definitely selling my summer place, and before the end of the year, will be able to afford to make some kind of a move. My next problem is to decide where to go. For years I have had my heart set on moving to New England—near Boston—but actually, except for Nora, Winifred, and Luise, I do not know people there, whereas in this area I know people.

However, if I stay here, I cannot shake off the family problem, so . . . ?

I have just recently discovered a friend who is keenly interested in a more intelligent approach to teaching music to children. She has spent two summers in Aspen, Colorado, studying music, and is very much impressed by the work of Aaron Bodenhorn[234] who, according to my friend, accomplished wonders with a class of children in eight weeks. He evidently gives them a very thorough basic training in theory and ear training so that when they are faced with "real music," they are very well prepared to hear and comprehend it. My friend, Mrs. Roberg,[235] is most eager to have me visit his classes in New York where he teaches during the winter. In fact, she is planning to go to NY early in the year and take several local teachers with her and hopes I can join them. She is a great music lover and sponsors many young musicians and

234 Aaron Bodenhorn (1898–1992) of Bronxville, New York (https://www.ancientfaces.com/person/aaron-bodenhorn/13351278).

235 Ruth Roberg, wife of Leo Roberg, photographer; Lucy Montgomery, wife of Chicago financier Kenneth Montgomery; Jean Evans, wife of professor, author, and TV host Bergen Evans; and Eleanor Martin, wife of architect Albert Martin, were key supporters of Chicago's Fine Arts Quartet. See Abram Loft, *How to Succeed in an Ensemble: Reflections on a Life in Chamber Music* (Cambridge, MA: Amadeus Press, 2003), 93.

musical activities. At present she is teaching my nephew Jimmy, and everything seems to be going very well. Her very deep desire to teach and see that music is taught intelligently to children springs from a great tragedy in her life. Her only son was killed by lightning about five years ago while at a summer camp. (One of the Lindbergh boys who was running behind the other boy narrowly escaped the same fate.) Mrs. Roberg feels that if she had only known what she knows now about music, she could have given her son a much greater joy in music than she did. She is most eager to hear any of your lectures and concerts you will give in the spring and to meet you. She has a nephew who is studying in Germany on a Fulbright scholarship (not music) and, as he is also a music lover and plays piano, she hopes he can go to Fontainebleau next summer. His name is David Harr, so if you hear from or about him, you will know who he is. I suggested that if he could get to Paris and meet you, it would be a good idea. I hope you will agree!

As I have only the vaguest idea of your plans for your United States visit, I hope I will be better informed before it is too late for me to plan, as I would be sick if I missed an opportunity to see you and hear you. Winnie said that you expect to be in this area part of the time, so I am all agog. Will you perhaps be at the Arts Festival at the University of Illinois? Maybe I will move down there if so! Please have someone let me know.

Oh, by the way, do you know a good musician in San Diego? Barbara and Jon have bought a house there, and I am trying to persuade Barbie to start Christine's music training as the child is very ready for it. She is only two and a half—well, soon three—very imaginative and bright, and ought to have ear training right now. Of course, it is Barbara who should have the solfège lessons and then she should work with the babies a little each day.

Your birthday party must have been a great success. I read about it in Time, and Annette sent me a clipping about it from a Swiss newspaper, and today I read further details about it in the Fontainebleau paper, which just arrived. I wish I could have been there!

It seems to me there were one or two other things I wanted to tell you. Oh yes—the University of Chicago, the Art Institute and the Chicago Symphony are giving an arts course this year to anyone who wants to join. I was tempted, but it was too expensive for me, especially as I could not count on being free to attend the classes each week. But two of the music lectures will be by Bob Middleton and Easley Blackwood[236] (in the spring, thought you would be interested. Perhaps YOU will be lecturing! Who knows!). We are having a marvelous Picasso exhibit at the Art Institute at present. Many people have come from NY to see it as they say it is so much better arranged here than at the NY museum.

All my love, I think of you always, Ruth

236 Robert Middleton and Easley Blackwood were students of NB's. Middleton (1920–2016) was chair of the music department at Vassar College from 1974 until his retirement in 1985. See "Guide to the Robert E. Middleton Papers, 1939–1954." Blackwood (1933–2023) was professor emeritus at the University of Chicago where he taught since 1958. "Blackwood's . . . tonal composition . . . stems from his groundbreaking research into the properties of microtonal tunings and his decades-long study of traditional harmony." "Easley Blackwood," Artists, Cedille Records, (https://www.cedillerecords.org/artists/easley-blackwood/. Russell Trapp, "In Memoriam: Easley Blackwood, Jr.," January 24, 2023, https://music.uchicago.edu/news/memoriam-easley-blackwood-jr.

Letter 57-8

31 December 1957

Dear Ruth,

Last hours of 57. How to stay without coming to you. Tasha is proud, I am touched. Love and little agenda:

Arrive April 3,
Philadelphia 16,
Boston 18
NY 25 or 26
??
Potsdam our P. May 5,
Carbondale May 12,
Urbana 20,
??
Oxford, Ohio June 2,
Smith College 8,
Boston 10,
14, on the Flandre.

Am so eager to see you. Love, wishes, and profound affection,

N.B.

1958

LETTER 58-1

17 JANUARY 1958

Dear N.B.,

I just found out something about my father that I never knew before. When he went to S. Africa as a young man, the first money he earned was for playing his violin in a café in Johannesburg to pay for his dinner! I never realized how romantic my background was! Love, Ruth

LETTER 58-2

21 JANUARY 1958[237]

Wishes—& wishes—& still more wishes. Am writing as a machine, have no more words nor mind but do still know that I pray the Lord to bless you, that I love you as ever, & am preparing

237 Le Palais Monaco. RR's 48th birthday.

to exhaust you. You may still be saved if I have to travel by night! So faithfully, with so many thoughts and hopes,

Yours, dear Ruth, so devotedly,

N.B.

August 6, 1958

Dear Mr. Novak,

I meant to get in touch with you before I left Concord, but my plans unexpectedly changed and I left quite a bit sooner than I had originally planned.

I will be back in Concord about the last week of August, and if you wish to talk to me about the solfège classes, I will see you any time you wish. As a matter of fact, I do not even know when classes begin, or when I am officially expected to be there.

Perhaps Miss Sanderson told you I visited her class and had a brief talk with her. I saw that the older pupils were doing elementary work, and she told me that the children worked the same way, but at a slower rate of progress, so I didn't feel it necessary to continue visiting the classes. I would like, however, to meet with the assistant solfège teachers (for the preparatory classes) so their work and mine will go along similar

In the fall semester of 1958, Ruth Robbins began teaching solfège at the Longy School of Music. She shows confidence in her ability to teach a course that Nadia Boulanger herself had chosen for her in a September 1951 letter of recommendation.

In her letter, Ruth identifies Paul Hindemith's Elementary Training for Musicians *as the text she will use for the class. First published in 1946,* Elementary Training *provides entry-level basics, starting with "Quarter-notes, Half-notes, and Whole-notes (and rests)" in chapter 1, while providing clear and in-depth discussion of meter and rhythm; changing tempi, dynamics, and expression; and chromatic scale in later chapters.*

[August 6, 1958, letter to Mr. Novak, courtesy of Longy School of Music Archives]

lines. I expect to use Hindemith's "Elementary Training for Musicians" a great deal, and if they are not acquainted with the book, it would be advisable for them to obtain copies for study.

Hoping that you are enjoying your summer vacation, I remain

Sincerely yours,

Ruth Robbins
3 Court Lane
Concord, Mass.

Phone-
EMerson 9-2555

LETTER 58-3

26 JANUARY 1958

Dear N.B.,

I had my interview with Mr. Smith,[238] and he is definitely going to give me a children's class in solfège in the fall. In the meantime, I will have to work like mad myself as I am très rusty. I have started working with Luisa[239] and find her an excellent teacher. She made it so clear and precise just what one should feel in the fingers as well as just what should be going on in the head at the same time that I could respond immediately, for the first time in my life! I am following her orders explicitly, and am to drop all my other work at the piano (sight-reading, transposing, etc.) and concentrate on pure piano technique for the next few weeks. I am not to work more than 20 minutes or a half hour at a time, but am supposed to repeat the work several times a day.

Last night we went to Brandeis University to hear the first of Noel and Paul's five concerts they will give for the next five weeks. Bach's C minor Sonata, Stravinsky's Duo Concerto, Beethoven's Kreutzer Sonata. They played beautifully. What a superb artist Paul is![240]

238 Melville Smith, NB's student from the 1920s, who was director of the Longy School of Music from 1941 to 1962.

239 Luise Vosgerchian (1922–2000) first studied with NB at the Longy School in 1945 and then after the war went to Paris to further her studies. She joined the music department at Harvard in 1959 and taught there until her retirement in 1990. See "Beloved Music Teacher Vosgerchian Dies at 77," *Harvard Gazette*, March 16, 2000.

240 Noël Lee (1924–2013), American pianist and composer, studied with NB at the Longy School of Music in the 1940s and later in Paris; he was a visiting professor of music at Brandeis University. Paul Makanowitzky (1920–1998), child prodigy violinist who had his professional debut in Paris at age nine and in New York at seventeen, had his soloist career interrupted by his volunteer service in the United States armed forces (he was a Swedish citizen). After the war, he was soon engaged as a soloist, leading orchestras under Pierre Monteux, Paul Paray, Vladimir Golschmann, and Serge Koussevitzky. In 1954, Makanowitzky met Noël Lee. As a duo, they concertized extensively between 1954 and 1964. The *Boston Herald*'s P. C. Brooks praised them as "the best ensemble playing to be found anywhere in the world." Norbeck, Peters & Ford (http://www.norpete.com/s0400.html).

I am listening to a recorded all-Chopin concert by Dinu Lipatti. What an artist he was, too!

I left my car at the Ford garage (here in Concord) to have it greased and the oil changed, and I told the man about how the old girl had lost all her youthful vigor when she had a major operation recently. He said he would check her and let me know what he found, but not go ahead with any repairs without consulting me as I had already spent a lot of money to have the trouble fixed, and it was not any better. Well, I waited for a phone call which never came, so finally I went to the garage. Well, my car, she was quietly waiting for me. I paid the bill (no charge for any repairs) and started off. She was her old self again!!! She leapt forward at the slightest touch of the accelerator, she flew along the road, she practically soared uphill! I am so happy that maybe now I will have her face lifted a little, but not too much as I do not want her to lose her real character. Perhaps just a new glass eye. You must come back and let her take you to California. She will reserve her best energy for one last final fling with you!

By the way, no news from the Quebec police as yet. But the Canadian "mounties" always "get their man," so they say, so I am not out of danger yet! But I will bet that when they realized I was to go right back over the same road and could check up on all those "30 mile" zones, they tore up the ticket pronto.

This paper does not like this pen and ink.

Lots and lots of love, Ruth

XOXOXOXOXO—please share some of these with Annette.

Letter 58-4

3 March 1958
36, rue Ballu
Paris, IXe

[From Annette Dieudonneé]

Dear Ruth,

I am sending you the schedule of N.B.'s trip. You will see at first sight that it implies lots of leisure and relaxation!

Well, I do hope she will, after all, survive, being of a strong constitution. It is the best one can hope, is it not?

I hope you will be able to see a good deal of her and to drive her. You know that you are the only person she likes to be driven by.

Bravo for your moving east; it is a wonderful idea.

With much love,

Annette

Letter 58-5

17 March 1958
36, rue Ballu
Paris, IXe

[From Annette Dieudonneé]

Dear Ruth,

N.B. is very, very sorry, but here is the schedule of her time in Chicago:

Coming from Potsdam, NY, she arrives in the morning, at an 11:00 a.m. lecture at the Arts Club.

Lunch at old Mrs. Shortall's whom N.B. wants absolutely to see.

At 3:00 p.m., other lecture at Rosary College and leaves Chicago evening for Carbondale.

As you see, it is absolutely impossible for her to even consider any addition to it. She regrets it deeply, but, what to do? If your ladies want very much to see her, you could suggest to them to go to Carbondale, Ill., where she will stay for several days. The best day for going should be—I do not know, excuse me. They should telephone to N.B. to know when to go to Carbondale. N.B. will be the guest of the president: President Delyte W. Morris, Southern Illinois University, Carbondale.

Please, excuse my "secondhand typewriting," and pray for our surviving to this trip and organization of it!

Much love, dear Ruth, Annette

Ans by telephone

September 12, 1958

Dear Mr. Smith,

I have finally found a house that will be suitable for my work, — right in the center of Belmont in an excellent location. It will not be available for three or four weeks, but in the meantime I must make arrangements for financing it.

The kind of mortgage I get will depend on my assured monthly income, so I'll have to know specifically what my Longy School wages will be.

I am going to Cape Cod for the weekend, but expect to be back Monday - I will phone you in the afternoon or Tuesday morning, and I will be very much obliged if you will give me definite information.

If there is any other matter you wish to see me about, we can arrange the time when I phone.

It is a great relief to have found a house, and my only regret is that I cannot be settled before school starts. But I don't see any reason that moving will interfere with my work -

Sincerely,
Ruth Robbins

The year 1958 was when Ruth Robbins freed herself from two decades of being the primary caretaker of her deaf mother (her father died in 1938). Her move to Belmont, Massachusetts, was also a significant move away from her family home in Highland Park, Illinois, where Robbins had resided since her early teens.
[September 12, 1958, letter, Longy School of Music Archives]

Letter 58-6

[Undated]

[This note refers to Boulanger's planned tour in the United States April–June 1958]

The "carnets" arrive regularly, & also ancient reports explaining need for fantasy! Land, God willing, on the 3rd of April. Shall come through Chicago on May 13. Hope to have seen R.R. before that. Despaired—too much to do but . . . well, let us hope. You will receive a new list including you to run around! From Illinois to Canada, to Ohio, to Mass., etc. Love, thanks.

Letter 58-7

20 June 1958
French Line
À bord Flandre

The last hours. May even land this evening! But empty head after these long, misty, smooth cold days.

Cannot imagine you will not be (at/on) rue Ballu tomorrow morning! The end of this kind of a legend is disheartening. But . . . it will never end really.

Tomorrow, Marian's wedding.[241] Wednesday my pilgrimage to

241 Likely Marian Baring-Gould, who, along with Georgette and Arthur Sachs's daughter, Marian, was one of "the two Marians" tutored at home so NB could have the company of children when she was a guest of the Sachses during the war years.

bring home Jean and Marie Blanche de Polignac.[242] And [in] life is there sorrow, joy, start, end.

Try to come back where you are needed and expected. Let me really say how grateful I am for your endless generosity.

From the depth of my heart,

I am your devoted, N.B.

Letter 58-8

11 September 1958

Dear N.B.,

Here it is, your birthday time again, and I am not there to give you my love and best wishes and wish you many happy returns of the day! I am sending this to Paris as I do not know where to reach you, although Marcelle wrote me a few days ago, telling me about your schedule for the next few weeks. It sounds almost as wild as the United States one was. How I wish I could be there for your concert in Turkey with Biret![243] Please give her my love and congratulations and tell her I hope she comes to Boston soon.

I have two great pieces of news—no, three! Barbara has a fine big boy born Sept. 2 named Lars Robbins Lindbergh! I have a new (used—1955) car, a Rambler Station Wagon. It is the loudest (color-wise) car in Concord, being a combination of chrome and cream-of-tomato-soup pink. You might be even more embarrassed to be seen in it than my old shabby Ford, but if you immerse yourself

---

242 Comte Jean de Polignac (1888–1943) and Comtesse Marie-Blanche de Polignac (1897–1958). Comtesse de Polignac had been great friends and financial supporters of NB's protégés. "My pilgrimage to bring home Jean and Marie Blanche de Polignac" is unclear. Was NB bringing Polignac ashes or artifacts back to Paris?

243 RR here refers to an upcoming 1958 concert in Turkey.

in a lot of "jive" and "be-bop" popular music, you will get into the spirit of the thing. Actually, it is very comfortable to drive and easy to handle, and simply does not use any gasoline at all!

The third piece of news is that I am buying a house! Right in the center of Belmont! That I can hardly believe, but it is true! It is not quite the ideal place that I had in mind when I started looking—a lovely 200-year-old house in an ideal location for my work with lots of room and in a charming country setting with brooks and stone fences. Well, the house is old, but merely 40 years or so, but the location is excellent for my work, and there is plenty of room.

I had to give up the charming country setting, but from my house on up the hill are lovely houses, some that are beautiful old New England houses, and the top of the hill is a very large estate owned by I have forgotten who. Perhaps you know the area. My address will be (after Oct. 15) 486 Concord Avenue, Belmont.

I hope you will return to Boston and be my guest. If you ever plan to spend a year here (as Mr. Smith tells me he is trying to persuade you to do) you can live at my house. Well, if I do not mail this in a few minutes, I am afraid you will not get it in time for your birthday.

All my love, and wish I could be with you, Ruth

LETTER 58-9

9 DECEMBER 1958
486 CONCORD AVE., BELMONT 78, MASS.

Dear N.B.,

In two weeks I will be in Aspen, Colorado, to spend the holidays with my family. They are all gathering from everywhere, and I suppose (if I took time to stop to count, you would never get this!) there will be around 25 of us, as I think all the Lindbergh family will be there, too. Now that I live so far from most of them, I am not likely to see them except on such occasions.

I have been so occupied with reorganizing my life and getting my house settled that I have practically ceased to know how to write letters, but I most certainly have not ceased to think about you! Especially as I see so many people who know you!

Mother was here for four weeks, and wore out my aunt who came with her (and stayed for two weeks), my aunt in Cape Cod, and me. It has taken me two weeks to pull myself together and arrange things the way I want them, and to catch up on business, organize my teaching, organize my house, and try to make a little preparation for the family Christmas.

Luise and I went to hear Soulima's concert (with Claire Richards)[244] at Harvard last night, and were greatly disappointed. Claire is no match for Soulima, and has no real rhythm. She managed to spoil all the exciting rhythmic effects by coming in just ahead of Soulima, and also by not hearing the quality of his or her playing. Poor Soulima tried to make the best of the situation, but his style of playing was very effectively killed in the combination.

244 Soulima Stravinsky and pianist Claire Richards were both on the music faculty at the University of Illinois.

I am very glad to hear by way of Winifred (by way of Marcelle, I think) that you and Annette are well. If only I were rich enough to hop on a jet plane and see you in time for breakfast tomorrow! But the way my life is scheduled now, I never have more than 24 hours free, so I really cannot plan any jaunts except at vacation time. It is probably just as well, however, as my house will absorb all my free time and ready cash for some time to come. Although it is a very attractive little house and just perfect for me, it has been very well used by a family of active children, and needs redecorating throughout.

Here it is, another day, and I am waiting for a pupil (the only one, so far, who comes to me). She decided to take lessons instead of her child, which I think is a good idea as she will understand what is going on when her child eventually starts. I am not very proud of my work at Longy so far. Handling a class of unruly American children is a special technique in itself, and just to keep them from drawing pictures and throwing chalk and fighting takes more skill than I have got, regardless of whatever method of teaching music is used! I never functioned well with more than one person at a time anyhow!

Here is my pupil, so I will stop.

Much love, Ruth

1959

LETTER 59-1

1 JANUARY 1959

Dear Ruth,

Since your letter arrived[245]—I am waiting, daring not say a word—but cannot stay so. Have to say how near I am, how anxious, praying with you from the depth of my heart.

Wait . . . under such circumstances is the most terrible trial one can face. You are right to keep hoping, decided to live . . . as if life were not mad. One wonders how the heart stands such a tension.

Thank you to have written. Your thought, at this moment is in itself such a sigh of affection.

We are ok, well and all, to hear you. United in this anxious waiting. Willing at any price to keep hope alive.

With so profound affection, your N.B.

245 This letter from RR is missing, but RR no doubt wrote NB about her brother Jim's December 1958 disappearance on a solo flight from Denver to Seattle in his twin-engine Piper Apache. Since he was an experienced aviator, there was extended search and rescue, and family members still held hope into January. The wreckage was not discovered until the following summer.

Dear Ruth, I am near you. I hope to write you and I pray with you.

With so much love, Annette.

Letter 59-2

11 January 1959

Dear Ruth,

Words are vain. What can they do? Please, feel only that I am with you, constantly try to keep hope alive—difficult indeed. And I feel, as if I were there, the courage you need to hide your anxiety. So little can be done. And waiting is so hard.

May the lord help you in this terrible trial.

What was said to your Mother?

With so profound affection, N.B.

Letter 59-3

21 January 1959

Dear Ruth,

More than ever, wish to be with you on the 21st. Words are useless. I am simply with you, from the bottom of my heart. And that is ok.

Pray the Lord to help you all in your terrible anxiety. What a trial.

So faithfully and tenderly with you, N.B.

Letter 59-4

26 January 1959

Just to be with you, dear Ruth—for, I never remain far. I know your courage, your determination not to give up—but, as the days go by, it is difficult to fight anxiety, not to foresee a reality one wants to deny. And your poor mummy, so old, so hopeless.

This "unknowing" is one of the most tragic trials one can have to stand. Permit me to share your fears, your hopes, and your sorrow. For, even if your brother comes back, the suffering will have been so heavy to all.

As ever, N.B.

Letter 59-5

5 April 1959

Dear Ruth,

So long I did not write—queer as I am thinking of you constantly. There are no words to say, but only submit to the will of God.

In spite of all your courage, I am afraid your long state of anxiety has been as hard on your health as on your body. Am so sad to be so far away and so useless.

Everybody has been gone. Marcelle just came back. My godchild Tadeusz[246] this evening. Annette tomorrow.

And life goes on, rather tragic in its implications but . . . we would

246 Tadeusz Jackowski (b. 1936), a Polish graphic designer and professor at the University of Arts in Poznań, Poland.

fall into despair if we did not concentrate on our own duty. And there, it is simple, evident, and it is as we can act still with some use.

Feel my affection, stronger than ever,

I am your, N.B.

How did this card arrive now? Unbelievable but in the mail. Strange as it is.

Letter 59-6

16 July 1959

Dear N.B.,

My two nieces (Susie and Mary Miller) are repacking for the last time before we leave for Montreal tomorrow. They sail Friday morning, and I would give anything to go with them. I am beginning to regret my job teaching at Longy as it will keep me tied up each year, except for the summers, and although I enjoy Fontainebleau, what I miss the most are the winter classes and lessons at rue Ballu.

My sister and nephew Jimmy sail from NY on August 14, and will go directly to Brussels to pick up a little car that will be waiting for them there. They will probably stop at Fontainebleau en route to Switzerland, and I hope it will be a day when there will be a concert which they can attend. That will be probably about August 20. The girls will spend about a month or more traveling through England and the Scandinavian countries, so will not get to Fontainebleau this summer, but you will no doubt see them in Paris before the year is over.

As you can see, I am feeling very unhappy about not going to Europe this year, but the anticipation of a visit with Marcelle in the fall and with you in the spring (???) will pull me through. If I could anticipate seeing Annette, too, I would be downright cheerful! Well, next summer will be along before I know it, and as soon as I find out the day Longy finishes for the year, I will make a reservation for the next day!

Although this summer has been and will continue to be quite broken up with trips here and there, I hope to accomplish something with my practicing. The lessons I had with Luise[247] last summer are still bearing fruit, and whenever I manage to do a few days of consecutive work, I am aware of a quality of sound that I never accomplished before, or heard for that matter. But do not be alarmed. I will never be a virtuoso, but it is gratifying to feel that there is still progress possible in this old bag of bones.

I think of you so much, and although I do not have much news, I want to tell you how much I miss you and wish I were there.

Please give my love to Annette, and loads of love to you, Ruth

---

Letter 59-7

25 August 1959

Dear Ruth,

How dear of you to let me know: Yes, it is better for your Mother and for you all, to, in your sorrow, have the certitude your brother died as he fell.[248] But . . . how sad.

---

247 Luise Vosgerchian (1923–2000) studied with NB in Paris from 1949 to 1956. She became full professor at Harvard in 1971 and was appointed chair in 1974. "Beloved Music Teacher Vosgerchian Dies at 77."

248 In the summer of 1959, the wreckage of his Piper Apache was discovered by a shepherd near a pass high in the Rocky Mountains. Jim's son Dick, with two companions, climbed to the crash site in the summer of 1959 to identify the plane and his father's skis. They concluded he had died upon impact.

You know I am with you more than ever.

The book did arrive. How did you find the time to remember my birthday? Will keep the book to read starting on Sept. 15th. The card is so touching too!

Forgive this hasty note. You cannot imagine what life is here. Not a minute free . . . but . . . we are so sad this session came to its end so soon.

Exacting and passionating. My students especially.

As ever, so deeply yours, N.B.

Letter 59-8

16 September 1959

Dear Ruth, how good you are. Thank you so much. We speak of you daily. Yes, Mont. Pelerin, but last year these unbelievable trips. You are so generous.

Shall be in Lausanne, course at the Conservatory 4, 5, 6 Oct. Will I have the possibility to search for your sister[249]—hope so?

Again so many thanks and courage for [unreadable].

God Bless you, N.B.

---

249 When RR's nieces Mary and Susie Miller told her sister Helen Miller that they planned to spend a college year abroad in Lausanne, Switzerland, Helen promptly made her own plan to spend the 1959–1960 academic year there.

Letter 59-9

6 November 1959

Dear Ruth,

What a joy to have your letter! Yes, was sad to miss the family, but . . . they had such a good time! And the green house?[250]

Better too soon than never. So here are wishes for a HAPPY CHRISTMAS, HAPPY NEW YEAR.

How I pray to see you again . . . on this earth of ours!

Deep affection, as always, from your N.B.

250 Although RR's letter is missing, she must have once again expressed disappointment at not being in Europe when her sister and family were there. NB alludes to a new greenhouse RR had added to her house in Belmont, Massachusetts.

1960

Letter 60-1

January 1960

Dear Ruth,

Your anniversary is on the way—and here are many warm wishes, coming from the bottom of my heart. I do love you so much.

Cannot answer your shining letters—am worn out after the Christmas wrapping, more or less alone but will soon recover!!! Your book seems most interesting and the almanac (my weakness—one of them) so lovely. Thank you so much. The night is already very shortened and by pity, for my soon-coming students feel wise to have some sleep!

As ever profoundly, your N.B.

Am thinking to poor Wendy![251]

Anne Lindbergh has disappeared. She came . . . and never

251 RR's niece Wendy suffered a tremendous trauma. She was in the hospital delivering her second child when her firstborn son, at home with his father, died of sudden infant death syndrome, or SIDS.

returned. Not a sign. Left also Mme Vergniaud very abruptly. Cannot understand but don't mention it to her mother.[252]

Annette is a little better, but, of course, heartbroken. She adored her Mother.

Letter 60-2

26 February 1960

Dear Ruth,

What a lovely surprise! You must have felt that I lost all my handkerchiefs, stolen in Geneva!! What a better one! And the enigmatic characters. But finally seen, and the mystery discovered.

Thank you so much.

Am leaving Sunday. Disorder is at its top and agitation exemplar. Hope however to be ready! Problem—reduce the size and the number of luggages and bring all the usual and useless things to Varsovie![253]

So, it is your turn to guess how looks the rue Ballu and its inhabitants.

Pray for me!

And be thanked of dear unknown, anonymous friend,

Nadia B.

---

252 She refers to "Ansie" Lindbergh, the elder of the two daughters of Charles and Anne Morrow Lindbergh.

253 Warsaw.

Letter 60-3

21 March 1960

Dear N.B.,

I am horrified to realize how much time has gone by since I last wrote you. I have been thinking about you so much, and as usual, intended to write, but . . . !

Next week I will drive to NY with Mother to meet my sister Jane and see them off to Europe. It hardly seems possible that the time has come. I still have quite a bit more ironing and sewing and various small jobs to do for Mother before next week, and then it will be April, and I will have to start preparing for my trip!

I have been thinking a great deal about Fontainebleau and have decided it would be crazy not to concentrate only on the work with you. What I really would like to do is come as a special student and just have private lessons with you. Would you accept such an arrangement, and if so, what arrangement do I make with the New York office when I apply?

At present my plans are more or less as follows (nothing settled, however): As soon as Longy is over, I will go to Europe and after a day or two in Paris, join my sister in Switzerland (around June 9 or 10). As she and the others will be returning to the States on July 8 (present plan), I will come to Fontainebleau at that time (if it is alright with you!).

This part of my plan is very indefinite: I will sell my car here and buy a little Volkswagen or Renault to use in Europe and then bring it back with me. In this way, I can manage to do quite a bit of sight-seeing (as well as perhaps be useful to you during the summer!). If I have a car, I could live in one of the more remote rooms from the school, and I think I would prefer having my meals elsewhere, too, as frankly, I want to avoid being too involved with Winnie. As Mother has given me money for the trip, it is not financially difficult, but I prefer being independent.

I will wait to hear from you before I write to the NY office.

With ALL MY LOVE and GREAT ANTICIPATION for the summer, Ruth

486 Concord Ave., Belmont 78, Mass.

P.S. Love to Annette, and Marcelle, too.

Letter 60-4

25 March 1960

Dear Ruth,

Do you realize what your coming is meaning?

Dared not believe in it. Must scream my joy!

Am perfectly hopeless, drowned under work, but so very happy!

As ever, your N.B.

LETTER 60-5

[UNDATED][254]

Dear Ruth,

Shall call your sister[255] in a minute. Here I am again [in] this tranquil spot, so lovely. Real country.

Hope to see the family at the Conservatoire.

As ever to miss you so much, dislike the traveling; dear Fontainebleau, so, so, so nice!

As ever your N.B.

LETTER 60-6

25 MAY 1960

[FROM ANNETTE DIEUDONNÉ]

Dear Ruth,

What a joy to think of you coming here so soon! This is, certainly, such good and wonderful news. You have nothing to do with the NY Committee, and no application to make. You will come as a free student simply to work with NB. She will ask Mlle Delécluse as a personal favor to find you a room for you and you will take care of your meals. Now, there is another solution if you will like it: you could have a room at the hotel where Maman lives. It is near the Station, just near the forest; they have [a] phone, the hotel is quite well kept up, the people awfully kind. It is a bit far

254 Likely April 1960, when RR rendezvoused in Paris with her sister and other family members.
255 RR's sister, Helen Robbins Miller, lived in Lausanne during 1959–1960.

from the Palace, but, if you have a car . . . and there is a bus. Mother, of course, would certainly not bother you, she lives quite apart. The question is, I don't know if they would accept to give a room without meals. Last year the whole boarding room and meals was 2500 f per day.

Will you, please, answer quickly, because it is difficult to have rooms in F.bleau.

With very much love, Annette

LETTER 60-7

12 SEPTEMBER 1960

Dear Ruth,

When I think you ought to be there, my heart is breaking. But . . . when had I seen you, as the summer has been really terrific. We love to complain and so . . . I do.

We were delighted with Anne Lindbergh. So nice and good willing. Do you consider I ought to ask her to attend Wednesday class or not?

We speak of you so often. Winnie will be here Thursday, but again will not see as much as I try to put some order in the mail. Am I not a fool to think it is ever possible?

With so much love, as ever N.B. —With love, dear Ruth, W.

Letter 60-8

16 September 1960
Lans-en-Vercors

You are so kind. The mission, your research, vain, in Santa Barbara—memories, and also hopes, for you cannot always postpone your return. Well, who knows, perhaps will I use the pink car before you come!

Thank you, love, deep love, N.B.

Much love, dear Ruth, to you. It is too bad you are not here. Hope you come soon. Annette

Ruthkins you rascal! See you soon! W.[256]

256 This somewhat cryptic postcard highlights the dynamics of women close to NB. Annette Dieudonné, among NB's first students, followed in NB's footsteps to teach at the Paris Conservatory and at Fontainebleau, serving as NB's musical assistant and constant companion. Winifred Hope Johnstone, from a wealthy musical family in Boston, provided NB a well-connected agent in the United States who went out of her way to help, as in her 1959 letter to Leonard Bernstein:

Dear Mr. Bernstein, I appreciate particularly your help and interest in the Lili Boulanger Fund, and want to join my personal thanks to the treasurer's acknowledgement of your generous contribution. You must have so very many appeals from music charities, but I do feel we are doing a rather special job both for music and for international friendship. If you have a moment, do read the enclosed information which I am taking the liberty of sending again, in case you have not the appeal at hand. I am terribly anxious to get the "De Profundis" performed over here, knowing that this is our dear friend, Boulanger's, greatest wish. Markevitch has just sent me the address of the company who did the recording: The Beloch Recording Co. 112 03, 14th Avenue, College Point 56, N.Y. I have written them for information as to the date of release as I have had many enquiries. Unfortunately the Lamoureux Orchestra would find it difficult to repeat the Salle Royal programs when they tour the United States next spring, lacking a chorus, etc. May I say how much your many Boston friends admire the splendid work you have been doing on T.V. and I shall never forget that evening in 1948 chez poor Marie-Blanche when you played at sight a fiendish Str. Score with Nadia! Again my thanks, very sincerely, Winifred Johnstone. 122 Bay State Road, Boston 15, Mass. April 16th 1959. (Letter, "Winifred H. Johnstone to Leonard Bernstein," April 13, 1959, Music Division, Box/Folder 9/21, Library of Congress.)

Annette and Winifred each provided NB crucial support—one on the music side, the other marketing communications. RR was incapable of providing such mission-critical services to NB. What RR provided was relaxed camaraderie, humor, and emotional support.

Letter 60-9

13 October 1960

Not yet anything settled,

But if—would go California, around Baltimore, and probably around Boston. Seems somewhat vague. May, maybe April.

Shall let you know soon as I know better. Count on pink or green or red to go around.

May address 122 B.S.R.[257] Don't you know!

As ever yours, N.B.

257 The residence of Winifred Johnstone in Boston.

1961

Letter 61-1

1 February 1961
486 Concord Ave.
Belmont 78, Mass.

Dear N.B.,

I do not know what your plans are, but here are mine:

I have again made tentative arrangements to go to Europe this summer, leaving here May 31 with a friend. After long deliberation, I decided not to land in Paris as our plan is to get a little VW in Germany, then go directly to Southern Italy, and then spend the month of June winding our way northward through Italy and Southern France. I was afraid that if we went directly to Paris, I would never be able to pull myself away, so avoiding it altogether until the end of the month was the best way to solve that problem. However, it will be painful to be on the same continent as you and not see you for a whole month!!! I understand you are not coming to the United States this year. Then I hope to go to Fontainebleau (as I planned last summer) and return to the United States with my VW when I run out of money or about Sept. 20, whichever comes first! My friend will travel a little more in July and then return to the US. This will probably be my last fling in Europe as Pres. Kennedy will no doubt spend my money if I do not—hence the urgency to carry out my plans this summer!

There is a very interesting course of programs on television just now—master classes of Casals' filmed in California. However, the program I am really wild to see is the one of your Wednesday class! Have not heard yet when it will be broadcast.

I have been having a very enjoyable winter with my sculpturing class. Our teacher this year is a M. Moranon, from somewhere in the South of France, I am sure. He has such a thick accent that it is difficult to understand him, but he is very witty and keeps us amused all the time. As my musical life consists entirely of teaching youngsters, many of whom do not want to study, and practically none of whom do any work, it is not very inspiring. The reason I enjoy the art work so much is that I myself am actively making "art" (??), and that is the most deeply satisfying thing in my life. That is why I miss you so much, and all the musical activity that goes with you. I hope that you do not mind that I enjoy sculpturing so much!! By the way, in my enthusiasm for bones, I miscalculated the number. There are only 27 bones in each hand, not 28 as I previously announced to you. I hope this grave error has not upset your life!

The book by Robert Henri[258] is one I heard about years ago, but has gone out of print. It has just been reprinted, and as he was noted

258 *The Art Spirit*, by Robert Henri (1865–1929), originally published in 1923.

as a most inspiring teacher, I thought you two would have much in common!

Mother will be here shortly for a few weeks while my sister Helen and her husband (Susie's parents) go to Ghana to see their son Tommy, who has been having a most interesting year teaching in a secondary school there. He spent the Christmas holidays visiting Nigeria, often in remote villages where no white man had ever been seen before. He and the other teacher with him were often greatly mistrusted at first, so, in order not to offend the tribal chiefs, they took part in rituals, ate whatever food was proffered, and even danced the native dances as best they could when asked! After winning the confidence of the natives, they were usually showered with gifts, mostly in the form of food (chickens, grain, etc.). They accepted everything as they felt the people would be insulted if they did not, even though they could see what a great sacrifice it was for many. As Tommy expects to attend Harvard Law School next year (if accepted), I hope you will have a chance to meet him when you are here. He is quite a person!

We have just had the snowiest, sunniest, coldest January in history, but my heart glows with warmth when I think of you!

All my love, Ruth

Letter 61-2

4 February 1961
36, rue Ballu
Paris IXᴱ, France
Tél: Tri 57-91

Dear Ruth,

What a letter—wonderful, and with such happy news. Do not change now. How would I stand another deception? Seeing you again will be such a joy.

Am in Paris in May, about June 1 to 12, gone Sept. 1 for Romania, God willing, back in November from Moscou. The Valentine makes me quite cheerful and your letter so glad.

Come back Thursday, am in despair (hardly too strong a word). So many things accumulating but do love you as ever so faithfully.

N.B.

Letter 61-3

27 March 1961

Dear Ruth,

Thank you so much. Happy Easter and welcome, even with chopped fingers. We will find you an activity anyhow. Know you are always with me and feel comfort in it.

So faithfully,

N.B.

Weather unbelievably radiant! A miracle. Annette sends love.

Letter 61-4

1 June 1961

Dear Ruth,

Well . . . well . . . fame and joy. The little Ruth . . . the sculpture sold.

Congratulations!

Leave tomorrow for England. Shall be back on the 13th and 14th. And for the time being, in despair . . . how will I be ready tomorrow?

But my heart shines of joy at the thought of seeing you soon, Dear One,

N.B.

What an irony. Must go to Southend just when you will leave yourself. We could—but no, I fall into dreaming, as to gain time I must take the train so . . . everything all right.

Letter 61-5

17 August 1961

Dear N.B.,

It is very sad that I will not see you at your classes tomorrow (however, we will be at the concert) and that there is only one more lesson for all my problems to be solved (musical ones, that is!), and that I have done nothing for you with my car (I would have driven you to the moon), and that I must deliver it to Paris on the 31st as the insurance expires, and I may have to settle my accounts with you after I am home, and lots and lots of other things!

When you return from Switzerland, I will be very happy to take a load of things to Paris for you before the 31st if you can possibly have anything ready.

I will meet you as planned on the 24th.

Love,

Ruth

P.S. I have a birthday present for you. I know it is hopeless to ask you for dinner, so I have not even tried! But maybe a miracle will happen??? XOXOXOX

Letter 61-6

7 September 1961

[Mailed to Boulanger's hotel in Bucharest]

Dear N.B.,

I wish your trip could have been as easy and pleasant as mine was to Boston. I left Paris at 11:30 a.m. (Orly, that is) and arrived in Boston at 1:15 p.m.! Luise and Kamil[259] met me at the airport, which was wonderful. After a nice visit with them while they had their dinner (I had mine on the plane), I came home and found everything just as I left it, except the garden. That will take two years to put back in order. There was three months of accumulated mail for me to go through, and it took me two days just to sort it. There were two very pleasant surprises: 1) your letter of June 1, which Luise had

---

259 Luise Vosgerchian (1922–2000) and her husband, Kamil Pagacik.

not known where to forward to find me, and even though it was three months late and I had seen you the day before, it was VERY welcome; 2) a letter from the Fine Arts Museum School notifying me that I had been awarded a PRIZE! Can you imagine?! I have decided to frame the check (five dollars) instead of cashing it. Now, are you not impressed!

I hope this letter will find you somewhere before the 16th, as it is a HAPPY BIRTHDAY[260] letter, and also to say what a wonderful summer it was to be with you at Fontainebleau!

Love and kisses,

Ruth

LETTER 61-7

29 OCTOBER 1961

Dear Ruth,

Congratulations . . . delayed but sincere. And a frightening responsibility which is to fall on you. For I do hope, yes. I dare hope that we will go on and for the starting very likely around March 12th New Haven, Boston, Exeter, Boston, Albany, Boston . . . until April 22 to Potsdam. To NY for May then Paris. What do you think of it? Do you laugh weep, revolt, wonder? Am rather anxious to know! May not be as real as it seems. But something within says: But why not.

With so great affection, N.B.

---

260 The Bucharest postmark indicates the letter arrived on NB's birthday, September 16.

From Nov. 5 to 10, Co. Mill Farnsberg, 14 Kalka Plan, Stockholm. Paris 12 to 16, Monaco Palais Principal 15 to 21.

LETTER 61-8

1 NOVEMBER 1961

[FROM ANNETTE DIEUDONNEÉ]

Dear Ruth,

How are you? How is the cleaning of the windows? The trip to Greece was marvelous. Such beauty. It was really refreshing.

N.B. will not tell you, but she is very sad to know that you will not be free although, of course, it is most natural. She had hoped to do all these trips in such a lovely way . . . and now . . . railways and time tables . . . this is sad.

But, my dear, don't worry. After all, it is quite normal and you can't help it. Life here is rather sad, and the future not bright. What a queer idea to have been born in such a time! We should have chosen better!

With so much love,

Annette.

Letter 61-9

[December 1961]

You see the gradation!! Is it not very impressive. Have written to Winifred; as many trips with R. who drives to my rythme[261]—small car—Therefore no company and silence assured.

How sad I am to go. G. Pinault so sick, a very dear friend too. Pasha not well, but I am happy too. God willing the 8th in France.

Address: Miss G. Robinson Smith, 1 Sutton Place South NY, 22 (Plaza 3-1880)

Letter 61-10

30 December 1961

Dear Ruth,

Thank you so much. What a nice case for my dear clothes! You have such amusing ideas, always. Am afraid your schedule grows but at some places relieved.

All my wishes are with you, so faithful, and I am already once more very grateful.

May the Lord guide us in this somber New Year.

Am devotedly yours,

N.B.

261 In this context, the word "rhythme" means "pace."

1962

LETTER 62-1

21 JANUARY 1962

Dear Ruth,

To celebrate the 21st in grand, official manner.

This said, receive wishes, thoughts, and the profound joy to see you soon. We will have to be good diplomats. Am learning and remember the value of silence!

Happy, happy birthday to you,

From your rather abusive,

N.B.

abusive: concient[262] of taking advantage of you—in the near future! This pretense to be: future!

262 In this context, "concient" means "aware."

LETTER 62-2

1 FEBRUARY 1962

Alas, there is no assurance that you will get this on the boat, so I am sending it to where I hope you will be!

Dear N.B.,

Welcome to the dear old USA. Guess what? I have just been told that Longy School has someone who will take all my classes for the rest of the school year and I will have the half-year leave of absence, after all! Even though I will miss that monthly paycheck, I feel as though I have been given a million dollars. My freedom and independence again! As a matter of fact, I have been thinking very seriously all winter that I would not go back to Longy next fall as Melville Smith is no longer with the school, and it is not the same place without him.

I am listening to a talk by Boris Goldovsky[263] and some of his young opera singers on the television program. You are right, I should have been an opera singer!

Several days later.

I just realized I must mail this at once if I want to be sure to catch you on the boat. Wish I could be there! I hope to see you at Luise's concert, if not before or after. I must find out when and where to meet you with my car, etc., etc., etc.

Also, love and kisses.

---

263 Boris Goldovsky (1908–2001) was a Russian-born conductor and commentator. As an opera producer, conductor, impresario, and broadcaster, he was prominent within the American operatic community from 1946 to 1985. See Anthony Tommasini, "Boris Goldovsky, 92, Musician and Opera's Avid Evangelist," *New York Times*, February 18, 2001, 41.

Your devoted chauffeuresse (chauffeuse?),

Ruth

P.S. XOXOXOXO

P.S. 2 I just read Virgil Thomson's article about you in The New York Times.[264] It makes me feel POWERFUL. Xoxoxo

In Boston in April during her 1962 American tour, Nadia gave Ruth this photo of Sviatoslav Richter kissing her hand. A few days earlier, Ruth drove Nadia to Washington, DC, for a luncheon with President John F. Kennedy and First Lady Jackie Kennedy. [Ruth Robbins Archives]

264 Virgil Thomson's February 4, 1962, *New York Times* article "Greatest Music Teacher—at 75" begins: "Nadia Boulanger, who will conduct the New York Philharmonic in four concerts beginning Feb. 15, and who will later this year celebrate her seventy-fifth birthday, has for more than forty years been, for musical Americans, a one-woman graduate school so powerful and so permeating that legend credits every United States town with two things—a five-and-dime and a Boulanger pupil."

Letter 62-3

7 May 1962
Cunard Line
RMS "Queen Mary"

Dear Ruth,

Which words would be adequate! You know I hope, what I do feel, so deeply. When I say thank you, so many things are meant. You have to have open ears and a receptive mind!

How strange it will be to go on without you—and how sad—but these weeks will always remain with me. Such a gift of one self is a blessing, and it has given to all these journeys a character of confidence, of rest, of intimacy quite unique.

We arrive after a calm sailing on the whole, by the darkest day—wind, mist, rain—a really gloomy atmosphere. And my solitude would be rather melancholic (in French use) were I not to find in Paris dear ones, and had I not such unforgettable memories. So much received, so much done, and surrounded by unbelievable gifts.

Hope Annette is not as sick as Marcelle makes me fear. This fear has rendered this trip full of anxiety.

And, may I confess, with Tasha[265] gone—well, dear Ruth, why would I darken your thoughts with my darkness?

Often I will feel "our" ideas, hoping she has forgotten her troubles. Impossible to leave you without. With real emotion, thank you. And to repeat, all this will remain with me as long as I am here.

Take care of yourself!

Yours, N.B.

265 Tasha was NB's beloved cat.

Letter 62-4

5 June 1962
Palais de Monaco

Dear Ruth,

How a long letter is needed, but I can hardly send these feverish lines—really difficult time—and so little help, in spite of Annette struggling more than she can.

Anyhow, have your letter and wonderful blankets, so warm and lovely with those pink lines. Thank you so much. Thank you for everything, as I do not know how to express. Do you feel it? Hope so and remain so devotedly yours,

N.B.

Letter 62-5

9 June 1962
36, rue Ballu
paris IXe
Tél: Tri 57-91

What an eloquent poet!

Indeed wish to write but have so much to do and so little help that the problems are unsolved—queer period, under, for all, such a pression! But everything remains present and I still bless "my" VW!

How big is our shrinked world—everywhere is everywhere—but you are there, and I am here! It makes the whole difference.

Going Tuesday to England: London —> Bath —> London —> Bath —> London —> around —> London. What a joy it would be, looking around!

And when I think how easy it could be! Pray for me—pray for these weeks to come. So heavy! And realize how much I have left in my VW.

With deep affection,

N.B.

Hope the lines [are] carrying loads of thanks for an "unvaluable" warm and light present reached you.

Letter 62-6

16 June 1962

Dear N.B.,

Two letters from you in three days is absolutely overwhelming! The last came first, the first came last, and if I had been a little more patient, I could have saved you a lot of trouble. Anyhow, now I am completely satisfied, and I would write you another "poem" if we were not having very hot weather at the moment.

Life for me has slowed down to a crawl. My pupils are all going off for the summer, and I have no plans beyond trying to bring my house and garden back into shape after so much neglect in the last year. Mother is well, but tires very quickly now (she is 88), so it is hard to find things she can do to occupy her time. I have plenty to do every minute of the day, but it is an awful fight to get myself to do it. Where do you get all your energy?

I watched Stravinsky's The Flood: A Musical Play the other night on television (composed especially for TV), but I wonder what kind of an impression it made on a nationwide audience. First of all, on almost any TV set music sounds not at all well as compared to a good radio, and secondly, it takes a rather special audience for such music, and thirdly, the visual effects combined with the ballet were far too elaborate for a small 20 inch screen, and no color. I kept thinking how superb it would be in a theater or as a first rate color moving-picture, but I will be very much surprised if the TV performance is considered successful. Perhaps I just wasn't in the right mood!

I know you are somewhere in London —> Bath —> London —> Bath, or some part in between, but I do not know where to mail this except Paris. Wish I could be there to transport you (with a little less luggage!) as I do not know England at all well.

Love and encouragement,

Ruth

Letter 62-7

29 July 1962

Dear Ruth,

Thank you for everything.

We are very sad. Mlle Roger[266] died yesterday. More than 50 years she helped us. We must submit—and I do—but the heart is heavy.

Devotedly with you,

N.B.

---

266 NB's housekeeper, perhaps?

LETTER 62-8

SEPTEMBER 1962

Again, thank you dear Ruth, oh, how I miss you too. But you force me to recognize that to attain 75 years is a great luck, with such friends.

So affectionately,

N.B.

Good news from Annette, now en route to Benares!

Sept. 1962

Hotel Richmond, Genève until Oct. 5th

LETTER 62-9

18 DECEMBER 1962

Dear Ruth,

Did I send a tiny message and was hoping it would go through the air? Anyhow here—remembrances of ours from place to place looking for hats and surprise food.

Well, maybe next year! Not out of question.

Think of you—do miss you. Had super concerts. Markevitch's works, Idil, Tchaikowsky, 3 Richter Recitals, and today a long visit. Why are you not there!!!

As ever with so much love,

Happy Christmas, N.B.

1963

Letter 63-1

21 Jan. 1963

Dear Ruth,

Soon your anniversary! How I wish I were there to prepare a real celebration! Instead I am alone, far away in my empty room! Well, a little bit of dream and I will soon really believe we are preparing a superb party.

Why is our shrinked world still so big, & I so queer as not to fly all around as a bird? Just could be but . . . is really not.

Hope nothing will prevent champagne to be drank to your health on the 21st.

Find here all my wishes and believe in my profound affection,

N.B.

Letter 63-2

11 Sept. 1963

Dear Ruth,

Your kind, thoughtful letter would render me very ashamed, if I had not the feeling that in spite of my silence, you have been the whole summer with us.

Terrific summer indeed—but lovable with the youngsters around—but now after two months of obliged sacrifice of the mail, I try to put some in order. And it is something atrocious—presto agitato through the world, writing everywhere without saying anywhere one is felt. Horrible betrayal. But if not so, the silence would be prolonged?

5 days here with Marcelle—tomorrow Paris. Annette leaves Sunday for Turkey, Iran, Hong Kong, Tokyo, and . . . more prosaically for Cannes. Was to be in Warsaw, but dates have been changed. I gave up what became really difficult and perhaps it is wiser as . . . well you can imagine one is rather exhausted! But the old machine is still solid, and I stood there months without losing the joy to feel awake and alert.

You are as always present. I am as always sad not to see you—and so does life go on.

Be sure your letter has given me a very great joy. You are so dear to me. Hope we will once more run around the world—where it would find me happy to be with you.

Were Annette here, she would join me in sending love. But, does she not always do?

Forgive the usual, more than ever haste and believe in my old faithful affection,

Lovingly, N.B.

Letter 63-3

24 November 1963

Dear N.B.,

I have been sitting before my television set[267] for several hours trying to take in the events of this incredible moment in history. At this moment, officials are awaiting the arrival of President de Gaulle. The prime minister of Japan has just arrived. Dignitaries from all over the world are expected to continue to arrive all night. I am absolutely drained emotionally from all I have seen. What looms more and more in my mind is the greatness and nobleness of Mrs. Kennedy, the president's widow. Her fortitude is overwhelming. Within two hours after the slaying of the president she stood calmly at the side of Lyndon Johnson in her bloodstained clothing for his swearing in ceremony as the new president.

At no time in the long, sad, two and a half days since the murder has she lost her composure. It has just been announced that she wishes to walk behind the cortège to the funeral rites tomorrow.

Hundreds of thousands of people are lined up to pass the casket in the Capitol. The most dramatic moment, and the likes of which I hope never to see again, was to witness, here in my little house in Belmont, the actual shooting of the president's assassin in the Dallas, Texas, police station by a man who managed to break through the heavy guard escorting the assassin to an armored car. It is all so unbelievable.

Now, it has just been announced that after the funeral

267 Written two days after the John F. Kennedy assassination.

tomorrow, Mrs. Kennedy will receive all the heads of state from all over the world.

Poor Idil![268] Her debut in the States has been completely pushed into the shadows by the momentous events. I was to have heard her last night, but the program was completely changed, and she did not play. She did play on Friday, however, and I was fortunate enough to finish my teaching in time to catch it on my radio.

It was so good to see her briefly at Nora's reception. Her cheerful countenance is the same, but gone is the little pudgy, fuzzy-haired Idil I remember! She is due to play again Tuesday night, and if Luise can get a ticket (she is playing also), I will hear and see her again.

I have thought so often these last two days of the happy occasion a year and a half ago when I drove up to the White House door with an important and renowned passenger in my little VW. What a contrast to the scenes of today!

I am worn out, but cannot tear myself from the TV screen. And tomorrow will be another tearful day, the official day of mourning. After that, life will return to "normal"—but who knows what the consequences of this dreadful tragedy will be?

With all my love and gratitude for the many, many happy times with you.

Love, Ruth

---

268 See "November 22, 1963" in Part 1 for a full description of Biret's American debut.

Letter 63-4

28 November 1963

Dear Ruth,

Your letter moves me most deeply. We are all so profoundly shaken—such a tragedy—a tragedy terribly monstrous and absurd. For nobody can gain anything: a beautiful, noble life has been taken, and everyone has lost what nothing can ever repay.

Thank you to have written—it is kind and generous and I love your sorrowful letter, so near our feeling.

Forgive this hasty message—everything is impossible these days but you are always present. If everything goes well, Annette will be here next Thursday.

Read the unwritten and believe in our complete understanding and in my great affection,

N.B.

1964

Letter 64-1

21 January 1964

Ah ah, Dear Ruth,

Great celebration here for the 21st—Dear Miss Robbins, all our wishes, all our joy. For in these heavy days, we must give all the meaning to the happy event.

And it is one!

How good to have to say our affection, our love, our expectations—for . . . something must be done to be together again.

May be next year, near the Pacific, why not . . . prepare yourself . . . but don't yet start.

All my wishes go to you with all my deep profound affection. Dear Ruth, God bless you.

N.B.

Letter 64-2

22 March 1964

Dear N.B.,

Spring has arrived, and here I am just now writing you a winter letter! Even though I live a rather uneventful life (except when you are around!), time goes whirling by.

I have just returned from Illinois where I helped to celebrate Mother's 90th birthday. Except for not being able to stay on her feet for long, she is in excellent shape, and more alert than ever. My sister and I took her to the Art Institute (which you would never recognize now, with new wings and complete remodeling) to see two exhibits: one a stunning exhibit of Northwest American Indian items, and the other a contemporary modern exhibit. She kept us laughing the whole time with her witty observations of both exhibits. She just returned from a 3000 mile motor trip to the southwest with Jane, and enjoyed every minute of it.

I am listening to and watching a very interesting "dramatized" performance of the St. Matthew Passion by the NBC Opera Company (Donald Gramm[269] singing bass). It is being sung in English, which, of course, causes it to lose something musically, but of the thousands of people listening all over the US, probably few are musicians, and the others would be lost if they could not understand the words. There is no "action" to speak of, but the photography is interesting and effective, and it is a very tasteful performance.

While I was at my sister's, she gave me a book called Black Like Me by a white man who had darkened his skin by medical treatment and spent several weeks as a "negro" in the Deep South in order to obtain a deeper insight into the nature and problems of the negro

269 Donald Gramm (1927–1983) was a virtuoso bass-baritone who performed primarily with the New York Metropolitan Opera in a wide variety of roles; his 230th Met performance was on March 3, 1983.

people. It turned out to be John Howard Griffin![270] The book certainly is an eye-opener, and one all Americans should read. I am sending you my copy as I think it will interest you, if you can ever find time to read it! If you already have a copy, give mine to someone else.

I have become a member of probably the most ancient and honorable profession of 4000 or more years of civilization—a pot maker! You cannot imagine what a fine feeling it is to take a lump of clay, spin a wheel, manipulate the hands a little, and lo and behold, there is a beautiful bowl! (Well, maybe not so beautiful at this stage of the game, but a fine feeling, just the same!) It is almost a miracle to watch. Little bowls aborning from the top of a large lump of clay until there is no clay left, but a row of exquisite (hopefully!) pots, instead. And playing with all that mud legitimately at my age! That is the most fun of all—my second childhood, I guess!

Take care of yourself, and what are your plans for next year? California? There are no trips for me to Europe for some time, I am afraid. Mother will be here with me all summer.

Barbara and her family are moving to Santa Barbara for at least six months and then no one knows where. They are looking for a ranch where her family and Susie and her family will live eventually somewhere out west. Wendy expects another child in September.

I have shoveled so much snow this winter that I dream of California for next winter. Who knows?

All my love to you. France still seems awfully far away even though it is now possible to fly there in less than two hours!

I miss you!

Ruth. XOXOXOXO

---

270 John Howard Griffin (1920–1980), the American journalist and social critic, was an accomplished pianist who at age fifteen went to France, where he studied literature, medicine, psychology, and music. Beginning at age nineteen, he worked as a medic in the French Resistance army. See Elizabeth Griffin-Bonazzi, "Griffin, John Howard (1920–1980)," (Texas State Historical Association, January 1, 1995, https://tshaonline.org/handbook/online/articles/fgr99).

LETTER 64-3

16 APRIL 1964

Dear Ruth,

Have received your letter, the book which seems so important—appreciate it all—but . . . since my return from Pologne,[271] everything is worse than ever.

And so, as deeply as I want to conscient[272] your letter, so rich and unrelenting, the book so heavily meaningful, I must beg you to read all the pages which go to you with such love and such sadness. Will you ever come . . . ???

In profound attachment,

N.B.

LETTER 64-4

8 MAY 1964

Dear Ruth,

Here is your letter . . . in advance—believe it or not! Thank you so much for the dear little card, very touching.

Annette has gone Monday evening—and leaves from Paris tomorrow. May the Lord protect her. Superb voyage—but exhausting. Delhi, Agra, Calcutta, Benares, Bangkok, Phnom-Penh, other places, excursions, and the 29th in Japan! Will she stand it? And however it would be a pity to lose such a unique opportunity.

271 Poland.

272 In this context, the word "conscient" means "be thoughtful of."

Am here, thinking, walking as no more can, with this stupid accident—well—not so serious. Shall be in Geneva for the competition and in Paris around Oct. 8th.

Don't take too hastily a decision to leave for California. I understand, but think it over.

As ever, missing you so much and feeling you so near.

N.B.

Letter 64-5

7 November 1964

What was in the air?? You felt what was to happen and on May 26th, arriving on The France. I hope to find my dear RR—to, from the boat, run to Potsdam, from Potsdam run to Chicago as to the place which connects rapidly P. to C.

What a joy it would be! Once more and I would presume the best, our crazy trips stopping at restaurants where we would not eat, losing patience!

Forgive this hasty message, it brings you hopes, wishes, thanks and all the affection of your,

N.B.

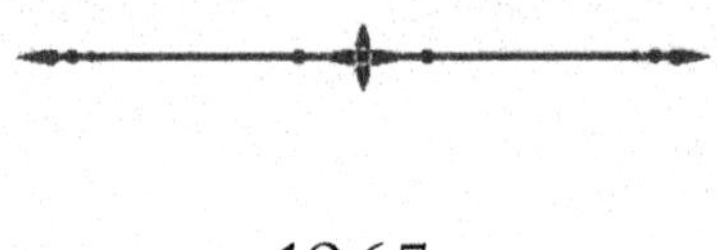

1965

Letter 65-1

21 January 1965

Dear Ruth,

For the 21st loads of wishes carrying a deep love—hasty lines—the state of disorder is here frightening—hopeless—not a card answered. So, read the unwritten and feel very rich. For here are bunches of love, thoughts, wishes,

N.B.

Letter 65-2

19 April 1965

Dear N.B.,

Help! Help! I am getting a teensy-weensy bit anxious to know dates and places and things. When do you arrive in NY? The 25th,

26th, 27th? Are you planning to start immediately for Potsdam, or the following day?

There are rumors that you are going to Toronto. Before or after Chicago? When do you expect to arrive in Chicago???

I saw W. Piston[273] for a second today. He said he heard I was meeting you in NY!!! It is time, n'est-ce pas???!

In case you did not get my last letter, I will be able to attend the Ravinia Concerts, after all, thank goodness. However, I will not return east until late in the summer. It is unlikely that Mother will be able to negotiate stairs when her cast is removed, so I cannot have her here in Belmont as usual this summer. I will stay on at my sister's to take over her care for several weeks.

WHY COULD I NOT HAVE BEEN TWINS?

Love, Ruth

P.S. I may return to Belmont after you arrive at Potsdam to pack the things I want to take to Chicago. I will not know how much room there will be until after I collect you and your paraphernalia. Will return to Potsdam, of course!

Letter 65-3

20 April 1965

Dear Ruth,

Well, well, your life is as hectic as mine. Hope we will nevertheless meet one day or one year somewhere, who knows how and when.

---

273 Walter Hamor Piston Jr. (1894–1976) was an American composer of classical music, music theorist, and professor of music at Harvard University who had studied with NB in Paris 1924–1926.

It is a beautiful hope gone—but it has been a dream—and has given me joy. So, am still grateful.

Shall arrive in Chicago, around the 11th or 12th. Things are still unsettled and will leave on the 18th for Toronto. On the 20th night for Washington—on the 22nd night for NY, and on the 23rd for France if I survive these trips and the heat!

Well—left to the will of God.

So devotedly, your, N.B.

Letter 65-4

5 May 1965

Arrive on board of France in NY on May 26th

Leave for Dartmouth on 27th early morning

From Dartmouth leave for Potsdam on May 28th, early

Will drive from Potsdam to Chicago on June 11th, perhaps 10th.

Sorry but, . . . everything was and remains so tragically connect[ed] with London where my beloved ones struggle with death. It is horrible. Am so hopeful we will once more go through towns and towns.

Love, N.B.

Dear Ruth,

Here are the answers you asked for. Thank you for your kind letter. I do wish to see you. Time is long.

With love, Annette.

Letter 65-5

12 May 1965

Dear N.B.,

Thank you for the information about arrivals, etc. I understand (from Winnie) that the boat arrives very early in the morning—in fact, the night before the 26th, so I will plan to be there at the crack of dawn, so to speak. If for any reason I should be delayed, I will notify you through the French Line. If such is the case, where can I get in touch with you in NY? (Fontainebleau Office)

The drive from Dartmouth to Potsdam will be beautiful, but I hope you will not be in too much of a rush. There are no direct fast roads and we have to go right through the heart of Adirondack State Park. Or go south and then north. It is somewhere between 225 and 250 miles as far as mileage goes, but it is rather slow going—about a six or seven hour drive. However, my map is an old one, and there may be a new faster road. I will find out exactly how far it is.

It will be wonderful to see you, but I will never be ready in two weeks!

Love, Ruth

P.S. My friend Helen Froehlich, who lives on the doorstep of Ravinia Park, says she will be delighted to receive you anytime.

Letter 65-6

16 May 1965

Dear N.B.,

I have just had a phone call from my sister in Illinois with the disturbing news that you have canceled the Ravinia Concerts due to a great personal tragedy.[274] I do not know what that means, but my thoughts are with you in this sad hour and I wish I could help in some way.

All my love, Ruth

274 NB was scheduled to conduct a concert at Chicago North Shore's Ravinia Park in Highland Park, Illinois. She canceled commitments in 1965 because of the death of Hélène Detroyat (née Bouwens). After NB's mother died, Hélène and her sister Jean Bouwens were NB's only living relatives—her half sisters. Their grandfather, architect William Bouwens, was a close friend of Ernest Boulanger's, and their parents, Richard and Marthe Bouwens, were close to NB's parents. It has now been established that Richard was Boulanger's biological father (see Francis, *Teaching Stravinsky*, 101–102). NB was extremely close with Hélène, thirteen years her junior, and was shocked by her death in an accident in London (email interview with Alexandra Laederich of the Centre international Nadia et Lili Boulanger, August 29–30, 2018).

1966

Letter 66-1

17 January 1966

Dear Ruth,

How dear you are. Yes, after such a year of unrepairable sadness. Preizen, 8 days after Mme Vagniaud . . . I feel it so deeply and it is good to have you here. I know you are always with me but your lines were and are comforting.

So deeply and faithfully, your,

N.B.

Letter 66-2

21 January 1966

In time? Alas, no. I know too well. But here are warm, deep wishes and all the affection of your devoted,

N.B.

Letter 66-3

13 September 1966

Dear Ruth,

Your letter is a joy—your wishes a blessing but . . . the time so scarce that I hardly know what I am doing. So, read, guess, wait, and understand what deep affection goes to you!

Try to come. Normally, not wise to wait too long . . . but who knows, perhaps am I still here for long!

I seem to laugh, but am so disheartened today. Intimate friends have lost a beautiful boy of 12. So rich of spirit, in gifts, in generosity. A stupid, tragic car accident and the little body lies there—the soul gone.

But I am happy in thinking of you whom I love so much. As ever, your,

N.B.

Letter 66-4

21 September 1966

Dear Ruth,

What an "avalanche" and what useful, intelligent presents and amusing too. How kind you are. Thank you a thousand times.

Realize how I do miss you and don't wait to come. Remember 1887 so . . . is there much time?

Well . . . who knows. With deep affection, always your devoted,

N.B.

Go to Leeds in a few hours and tomorrow, again full speed Competition 3 meetings a day. Had appreciated a few peaceful days. Welcome the busy ones!

1967

Letter 67-1

16 January 1967

Dear Mrs. Robbins,[275]

How good of you—and how pleasant and useful. Thank you so much. I am really very touched. Happy to hear you are so well and to send you my very best wishes and warmest thoughts.

Nadia Boulanger.

Letter 67-2

19 January 1967

Happy Birthday . . . but . . . delayed alas.

Forgive, realize always with you in deep affection.

275 This note is addressed to RR's mother, Sophie Snowell Robbins.

And again so many thanks,

Your,

N.B.

In principle for the 19th January 1967

Letter 67-3

28 June 1967

[From Annette Dieudonneé]

Dear Ruth,

N.B. was simply delighted to receive your letter. She thinks of you every day! But . . . if you saw what life is like! Much worse than ever. In fact, simply crazy and I wonder how she can stand it.

So, my dear, maybe one day she will write to you. But don't expect it too much.

How I should like to see you. Will you not come one day?

With much love,

Annette

Letter 67-4

12 August 1967

Dear Ruth,

So happy to read you, but so sad for your leg!

As ever in so profound affection,

your (under crazy pressure)

N.B.

Letter 67-5

1 September 1967

Thank you, Dear Ruth,

Your letters are so wonderful, so witty—how good to receive them. Hope all these breaks will soon be over and your body follow the lighting of your mind.

Tomorrow—Bucarest. Today despair and emptiness!! But you cheer me up.

So affectionately, your,

N.B.

Do come back, don't wait! Time goes, and we too.

Letter 67-6

10 December 1967

Dear N.B.,

My thoughts are certainly full of YOU at this moment, partly because I have just been reading the little Fontainebleau news bulletin with all the news about your 80th birthday party. I do not suppose that even your ears could hear me some 3000 miles away singing "Happy Birthday," but you might have! Anyhow, I was there in spirit (which, I might add, is not at all a satisfactory substitute for the flesh!).

I also think of you all the time, with so much gratitude for all the enlightenment in music and teaching that you have given me.

I do not know exactly how to say what I mean, but I think it is the attitude towards all the arts—the sense of craftsmanship, the sense of honesty, the sense of the essential, and of course, the sense of beauty.

All my studies with you and all those wonderful excursions with you—the Pyrenees, Rome, Angoulême, Poitiers, Tours (mostly in the middle of the night!), Dumbarton Oaks,[276] the White House (at least to the door)[277]—too many places to recall at this moment. Oh dear! I will have to stop writing about all those wonderful times. I cannot stand it!

I have lots of pupils this year to keep me busy. Several of them are quite musical and are also good workers, which is very gratifying. The rest pay my taxes. But I enjoy working with even the least of the children when he masters anything!

I hope you have a Merry Christmas and a Happy New Year, but if the new year does not give me a visit with you IN THE FLESH, I will never forgive it!

All my love, Ruth, XOXOXOXOXO

---

276 RR drove NB on many excursions in Europe and in the US. On May 8, 1958, RR drove NB to conduct a performance of Stravinsky's Concerto in E-flat, "Dumbarton Oaks" on the occasion of the fiftieth wedding anniversary of Robert Woods Bliss (1875–1962) and his wife, Mildred Barnes Bliss (1879–1969), owners of the magnificent Dumbarton Oaks estate in the Georgetown section of Washington, DC. This was also the twentieth anniversary of the world premiere of the concerto, which was originally commissioned by Mildred Bliss for their thirtieth anniversary. NB had conducted its premiere on May 8, 1938. During the time between the two performances, the estate gained global fame with the 1944 Dumbarton Oaks Conference" which created the proposals adopted in the United Nations Charter in San Francisco in 1945.

277 In 1962, NB was invited to the White House to meet Jackie and John F. Kennedy, the first Catholic United States president. RR related to her family how she drove Nadia down from New York for the White House luncheon. She described how the old "Bug" wended its way through the streets of Washington, DC, to the White House gate, where it startled the secret servicemen accustomed to sleek black limousines. While NB had lunch with Jackie Kennedy, RR joined the chauffeurs and limo drivers in their waiting lounge.

1968

Letter 68-1

21 January 1968

21st of January!! 19 . . . 68!

I salute the new born little Ruth and feel she has grown pretty fast. I send her tender love, deep wishes, and such affection,

More than she can believe,

Hurrah for "our" Ruth, N.B.

Letter 68-2

24 January 1968

Have I, dear Ruth, sent wishes as intended? Who would even know in this turmoil reigning here? So, here are these maybe delayed wishes going to you with such affection. Missing you so much!

Hope you have forgotten the traitorous staircase by now!
As ever so profoundly yours,
Nadia Boulanger—for Jan 21st—but already 24th 1968.

LETTER 68-3

31 JANUARY 1968

Dear N.B.,

Two letters from you in one week is superb! Too good to be true! But here they are, right in my hand! What a wonderful birthday present! And besides the letters, I have had two glimpses of you recently on television: once tonight (a photograph) on a program of Ashkenazy and Barenboim playing Mozart's Concerto for Two Pianos in E♭ and two or three weeks ago on a program about Menuhin.

It now seems like a dream, but I was present when Barenboim[278] first played for you when he was about to take up his studies with you—10 years ago, or 12? It makes me sick to realize how many years it has been since I have been able to go to France. Seeing Marcelle last summer helped enormously as she had not changed a bit.

I have another grand-niece, born about two weeks ago. That makes the 18th great-grandchild for my mother, I think! We have lost track. There is one more due in a few weeks. Our Christmas holiday started out well with about 18 of the family present, but afterwards people started getting the flu and strep throat, and Mother ended up with pneumonia in the hospital. All are well now, but my sister and I had our hands full for a couple of weeks nursing

278 Pianist and conductor Daniel Barenboim (b. 1942) studied with NB in Paris in 1955.

one person or another. Here everyone had counted on this great family reunion, and it ended up with everyone having to keep away from everyone else! (Except for Mother's illness, it was not as bad as it sounds, but it was very disappointing for the children not to be able to play together.)

I have quite a good class of pupils this year, 26 in all, and about six of them are very promising—mostly Armenians! However, as they each have one forty-minute lesson a week to learn everything about music, the progress is not spectacular with even the best of them. And that is the limit of their music education, except for a few who play another instrument in their school orchestras. The only way I can cope with things is to stress one or two aspects of the work for a few weeks and then shift to something else for a while, hoping that eventually everything will fall together and produce a fairly well-rounded little musician.

For the ungifted ones, it is a rather hopeless situation, and I should probably just let them learn a few pieces and let it go at that. But my conscience keeps pricking me, so I keep trying! Who knows? There may be one among them who, like me, would forever regret not having had the world of music opened up to them at an age when it was not too late to master something.

So, with that parting bit of philosophy I will say goodnight, and as you are still the busiest person on earth, I doubly appreciate the birthday letters. Many many thanks!

All my love,

Ruth

XOXOX

Letter 68-4

10 February 1968

Dear Ruth,

How touching an idea. Cannot thank you properly, but I do profoundly. So dear memories, and Mrs. Bliss still alive but already gone.[279]

Most lovingly your faithful, N.B.

Letter 68-5

18 August 1968

Dear Ruth,

What a sad letter.[280] I realize what must be for you the sight of you from Mother. Want you to know at once that I am with you, as is Annette.

Forgive the hasting haste but the summer is as interesting as exhausting.

Read the unwritten going so deeply to you.

With all our love,

Your, N.B.

Dear Ruth,

I think of you with so much love in these sad days.

Annette

279 Mildred Bliss, married to prominent diplomat Robert Woods Bliss, had been an ardent supporter of NB's. Already senile, she was to die in 1969.

280 RR's mother, Sophie Snowell Robbins, died in July 1968. The second sentence, with somewhat convoluted grammar, appears to mean that NB can visualize RR's suffering because of experiencing her own mother's death. Both RR and NB had complicated relationships with their mothers, and both tended their mothers' final years. RR's responsibility was shared with her sisters, however, while NB alone took full responsibility for her mother.

1969

Letter 69-1

21 January 1969

Have I sent the wishes which flow to you, dear Ruth?

So . . . great demonstration of festivity. . . . Hurrah, hurrah for R.R. our R.R.

I do from the depth of my heart and ever, your,

N.B.

Dear Ruth . . . Hello . . . happy, happy birthday to you,

Love,

Annette

1970

Letter 70-1

10 March 1970

Dear Ruth,

What a sorrow, when you arrive in Paris, I shall be in Monaco in the Jury, and busy the whole day.

I can hardly admit such an idea, but what can be done?

I leave Paris on the 18th and shall come back only the first days of May, leaving for England very likely on the 8th.

Imagining that you are coming finally and will not be there is heartbreaking.

With so much love,

N.B.

Letter 70-2

4 April 1970

[From Annette Dieudonneé]

Dear Ruth,

Thank you for your nice card. I will certainly be home in the beginning of May, but N.B. asks me to tell you that she will be back on the morning of May 2nd, but will leave again for London on the 5th. So that she will be "available" on May 2, 3, and 4. This is, of course, very short, but she hopes it will fit with your schedule, because she would simply be in despair and (maybe) commit suicide if she did not see you.

So, until very soon now, my love and heartiest wishes for your trip.

Annette

Letter 70-3

8 June 1970

Dear Ruth,

Indeed, I would give very much to have you there in August to support Annette morally and physically, and to bring us both your affectionate presence, but I can see how difficult it would be and so do not think of it anymore, one can do so much and no more, and keeping the decision not to see you, I will feel that in spirit you came.

As ever, your

N.B.

Letter 70-4

19 June 1970

Dear Ruth Robbins,

It is really heartbreaking having such a letter as yours.[281] Such an open possibility and be stopped by a miserable question of money. Please do not worry about it. You know what a joy it has been and a help too, but the circumstances make it impossible. I hardly have the courage to write that but I depend finally on the administration of the School. I cannot take a decision which is only concerning me.

Forgive the hasty note. We are all overworked and rather hopeless, but with the same profound affection with you, dear Ruth.

[Handwriting]

I hardly dare suggest that the half of the restaurant tuition could be found, which means the 300 fr. would remain at your own expense. It is really hard to state it but . . . forgive me!

[Unsigned]

Letter 70-5

15 July 1970

Dear Ruth,

Nobody is more thoughtful than you. I am not too sure to run after a new discovery of a "fatal" weakness, but I am so touched that you were thinking of it, that it makes me so cheerful and helped.

281 RR's letter she refers to must have canceled summer plans to go to Fontainebleau.

Remain so sad you are not coming, but propose yourself to come next year for it is unconceivable that you could miss the 50th anniversary of the School. Do not eat anymore and with the money taken from the disappearance of your body, you will make a fortune.

Annette is really not bad and if she accepts to take the necessary hours of rest, will maintain her classes till the end of this session.

Winifred is the shadow of herself but seems really a little better. What an energy she displays.

As always in deep affection, your N.B.

Letter 70-6

22 September 1970

Dear Ruth,

Not only wishes, but wit, love, and fantasy. You are a real Epistolian,[282] and I, drowned in endless and wonderful mail, remain your devoted

N.B.

P.S. Count on you in July 71 for the Jubilee of the School. Unbelievably beautiful concerts!

---

282 One who writes literature in the form of a letter.

Letter 70-7

9 November 1970

Dear Ruth,

Could it be true? I hardly dare hope—but what a joy it would be. Too beautiful to be true. Forgive this strange handwriting. Well . . .

Thank you for your letter. All my love left here, deep and faithful.

As ever,

N [?][283]

283 What follows "As ever" is a felt-tip mystery. Her typical sweeping "N" begins a signature, but what follows is indecipherable; perhaps "Nadjida," a Russian variant of Nadia?

1971

LETTER 71-1

15 JANUARY 1971

Dear Ruth,

What a deception, it was such a joy! The hope has given illusion. Hopes, now . . . wait . . .

With so much love,

N.B.

LETTER 71-2

19 JANUARY 1971

Happy Birthday, Ruth Dear. Am late, hurried, but full of warm feelings which surround you in flammes.[284]

As ever, for my ever, your,

N.B.

for January 21

284 In this context, "flammes" means "flames."

LETTER 71-3

5 MARCH 1971

[WRITTEN ON PALAIS DE MONACO STATIONERY]

Dear Ruth,

Your wishes joined me on my return from the clinic, after an eye's operation. Nothing too serious—but nearly forced by Prince Rainier to accept the aventure[285] and it must be hoped that after this progress is obtained. I feel only ashamed of myself.

Annette, with her endless heart [unreadable] remained here the whole time, regardless the damage it caused her. We return to Paris tomorrow, and life will come back to its usual rhythm. Find here all what goes to you,

—With so much love and wishes, as ever, your,

N.B.

285 In this context, "aventure" means "adventure."

1972

Letter 72-1

10 January 1972

Dear Ruth,

Had you not written, I would know you are there at any time. Forgive this crazy haste—but have the ambition to answer all the Christmas cards. We are all out of breath.

But I am near you. Love the pictures and dream you are soon to come in!!

N.B.

Letter 72-2

21 January 1972

In great ceremonial, here are wishes, thoughts, hopes, for . . . I refuse to admit going away without seeing you again. Could write pages and pages, but I['m] running a few minutes late, to save seconds so much and have better to let you write all the unwritten,

So faithfully, so expectantly,

Happy Birthday,

N.B.

Letter 72-3

27 September 1972

Dear Ruth,

Thank you. So good to have your letter, your wishes, and news through Marcelle.

Strange summer indeed: Winter in fact, session most interesting, so great sadnesses Nora passing away, several dear friends disappearing, and now Robert Casadesus[286] . . .

And life blooms, children are born, works achieved, the whole lost in violence, destruction, young men of value . . . and so it goes.[287]

Need to believe I will still see you, dear Ruth—waiting—I remain devoted.

Your, N.B.

286 Robert Casadesus, who with NB was the originating force of the Fontainebleau school, died on September 19, 1972.

287 In 1972, the deceits, misbeliefs, and horrors of the United States involvement in Vietnam dominated international news. This reflection on life, creativity, destruction, and death was made while the war was still being waged and bombs dropped. The Paris Peace Accords were signed in January 1973.

1973

LETTER 73-1

19 JANUARY 1973

Well, well . . . soon your birthday, and we will not celebrate together. It is sad—and how absurd. The time goes and as says Ron[s] ard[288]: Alas, We are going and soon it will be over. So, once more, through the oceans, wishes fly and mean to be there on the 21st.

Everything goes pretty well in this mad world, but what we live for stands and keeps us united.[289]

As ever with love, in deep attachment,

N.B.

288 Although NB's handwriting is unclear and the "s" appears to be missing, she is likely referring to the sixteenth-century poet Pierre de Ronsard, who often alluded to the ephemerality of life, love and beauty in his poems.

289 "What we live for stands and keeps us united" refers to their shared humanitarian values.

Letter 73-2

18 September 1973

Dear Ruth,

Marcelle describes me Sunday for visit her chats with you, and your letter receive from this living report and kind of active life.[290] Thank you so much for all that your letter brings, and understand why mine is dictated and short. But so warm, so full of all what is employed that it permits these poor little moves to carry a treasury of affection.

As ever, your old devoted, N.B.

Letter 73-3

16 December 1973

Dear Ruth,

You know how frequently you are in my mind. I miss you so much, but a special thought goes to you for the 18th. Feel present here affectionate memories, need of exchange, and understand how faithfully I am your,

Nadia Boulanger

290 This letter was dictated in English by NB and written down by a nonnative speaker of English, thus the sinuous, free-form grammar and spelling. NB wrote the final words in her own hand "your old devoted, N.B."

1974

LETTER 74-1

4 JANUARY 1974

Dear Ruth,

Have I, or not, sent you the wishes which bloom in my heart? You are so near . . . and so far . . . I feel you present—and miss you badly. Year marked by the death of very close friends, very difficult to stand. And one needs to [unreadable[291]] with the ones who are there. Great affection from your N.B.

291 Nearly 87 when this letter was written in January 1974, NB's handwriting is faltering. The unreadable word clearly means something like "value more" or "stay close" with the loved ones who are still alive. The closing phrase I have extrapolated to read "Great affection from your N.B.," as it was written partially on the stationery and (evidently) partially on the blotter beneath, with only the first couple letters of each word visible.

Letter 74-2

7 January 1974
Paris

Dear Ruth,

What a joy brings your letter!

I also keep present our adventures, the vain search for one pleasant place to have lunch on the highway, and hundreds and hundreds of details, always present. Alas! Many sad memories exist, as well. You probably did not hear of the passing of Barbara Trask,[292] which causes me great sadness.

With her, too, so many evocations of the past have abolished the distance between California and Paris.

With you, I keep on and keep on dreaming that you will announce your arrival tomorrow, for just half a day, but it would mean seeing you and going on hoping and thinking of you so profoundly, so tenderly, so affectionately, so faithfully.

I remain your poor old half broken,

Nadia Boulanger

And alas, Annette fell last Saturday and broke her wrist. It seems not to be very severe, but she can do nothing with her right arm and her life is quite impossible for the time being. Were she here today, she would join me in sending wishes and all our attachment, so great as you know, without forgetting your anniversary on January 21.

---

292 Barbara Trask was an American student of NB's; three of her compositions are in the Boulanger collection at Harvard's Loeb Music Library, Isham Memorial Library.

Letter 74-3

15 January 1974

Well, well, the great day is near, and one prepares to celebrate!

Happy, happy birthday.

Love has a new meaning, now that we can no more escape to understand. And in this rather frightening period, new light is shining. Will we be strong enough to deserve the trial which may still save us our poor world, so sick, so blind?[293]

Thank you for your letter, your wishes, all the thoughts which abolish time and space.

We feel you present but miss you more and more, hoping to see you again.

We must be confident and keep burning the light of love.

With so warm wishes,

N.B.

Letter 74-4

22 February 1974

Dear Ruth,

You know how to put many news in few words, and so I can follow you in detail. Would so much like to expose you all [to] what is going on here but that will be in a further occasion.

As far as today, let simply profound affection go to you as ever,

293 In the last months of 1973, the Yom Kippur War broke out between Israel and Egypt/Syria, and the United States Watergate scandal was at its height. NB seems to be hoping that love, even just between individuals, can conquer the evils of the world.

Hope,
Ever your,
N.B. Nadia Boulanger

Letter 74-5

19 September 1974
Vevey

Dear Ruth,

Here is one of your rich, amusing, and meaningful letters. Thank you so much, I follow you all and so feel somewhat less faraway.

After a session, very really nice with youngster hardly prepared, but very willing. Annette and I [were] very exhausted and arrived here . . . well, in a rather pitiful state. The care of Mrs. Makevitch and her daughters accepted us as the "nothing" we were, and helped us, so kindly, to come back to a more or less normal state. Winifred in B[oston] stays alone, and aging. A and I will be in Paris towards the end of Sept. Very much in this [illegible] especially awful if we go on.

With much love, as ever,
N.B.

1975

Letter 75-1

6 January 1975

Dear Ruth,

Thank you for your lovely card. The most extraordinary news is about your nephew Dick. How is it possible to walk off unscathed after such a crash! And what an experience for him.

I wish you a very good new year. May 1975 be affectionate to you, and good, and nice, and full of inspiration for your sculptures. I am sending you a book, which I hope shall interest you. As the mail seems to function slowly, I do not want to wait any longer. I wanted to send it to you two months ago. May it reach you before 1976!

Jolanda[294] is here back from India and shall leave for America when it suits her. It is awfully nice to have her here, as you may well imagine.

Well, dear Ruth, lots of love, and my faithful affection,

Marcelle

N.B. is still going strong!

294 "Jolanda" is unidentified.

LETTER 75-2

21 SEPTEMBER 1975

Dear Ruth,

Your wishes, your letter, your affection coming here in this calm village with Anna and Cecile Dungler [unreadable] you may have known. But one of the [godchildren?] mother of five little girls is in great danger. Facing death—or, what a recovery. I can no more be of any help. Wait, and it is all!

Thinking of you brings peace and sustains me.

Most faithfully, and in profound attachment,

N.B.

1976

LETTER 76-1

JANUARY 1976
PARIS

Dear Ruth,

Soon it will be the 21st of January, and I fear I shall be late, and it causes me real trouble, for you know you are so often on my mind.

Life goes on here as usual, unbearable to everybody, even for me, but I still survive.

What is most sad is the news about Sister Ignatia I received through Mrs. Chapman. She seems to be in good health but completely absent minded, having forgotten about Lamarr's death, about us. It is so painful. Our dear Sister Ignatia, enlightened by such an inner, vivacious, deep personality.

Marcelle is still in the States, but comes back next week, and told you all that goes on here.

Seem to be dominated by a hope to have the mail in order, all answered, and that enters already in the field of impossibility, but the mind remains free, and I am often with you, thinking, hearing, remembering, and it would not be fair to say that you are absent. Unseen, yes—but absent, no, by no means. And with deep affection I send you wishes. I hope you go through the turmoil spread over the whole world, sufficiently absorbed in your own activities, that you perceive the necessity to pursue our own efforts more than ever.

Winifred would certainly have joined, had she known I was writing you, and Annette does from the depth of her heart.

Forever and for my ever, yours, N.B.

LETTER 76-2

MARCH 1976

[HANDWRITTEN AROUND BOULANGER'S PRINTED NAME ON THE BACK OF AN INVITATION TO A MARCH 15, 1976, LILI BOULANGER MEMORIAL SERVICE]

So touched by such faithfulness,
NADIA BOULANGER
begs you to receive thanks,
wishes, and hopes.
N.B.

Letter 76-3

20 August 1976
Fontainebleau

Dear Ruth,

Needless to say that who comes introduced by you is welcomed.

But here is coming the last week in Fontainebleau, and immediately after departure for a whole month of September on holiday. It is quite impossible to see your protégée before my coming back to Paris. Will you be kind enough to tell her to write Place Lili Boulanger end of September to arrange an appointment, and whatever I can do, I will do my best to do.

We are overloaded with work, but this does not change our constant thoughts.

Most affectionately, N.B.

1977

Letter 77-1

[1977]

Dear Ruth,

Already 37 years,[295] and present as if it were yesterday. Feel you are often present here and remembering so many memories, so often brought to light. Find here thoughts, wishes, and the great attachment of your,

Nadia Boulanger

295 RR first met NB in 1940; the correspondence that has been preserved commences in the summer of 1941.

LETTER 77-2

20 JANUARY 1977
PARIS,

Dear Ruth,

Why in my craziness did I settle as your anniversary February 21? Anyhow, here I am hands full with wishes and the heart burning with affection.

Nadia Boulanger
ADRESSE PERSONNELLE: 3, PLACE LILI BOULANGER - ANC[T] 36, RUE BALLU, 75009 PARIS

LETTER 77-3

15 SEPTEMBER 1977

[DICTATED AND HANDWRITTEN BY ASSISTANT]

Your letter arrives, just in order to celebrate what you all make a wonderful day. In fact, the day is as beautiful as it is difficult on account of general decay. Yes, all that you awake is still present: Bordeaux, Chartres, Chicago, Baltimore, etc., etc., and I do miss you more and more. Time passes, but I want to see you at least once more. Am trying to answer some of the numerous messages; even in choosing, it is hard to keep up, obliged as I am to dictate. Read the unwritten, feel what part I take in all that concerns you, and believe in my profound faithful affection. Live with your "chemisette" in French; they are keeping quite willingly with the terrible rhythm to which they are submitted. So do the flannel [?] couverture!

Letter 77-4

24 December 1977

Dear N.B.,

How I wish I could turn back the clock 37 years and start my lessons with you all over again!! Only I would like to start out with a more solid musical background. Do you know I had never even heard of counterpoint until I worked with you! I would not want to relive all those years, but I would have an awful time deciding which ones to leave out!

I hope you are well and are having a Merry Christmas, and will have a VERY Happy New Year.

I miss you! And love, Ruth

1978

Letter 78-1

10 January 1978
Paris

Dear Ruth,

Well, in time I shall not be, but nevertheless with you very often and especially on January 21. Read what I should have liked to have written, and believe in my endless affection.

Nadia Boulanger

LETTER 78-2

10 SEPTEMBER 1978

[DICTATED AND HANDWRITTEN BY ASSISTANT]

Dear Ruth,

You are always with me, more especially on the Feast days, in memory days. Your sweet little message means so much and I can assure you that even if you did not state it, I would hear it. Knowing that you are always here.

The summer was very difficult, but ended with no deficit in spite of our fears. I am the only one who has to stand sacrifices, and lately a rather long séjour in hospital with only one problem: old age.

Let me say that it is a hard one, because nobody can bring a remedy to it. Anyhow, it is wonderful to feel oneself spoiled and surrounded by so many friends. Something miraculous about it!

Feel me very near and very moved by so much love. N.B.

LETTER 78-3

CHRISTMAS 1978

[NADIA WROTE HER LAST WORDS TO RUTH IN HER OWN HAND, "HAPPY CHRISTMAS, FAITHFUL WISHES, NADIA BOULANGER;" THE REST WAS DICTATED AND HANDWRITTEN BY A FRIEND]

Thank you so much for your letter, dear Ruth. It is so good to hear from you, though it would be so much better to see you. Well, dreams sometimes come to realization!

With love and hopes,

Happy Christmas, Faithful wishes, Nadia Boulanger

1979

Letter 79-1

4 September 1979

[Ruth's last letter to Nadia, written six weeks before Boulanger's death on October 22, 1979]

Dear N.B.,

I am almost too embarrassed to write you after letting so much time go by since the last letter. I am in a tremendous upheaval as I decided to move to California to be near my sister and her family. The movers will be here next week, and I have been frantically going through things to dispose as much as possible.

Among the wonderful treasures are so many reminders of you! Programs, letters, photos, music, and, yes, a bowl full of stones you collected in Santa Barbara.

I am very reluctantly giving up rocks I have collected from Montana, Colorado, and California, but yours I will keep to be reminded of so many wonderful times with you.

With love and kisses and wishes for a VERY HAPPY BIRTHDAY. From Ruth

Appendix: Music by Ruth Robbins

Short Pieces, Exercises, and Sketches
Written for Nadia Boulanger and Francis Poulenc

Companion website:
ruthrobbinsmusic.com

INTRODUCTION

Ruth Robbins studied composition with two of the greatest musicians of the twentieth century, Nadia Boulanger and Francis Poulenc. Her work as a composer is fragmentary. It consists of three exercises written under the direction of Nadia Boulanger when Robbins was a student at the Longy School of Music in the early 1940s. These were found in the Isham Memorial Library at Harvard's Loeb Music Library, to which Boulanger donated a trove of student compositions.[296] The remainder consists of brief passages and fragments in three notebooks discovered after her death, all likely written during and after her composition study with Poulenc in 1953.

As a nonmusician, I had no way to assess or even understand my aunt's forays into composition. Fortunately, I was introduced to a kind and patient musician who took the time to review the materials and explain them to me. He also engraved my aunt's handwritten

296 Isham Memorial Library, part of Harvard's Loeb Music Library, is a collection of rare original books, scores, and facsimiles of musical sources.

scores and provided me an audio file of each.[297] For all this, I owe a tremendous debt of gratitude to Jan Krzywicki. He studied composition with Nadia Boulanger at Fontainebleau in 1967, is a composer, and teaches composition at Temple University's Boyer College of Music and Dance. So Professor Krzywicki was an ideal informant to review Robbins's work.

Likewise, I owe a debt of gratitude to tenor Sean Christensen,[298] who reviewed the materials and made many incisive observations, this time from a vocalist's perspective.[299]

When I first listened to Krzywicki's audio files, I felt a surge of emotion. A window into my aunt's soul, never before available, opened for the first time as I actually heard what was in her mind as she composed these pieces. I listened, and even with an untrained ear, I felt something interesting and attractive about Robbins's exercises in composition.

By no means was Robbins a virtuoso pianist; at best, her performance was average. Yet she was highly intelligent, sensitive to nuance, and a hard working student. It is not surprising that she grasped the principles of composition and applied them in her own work.

These passages may be of interest to musicologists because of her close association with Nadia Boulanger and her studies with Francis Poulenc, and they may have intrinsic value of their own. Idil Biret said of Robbins's compositions,

> It is a pity our teacher never encouraged her lady students in the art of composition. She would always say her own compositions were "useless" (*inutiles*), which gives an indication about her way of thinking. Your aunt's compositions

297 Since RR does not indicate the tempo of any of the music included here, the MIDI realizations of the musical examples are open to question.

298 Sean Christensen, Tenor (website), http://www.tenorseanchristensen.com/.

299 The observations of Jan Krzywicki and Sean Christensen are from Zoom interviews in July 2021. Rather than encumber this chapter with numerous quotes and attributions from these two generous musicians, let me here assure the reader that everything of value in this section is from them, and all errors are mine.

> have a lot of interest—in the way she uses uneven rhythms, for instance. She could have developed this talent she obviously had.[300]

Elsewhere, Biret notes,

> [Nadia Boulanger] was wary of females. She would often say, speaking of children's voices in choirs, "the purity of young boys' voices can never be found in the voices of young girls." Then she would generalize in a way I did not like, "it is because a young boy has much more innocence than a girl who is, by her very nature, crafty and inclined to be vain." She did not say "impure" but probably thought it. I admired Mlle Boulanger a lot, but the arbitrary attitudes she was capable of having always surprised me.[301]

Biret felt constricted by Boulanger's rigidity, but Nadia herself had been a serious composer; she was awed by her sister Lili's compositional talent, and Louise Talma thrived as a composer under Boulanger tutelage, so she clearly had nothing against female composers! We might fairly say that composition was a sensitive area close to her heart because of her own aspirations and disappointments in composition. Boulanger likely chose not to encourage students to compose unless she believed it was the highest and best use of their talent—male or female. Moreover, Robbins' classmates in Boulanger's 1940–1943 tenure composition class at Longy included five youthful, talented composers: Harold Shapero (1920–2013), American composer and pianist; Robert Middleton (1920–2016), chair of the music department at Vassar College from 1974 until his retirement in 1985; Paul Des Marais (1920–2011),

300 Idil Biret, interview by James Miller, December 2019, Cordes-sur-Ciel, France.
301 Xardel, Idil Biret, 38.

composer; Claudio Spies (1925–2020), composer on the music faculty at Harvard, Vassar, Swarthmore, Princeton, and the Juilliard School; and composer Irving Gifford Fine (1914–1962).

To the extent Robbins had compositional talent, how could it stand out in this class? So her work was not fed with encouragement, nor was it watered with recognition. Despite barren soil, these few sprouts emerged.

The exercises and sketches described here, brought to light and placed in the context of her life and times, provide insight into both midcentury compositional styles and Ruth Robbins's personality. You can listen to them at this book's companion website: www.ruthrobbinsmusic.com.

"Ave Maris Stella," set in Ruth Robbins's hand (including her error in the title), composed as an exercise for Nadia Boulanger's composition class, Longy School of Music, 1943 [Isham Memorial Library, Loeb Music Library], Harvard

WORKS FROM THE ISHAM MEMORIAL LIBRARY

"AVE MARIS STELLA"[302]

Ave Maria Stella

302 Engravings of RR's handwritten scores in this section are the generous contribution of Jan Krzywicki, professor of composition, Boyer College of Music and Dance, Temple University.

The tradition of medieval plainchant (or "plainsong," from the Latin *cantus planus*) is characterized by a single melodic line and unmeasured rhythm. The origin of this simple style was to provide guidance for monks to chant their Latin prayers. The Gregorian chant is a form of plainchant.

Sung without musical accompaniment, plainsong rhythms are freer than the metered rhythm of later Western music, allowing—in fact, necessitating—singers and choirs to interpret the score with their own preferences and styles. A foundational hymn in the Western canon, "Ave Maris Stella" has been set to music frequently throughout its history by Renaissance composers Giovanni da Palestrina and William Byrd; Baroque-era composers Claudio Monteverdi and Marc-Antoine Charpentier; Romantic composers Dvorak, Grieg, and Liszt; and many modern composers.

In her exercise, Robbins made a beginner's error. She misread or misunderstood "Maris" (two syllables) to be "Maria" (three syllables) throughout. Whether this lapse reflects on the quality of Latin instruction at Pine Manor Junior College or whether she had a momentary brain freeze matters little. She was not brought up in the Catholic Church, but in any case, this error is a venial sin, not a mortal one, and for our purposes can be ignored.

Perhaps "Ave Maris Stella" was an exercise in melodic writing and text setting—that is, creating good melodic shapes with good prosody and correctly setting strong and weak syllables. It may have been written for some sacred occasion, since an unaccompanied chant would not have much likelihood of performance in any other situation. This handwritten score might be Robbins's first attempt at any kind of composition—all the more reason to excuse her error.

This exercise is well-constructed, with multiple returns to clear themes, but it lacks variety and direction. The repeated patterns allow singers to latch on easily. This style of chant is more a vehicle for text than a vehicle for music.

"Ave Maris Stella" in Latin and English

Ave, maris stella,
Dei mater alma,
atque semper virgo,
felix cœli porta.

Sumens illud «Ave»
Gabrielis ore,
funda nos in pace,
mutans Evæ nomen.

Solve vincla reis,
profer lumen cæcis,
mala nostra pelle,
bona cuncta posce.

Monstra te esse matrem,
sumat per te precem
qui pro nobis natus
tulit esse tuus.

Virgo singularis,
inter omnes mitis,
nos culpis solutos
mites fac et castos.

Vitam præsta puram,
iter para tutum,
ut videntes Jesum
semper collætemur.

Sit laus Deo Patri,
summo Christo decus,
Spiritui Sancto
tribus honor unus. Amen.

Hail, star of the sea,
Nurturing Mother of God,
And ever Virgin
Happy gate of Heaven

Receiving that "Ave" (hail)
From the mouth of Gabriel,
Establish us in peace,
Transforming the name of "Eva" (Eve).

Loosen the chains of the guilty,
Send forth light to the blind,
Our evil do thou dispel,
Entreat (for us) all good things.

Show thyself to be a Mother:
Through thee may he receive prayer
Who, being born for us,
Undertook to be thine own.

O unique Virgin,
Meek above all others,
Make us, set free from (our) sins,
Meek and chaste.

Bestow a pure life,
Prepare a safe way:
That seeing Jesus
We may ever rejoice.

Praise be to God the Father,
To the Most High Christ (be) glory,
To the Holy Spirit
Honor the Three as One. Amen.

"In Manus Tuas"

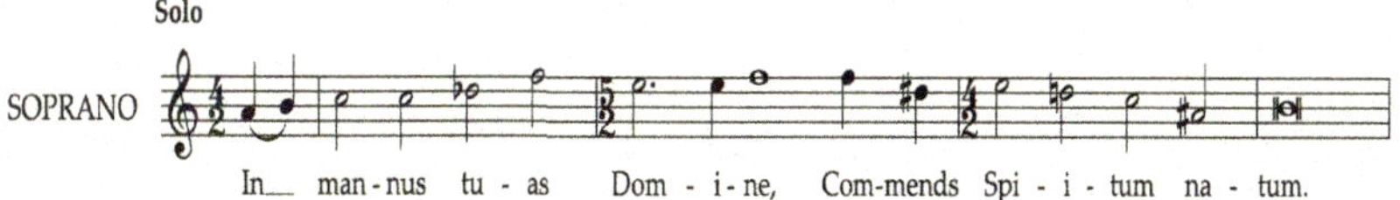

Ruth Robbins's handwritten notations, engraved courtesy of Professor Jan Krzywicki

Also based on a short Latin text, "In Manus Tuas" similarly has been set by numerous composers over the ages. The seven words "In manus tuas, Domine, commends spiritum natum" ("Into thy hands, O Lord, I commend my spirit") were Christ's last words on the cross. While Robbins's "Ave Maris Stella" is a simple soprano solo, her "In Manus Tuas" is a four-part choral setting, including a soprano solo.

Likely completing it as a class assignment, she set only five measures for the first line of the prayer. This may be an exercise in *cantus firmus* (firm chant) composition, using a single line of melody to build a four-part choral setting. Stretching out the first measure of the bass line while the three other voices hold the original melody introduces polyphonic composition to the underlying melodic foundation.

She probably composed the treble line—or had it given to her—and then harmonized it using some of the same chromaticism that is in the melody. The use of half-note meters (rather than quarter-note meters) is common to sacred choral music.

Interestingly, she varies the meter in the second, third, and fourth measures, from 4/2 to 5/2 and back again, a technique Stravinsky and Bartók were using from the early part of the century onward. In the summer and autumn of 1944, Robbins stayed with Boulanger at the Sachses' residences in Montecito and Lake Tahoe. Stravinsky was a frequent visitor, and Robbins turned pages for the two as they rehearsed side by side for the introduction of new Stravinsky works at Mills College in an October program. Stravinsky's notes and Boulanger's comments about them were in the air continuously during his visits, and background information was no doubt absorbed by Robbins.

"November 18, 1945"

The third fragment from the Isham collection is simply labeled "November 18, 1945." Only fourteen measures, it is defined by a lively rhythm alternating between 5/8 and 4/8, reminiscent of the folklike pieces by Stravinsky and Bartók. Even if it is only fourteen measures long, it does have a sense of beginning and ending, and so it could function as a children's piece. The play between diatonic and chromatic, between major and minor, indicates that she is trying to move out of traditional writing.

Ruth Robbins's Notebooks

Three music notation notebooks were found in Ruth Robbins's effects. While the above Isham collection compositions are indisputably from the 1940–1943 period when Robbins was Nadia Boulanger's student in the US, her notebook compositions and fragments cannot be dated but are likely to be from the 1950s or the early 1960s. During this period, Robbins traveled to France several times to study with Boulanger at Fontainebleau, where she also took a composition course with Francis Poulenc in 1953. Robbins's "later works" show some development of composition skills.

"Cahier de Musique"

This oversize (9.5 x 12 in.) notebook contains a partially completed composition of nineteen measures on the first page and three measures on the second. In the last (twenty-second) measure, only the bass clef has been set, indicating Robbins left this uncompleted. The rest of the book is blank. The sheer scale of the notebook itself, the meticulous precision of notation, and the complexity of changing key signatures and tempos perhaps hint that this was the beginning of a work of some ambition.

Two things are puzzling about this passage. First, she does not write down the meter, which is 5/8, clearly. Second, she writes on three separate staves, perhaps for three separate instruments? But no instrument can play the first two measures of the second line. Furthermore, instruments are not indicated for any of the three staves. And even when the music is compressed into two staves for piano, the span in the first measure (third note) is too wide for the hands. No instrument or voice type (soprano, alto, tenor, bass) can perform the notes in measures seven and eight as written. At this point, therefore, she was thinking abstractly and would probably have adjusted the music for a particular medium at some point.

The French, in their training, would often have students work on separate staves as a way of improving their facility with different clefs. This is typical of French training, to write on separate lines so you become especially aware of what all the voices are doing—you can lose track when it is only on two staves.

"Cahier de Musique"

"Composer's Manuscript Folio"

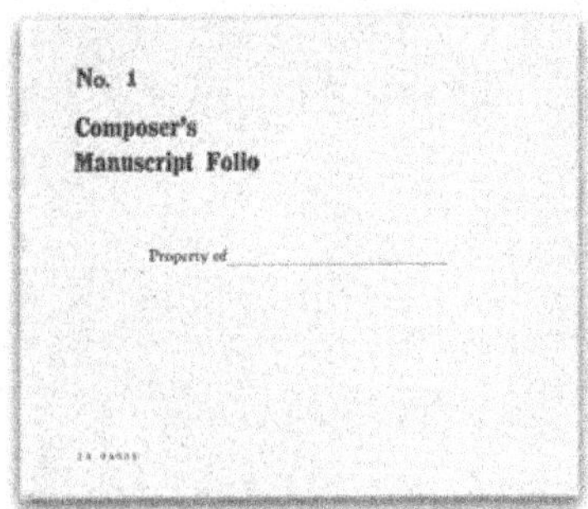

This notebook contains four looseleaf sheets plus two notebook pages of composition. The "manuscript folio" itself, as well as the loose sheets, may be Robbins's work in a composition class taught by Francis Poulenc at Fontainebleau in the summer of 1953.

These loose sheets appear to be early drafts of the "Cahier de Musique" passage.

Loose Leaves 1 – 2

Loose Leaves 3 – 4

Robbins's notation "as other but in G" implies this score is related to another one, but alas, nothing fitting was found in her notebooks.

The bottom two lines of the next fragment (Loose Leaves 3–4) employ the technique of invertible counterpoint—that is, a way of composing whereby the vertical placement of the instruments can be exchanged. If we call the top stave A, the middle B, and the bottom C, note how the melodic line in the first measure of stave A is repeated in the second and fourth measures of stave C, then back up to A for measures seven and eight. Measures nine and ten are crossed out, most likely because it didn't work as well as the ensuing inversion (mm. 11–12) and/or because three statements of the material were too repetitive. The last two measures bring the melodic line back down to C.

Composer's Manuscript Folio p. 1

The first of the "Manuscript Folio" pages shows the continuing interest in 5/8 meter. It might have been intended as part of the foregoing sketches as a possible middle or subsidiary section. It is in a related tonality but is more modal. The style is quite like some Stravinsky works, whereas the foregoing sketches are quite like Poulenc's. This fragment is attractive, but it is just the first couple phrases of a piece, not by any means complete.

Composer's Manuscript Folio p. 2, "Study in Fourths"

The second page, titled "Study in Fourths," is an exercise in quartal harmony—that is, the use of intervals of a fourth instead of the more traditional thirds used in triads. The effect, like in several of Robbins's sketches, is decidedly French in flavor, rather like Honegger or Poulenc.

Original Ideas notebook

"Original Ideas"

The third of Ruth Robbins's notebooks has a handwritten title: "Original Ideas." One could speculate that following her composition class with Poulenc, Robbins was emboldened to set her own course as a composer. If this is the case, these works date from the mid-1950s. This notebook has six pages of notation. Pages 4 and 5 are titled "Study in Appoggiaturas."[303] Other pages are untitled.

Original Ideas Notebook, pp. 1 – 2

303 An appoggiatura is a nonchord tone on the beat that resolves down a step to a chord tone; it derives from the Italian "to lean, "— that is, a dissonance is "leaned on" before resolving down to a consonance.

The first fragment has a decidedly neoclassical flavor, the cadence at measure 8 clearly Baroque. It also sounds like the music of Poulenc and other French composers. Once again, it is the start of an attractive piece that one wishes she had continued.

Original Ideas Notebook, Study in Appoggiaturas

Original Ideas Notebook, Untitled A

Original Ideas Notebook, Untitled B

This last setting is another folklike dance in A minor, rather like a children's piece, following the "November 18, 1945" piece. This can be viewed as a short, complete piece with an opening, a continuation, and a return to the opening material. Thus, it is modal: it begins and ends in the Aeolian mode, a scale that historically preceded the use of major and minor scales but had a comeback in the late nineteenth century and enjoyed much use in the twentieth century.

These pieces were written in a student mindset, but they do not feel like homework. She puts soul into her work. She cares about the melodies and harmonies she is trying to create. Even in the simplest ones, like the parallel-fourths exercise, she uses rhythm in a specific way. She is particular about her choices. She creates playful expectations for the listener in just a couple of bars.

Her work might be compared to that of contemporary composers who create an atmosphere in their compositions. Mozart and other composers are melodic, creating strong, structured statements meant to stand on their own. Contemporary composers—think of film scoring—often create an ambient atmosphere, a background mood for a story. She is good at creating a mood, and does it in just a few measures.

Ruth Robbins's talent as a musician may well have been for composing, not performance. She lacked natural artistic talent as a performer, but she was intelligent, understood music theory, had a good ear, and had a feel for bringing life to her compositions. None of these works are overwhelming, yet they show how an earnest student absorbed the understanding of music imparted by Nadia Boulanger and Francis Poulenc. One wishes that several of Robbins's sketches had been developed into full-fledged pieces of whatever size, that she had spread her wings a bit as a composer.

She was not encouraged or, apparently, motivated to commit herself to composition, but at least we have a glimpse at what might have been. And from her perspective, studying composition with Nadia Boulanger and Francis Poulenc, two of the greatest musicians of the twentieth century, was in itself a gift beyond measure. No doubt her appreciation of music was immensely enhanced by what she learned in these exercises.

Robbins advised her grandniece Gabby to listen to music carefully and every day. This indeed was Robbins's daily practice, her enjoyment greatly deepened by what she had learned from these two masters. By studying composition, Robbins gained understanding and skills that gave her rich rewards each day for the rest of her life. After she completed composition studies with them in 1953, God granted Robbins more than an additional half century of life to enjoy the invaluable gifts from her mentors.

BIBLIOGRAPHY

BOOKS

Bambrough, Renford. *The Philosophy of Aristotle*. New York: Mentor Books, 1963.

Barnes, Julian. *The Man in the Red Coat*. New York: Alfred A. Knopf, 2020.

Biret, Idil. *Idil Biret: Life and Music*. Philadelphia, Chestnut Hill Press, 2023.

Boulanger, Nadia. *Lectures on Modern Music: Delivered, under the Auspices of the Rice Institute Lectureship in Music, January 27, 28, and 29, 1925*. Houston, Texas: Rice Institute, 1926.

Bowra, C. M. *The Romantic Imagination*. New York: Oxford University Press, 1961.

Brooks, Jeanice. *The Musical Work of Nadia Boulanger: Performing Past and Future between the Wars*. Cambridge: Cambridge University Press, 2016.

———, ed. *Nadia Boulanger and Her Work*. Chicago: University of Chicago Press, 2020.

Campbell, Don G. *Master Teacher: Nadia Boulanger*. Washington DC: Pastoral Press, 1984.

Chan, Wing-tsit, ed. *A Source Book in Chinese Philosophy*. Princeton: Princeton University Press, 1963.

Conrad, Doda. *Grandeur et mystère d'un mythe: Souvenirs de quarante-quatre ans d'amitié avec Nadia Boulanger* [The grandeur and the mystery of a myth: Reminiscences of forty-four years of friendship with Nadia Boulanger]. Paris: Buchet-Chastel, 1995.

Finkel, Caroline. *Osman's Dream: The History of the Ottoman Empire*. New York: Basic Books, 2005.

Francis, Kimberly. *Teaching Stravinsky: Nadia Boulanger and the Consecration of a Modernist Icon*. New York: Oxford University Press, 2015.

———, ed. *Nadia Boulanger and the Stravinsky: A Selected Correspondence*. Rochester: University of Rochester Press, 2018.

Gallois, Jean. *Les Polignac, mécènes du XXe siècle* [The Polignacs, patrons of the twentieth century]. Monaco: Éditions du Rocher, 1995.

Govea, Wenonah. *Nineteenth- and Twentieth-Century Harpists: A Bio-critical Sourcebook*. Westport, CT: Greenwood Press, 1995.

Harmon, William, ed. *Classic Writings on Poetry*. New York: Columbia University Press, 2003.

Howard, Douglas. *A History of the Ottoman Empire*. Cambridge: Cambridge University Press, 2017.

Jung, C. J. *The Essential Jung*. Compiled by Anthony Storr. Princeton: Princeton University Press, 1983.

Kahan, Sylvia. *Music's Modern Muse: A Life of Winnaretta Singer, Princesse de Polignac*. Rochester, NY: University of Rochester Press, 2009.

Kendall, Alan. *The Tender Tyrant, Nadia Boulanger: A Life Devoted to Music; A Biography*. Wilton, CT: Lyceum Books, 1977.

Kerr, Philip. *Metropolis*. New York: G.P. Putnam's Sons, 2019.

Kinross, Patrick. *Atatürk: The Rebirth of a Nation*. London: Weidenfield & Nicolson, 2001.

Laederich, Alexandra. *Nadia Boulanger et Lili Boulanger: Témoignages et études* [Nadia Boulanger and Lili Boulanger: Testimonials and studies]. Lyon: Symétrie, 2007.

Lindbergh, Anne Morrow. *Against Wind and Tide: Letters & Journals, 1947–1986*. New York: Pantheon Books, 2012.

Loft, Abram. *How to Succeed in an Ensemble: Reflections on a Life in Chamber Music*. Cambridge, MA: Amadeus Press, 2003.

Mango, Andrew. *Atatürk: The Biography of the Founder of Modern Turkey.* New York: Overlook Press, 2000.

Menuhin, Yehudi. Introduction to The Tender Tyrant, *Nadia Boulanger: A Life Devoted to Music; A Biography*, by Alan Kendall, xv–xvi. Wilton, CT: Lyceum Books, 1977.

Monsaingeon, Bruno. *Mademoiselle: Conversations with Nadia Boulanger.* Translated by Robyn Marsack. Manchester, UK: Carcanet Press, 1985.

Nelson, James, ed. "Nadia Boulanger." In *Wisdom for Our Time*, 257–266. New York: W. W. Norton, 1961.

Nichols, Roger. *Poulenc: A Biography.* New Haven, CT: Yale University Press, 2020.

Plato. *Symposium*. Translated by Walter Hamilton. Harmondsworth, Middlesex, UK: Penguin Classics, 1951.

Potter, Caroline. *Nadia and Lili Boulanger*. London: Routledge, 2016.

Powell, Alex. "Organizational Identity in the History of the Longy School of Music." PhD diss., Boston University, 2014.

Preminger, Alex, ed. *Encyclopedia of Poetry and Poetics*. Princeton: Princeton University Press, 1965.

Robbins, Percy Arthur. "Autobiography of Percy Arthur Robbins." Unpublished typescript, n.d.

Roger-Ducasse, Jean. *Lettres à Nadia Boulanger: Présentées et annotées par Jacques Depaulis* [Letters to Nadia Boulanger: Introduced and annotated by Jacques Depaulis]. Sprimont, Belgium: Mardaga, 1999.

Santayana, George. *The Sense of Beauty: Being the Outlines of Aesthetic Theory*. New York: Dover, 1955.

Sidney, Philip. "The Defense of Poesy." In *Classic Writings on Poetry*, ed. William Harmon, 138–139. New York: Columbia University Press, 2003.

Spycket, Jérôme. *Nadia Boulanger*. Lausanne: Lattès Payot, 1987.

———, ed. *Nadia Boulanger*. Translated by M. M. Shriver. Stuyvesant, NY: Pendragon Press, 1992.

Steiner, George. *Lessons of the Masters: The Charles Eliot Norton Lectures, 2001–2002*. Cambridge, MA: Harvard University Press, 2005.

Tansman, Alexandre. *Igor Stravinsky: The Man and His Music*. Translated by Therese and Charles Bleefield. New York: G.P. Putnam's Sons, 1949.

Walsh, Stephen. *Stravinsky: The Second Exile*; France and America, 1934–1971. Berkeley: University of California Press, 2008.

White, Eric Walter. *Stravinsky: The Composer and His Works*. 2nd ed. Berkeley: University of California Press, 1979.

Xardel, Dominique. *Idil Biret: A Turkish Pianist on the Concert Stages of the World*. Translated privately by Idil Biret Archive. Idil Biret Archive, 2009.

Xardel, Dominique. *Une pianiste Turque en France* [A Turkish pianist in France]. Paris: Buchet-Chastel, 2006.

Zhuangzi. *Chuang Tzu: Basic Writings*. Translated by Burton Watson. New York: Columbia University Press, 1964.

Periodicals & Other Sources

Dada Manifesto, (1916 , Hugo Ball). https://en.wikisource.org/wiki/Dada_Manifesto_(1916,_Hugo_Ball).

Damrosch, Walter, and James Beck. "American Friends of Musicians in France." *Pacific Coast Musical Review* 33, no. 23 (March 1918).

DeVoto, Mark. "Melville Smith: Organist, Educator, Early Music Pioneer, and American Composer." In *Perspectives on American Music, 1900–1950,* edited by Michael Saffle, 265–300. New York: Routledge, 2000.

Driver, Paul. "Review of Mademoiselle: Conversations with Nadia Boulanger, by Bruno Monsaingeon." *Tempo*, New Series 157 (June 1986): 33–34.

Dyer, Richard. "Pianist Idil Biret Is Unparalleled in Playing and Recording." *Boston Sunday Globe*, September 24, 2000.

Forbes, Elliot, David Hughes, Leon Kirchner, and John Stewart. "Luise Vosgerchian: Faculty of Arts and Sciences—Memorial Minute." *Harvard Gazette*, February 8, 2007.

Greven, Corina, Francesca Lionetti, Charlotte Booth, Elaine Aron, Elaine Fox, Haline Schendan, Michael Pluess, Hilgo Bruining, Bianca Acevedo, Patricia Bijttebier, and Judith Homberg. "Sensory Processing Sensitivity in the Context of Environmental Sensitivity: A Critical Review and Development of Research Agenda." *Neuroscience & Biobehavioral Reviews* 98 (January 2019): 287–305.

Guerry, Jack. "Review of Mademoiselle: A Portrait of Nadia Boulanger, by Dominique Parent-Altier." *American Music Teacher* 38, no. 3 (January 1989): 57–59.

"Guide to the Robert E. Middleton Papers, 1939–1954." Archives and Special Collections Library, Vassar College Libraries.

Harvard Gazette. "Beloved Music Teacher Vosgerchian Dies at 77." *Harvard Gazette*, March 16, 2000.

Hoover, Suzanne R. "Teaching: Nadia Boulanger." *American Scholar* 46, no. 4 (Autumn 1977): 496–502.

Hughes, Allen. "Nadia Boulanger, Teacher of Top Composers, Dies." *New York Times*, October 23, 1979, https://www.nytimes.com/1979/10/23/archives/nadia-boulanger-teacher-of-top-composers-dies-onewoman-graduate.html.

Karlstrom, Paul J. "Alfred Victor Frankenstein, 1906–1981." *Archives of American Art Journal* 21, no. 2 (1981): 23.

Lewis, Anthony. "Review of *The Tender Tyrant: Nadia Boulanger*, by Alan Kendall." *Music & Letters* 58, no. 2 (April 1977): 228–229.

Miller, Margo. "Tribute to Kennedy Is Solace in Music." *Boston Globe,* November 23, 1963, 22.

Moevs, Robert, and Ellen Rosand. "Nadia Boulanger (1887–1979)." *19th Century Music* 3, no. 3 (March 1980): 276–278.

New York Times. "Jean Casadesus, Noted Pianist, Dies in an Auto Collision at 44." *New York Times*, January 22, 1972. https://www.nytimes.com/1972/01/22/archives/jean-casadesus-noted-pianist-dies-in-an-auto-collision-at-44.html.

Orledge, Robert. "Musical Idealism." Review of *Mademoiselle: Conversations with Nadia Boulanger*, by Bruno Monsaingeon. *Musical Times* 127, no. 1718 (May 1986): 277.

Ponsonby, Robert. "Obituaries: Rafael Kubelik." *Independent*, August 12, 1996.

Termini, Olga. "Great Teachers in Music History." *American Music Teacher* 43, no. 3 (December/ January 1993/94): 22–23.

Thomson, J. M. "Nadia Boulanger." *Early Music* 8, no. 1 (January 1980): 16.

Thomson, Virgil. "Greatest Music Teacher—at 75," *New York Times*, February 4, 1962.

Tommasini, Anthony. "Boris Goldovsky, 92, Musician and Opera's Avid Evangelist." *New York Times*, February 18, 2001. https://www.nytimes.com/2001/02/18/nyregion/boris-goldovsky-92-musician-and-opera-s-avid-evangelist.html.

Vitello Paul. "John LaMontaine, Pulitzer-Winning Composer, Dies at 93." *New York Times*, May 14, 2013. https://www.nytimes.com/2013/05/15/arts/music/john-lamontaine-composer-dies-at-93.html.

"Vittorio Rieti, Prolific Composer in Neo-Classical Style, Dies at 96." *New York Times*, February 21, 1994. https://www.nytimes.com/1994/02/21/obituaries/vittorio-rieti-prolific-composer-in-neo-classical-style-dies-at-96.html.

Ward-Steinman, David. "On Composing: Doing It, Teaching It, Living It." *Philosophy of Music Education Review* 19, no. 1 (Spring 2011): 5–23.

Whitman, Alden. "Lotte Lehmann Dies at 88; Diva and Lieder Specialist." *New York Times*, August 27, 1976. https://www.nytimes.com/1976/08/27/archives/lotte-lehmann-dies-at-88-diva-and-lieder-specialist-lotte-lehmann.html.

Wooddell, Glenn. "The Musical Godmother." *Music Educators Journal* 69, no. 4 (1982): 16–17.

Yeoland, Rosemary. "Nadia Boulanger et Camille Mauclair." *International Review of Aesthetics and Sociology of Music* 45, no. 1 (June 2014): 63–76.

Index